Feel-Bad Postfeminism

Library of Gender and Popular Culture

From *Mad Men* to gaming culture, performance art to steampunk fashion, the presentation and representation of gender continues to saturate popular media. This series seeks to explore the intersection of gender and popular culture, engaging with a variety of texts – drawn primarily from Art, Fashion, TV, Cinema, Cultural Studies and Media Studies – as a way of considering various models for understanding the complementary relationship between 'gender identities' and 'popular culture'. By considering race, ethnicity, class and sexual identities across a range of cultural forms, each book in the series adopts a critical stance towards issues surrounding the development of gender identities and popular and mass cultural 'products'.

For further information or enquiries, please contact the library series editors:

Claire Nally: claire.nally@northumbria.ac.uk
Angela Smith: angela.smith@sunderland.ac.uk

Advisory Board:
Dr Kate Ames, Central Queensland University, Australia
Dr Michael Higgins, University of Strathclyde, UK
Prof Åsa Kroon, Örebro University, Sweden
Dr Andrea McDonnell, Emmanuel College, USA
Dr Niall Richardson, University of Sussex, UK
Dr Jacki Willson, University of Leeds, UK

Published and forthcoming titles:

The Aesthetics of Camp: Post-Queer Gender and Popular Culture
By Anna Malinowska

Ageing Femininity on Screen: The Older Woman in Contemporary Cinema
By Niall Richardson

All-American TV Crime Drama: Feminism and Identity Politics in Law and Order: Special Victims Unit
By Sujata Moorti and Lisa Cuklanz

Are You Not Entertained?: Mapping the Gladiator across Visual Media
By Lindsay Steenberg

Bad Girls, Dirty Bodies: Sex, Performance and Safe Femininity
By Gemma Commane

Beyoncé: Celebrity Feminism in the Age of Social Media
By Kirsty Fairclough-Isaacs

Conflicting Masculinities: Men in Television Period Drama
By Katherine Byrne, Julie Anne Taddeo and James Leggott (Eds)

Fat on Film: Gender, Race and Body Size in Contemporary Hollywood Cinema
By Barbara Plotz

Fathers on Film: Paternity and Masculinity in 1990s Hollywood
By Katie Barnett

Film Bodies: Queer Feminist Encounters with Gender and Sexuality in Cinema
By Katharina Lindner

From the Margins to the Mainstream: Women On and Off Screen in Television and Film
By Marianne Kac-Vergne and Julie Assouly (Eds)

Gay Pornography: Representations of Sexuality and Masculinity
By John Mercer

Gender and Austerity in Popular Culture: Femininity, Masculinity and Recession in Film and Television
By Helen Davies and Claire O'Callaghan (Eds)

Gender and Early Television: Mapping Women's Role in Emerging US and British Media, 1850–1950
By Sarah Arnold

The Gendered Motorcycle: Representations in Society, Media and Popular Culture
By Esperanza Miyake

Gendering History on Screen: Women Filmmakers and Historical Films
By Julia Erhart

Girls Like This, Boys Like That: The Reproduction of Gender in Contemporary Youth Cultures
By Victoria Cann

'Guilty Pleasures': European Audiences and Contemporary Hollywood Romantic Comedy
By Alice Guilluy

The Gypsy Woman: Representations in Literature and Visual Culture
By Jodie Matthews

Love Wars: Television Romantic Comedy
By Mary Irwin

Male and Female Violence in Popular Media
By Elisa Giomi and Sveva Magaraggia

Masculinity in Contemporary Science Fiction Cinema: Cyborgs, Troopers and Other Men of the Future
By Marianne Kac-Vergne

Paradoxical Pleasures: Female Submission in Popular and Erotic Fiction
By Anna Watz

Positive Images: Gay Men and HIV/AIDS in the Culture of 'Post-Crisis'
By Dion Kagan

Postfeminism and Contemporary Vampire Romance
By Lea Gerhards

Queer Horror Film and Television: Sexuality and Masculinity at the Margins
By Darren Elliott-Smith

Queer Sexualities in Early Film: Cinema and Male-Male Intimacy
By Shane Brown

Screening Queer Memory: LGBTQ Pasts in Contemporary Film and Television
By Anamarija Horvat

Steampunk: Gender and the Neo-Victorian
By Claire Nally

Television Comedy and Femininity: Queering Gender
By Rosie White

Tweenhood: Femininity and Celebrity in Tween Popular Culture
By Melanie Kennedy

Women Who Kill: Gender and Sexuality in Film and Series of the Post-Feminist Era
By David Roche and Cristelle Maury (Eds)

Wonder Woman: Feminism, Culture and the Body
By Joan Ormrod

Young Women, Girls and Postfeminism in Contemporary British Film
By Sarah Hill

Feel-Bad Postfeminism

Impasse, Resilience and Female Subjectivity in Popular Culture

Catherine McDermott

BLOOMSBURY ACADEMIC
LONDON • NEW YORK • OXFORD • NEW DELHI • SYDNEY

BLOOMSBURY ACADEMIC
Bloomsbury Publishing Plc
50 Bedford Square, London, WC1B 3DP, UK
1385 Broadway, New York, NY 10018, USA
29 Earlsfort Terrace, Dublin 2, Ireland

BLOOMSBURY, BLOOMSBURY ACADEMIC and the Diana logo
are trademarks of Bloomsbury Publishing Plc

First published in Great Britain 2022
This paperback edition published 2024

Copyright © Catherine McDermott 2022, 2024

Catherine McDermott has asserted her right under the Copyright, Designs and Patents Act, 1988, to be identified as Author of this work.

For legal purposes the Acknowledgements on p. x constitute an extension of this copyright page.

Cover design by Jess Stevens
Cover image: *Girls* series two, 'It's a Shame About Ray' (02-02-13)
(© Apatow Productions/HBO Entertainment/Photofest)

All rights reserved. No part of this publication may be reproduced or transmitted in any form or by any means, electronic or mechanical, including photocopying, recording, or any information storage or retrieval system, without prior permission in writing from the publishers.

Bloomsbury Publishing Plc does not have any control over, or responsibility for, any third-party websites referred to or in this book. All internet addresses given in this book were correct at the time of going to press. The author and publisher regret any inconvenience caused if addresses have changed or sites have ceased to exist, but can accept no responsibility for any such changes.

A catalogue record for this book is available from the British Library.

A catalog record for this book is available from the Library of Congress.

ISBN: HB: 978-1-3502-2498-8
PB: 978-1-3503-2671-2
ePDF: 978-1-3502-2500-8
eBook: 978-1-3502-2499-5

Series: Library of Gender and Popular Culture

Typeset by Newgen KnowledgeWorks Pvt. Ltd., Chennai, India

To find out more about our authors and books visit www.bloomsbury.com and sign up for our newsletters.

Contents

List of Illustrations	viii
Acknowledgements	x
Series Editors' Introduction	xi
Introduction	1

Part 1 Impasse

1	Feel-bad postfeminism in *Gone Girl*	31
2	Postfeminist impasse and cruel optimism in *Girls*	56
3	Searching for belonging in *Appropriate Behaviour*	83

Part 2 Resilience

4	Suffering, resilience and defiance in *The Hunger Games*	115
5	Relationality and transformation in *Girlhood*	142
6	Feel-bad femininity in *Catch Me Daddy*	169

Conclusion	202
Notes	213
References	227
Index	257

Illustrations

1. Young adult novel *Haunting Violet* (Harvey 2011), featuring a beautiful dead girl as its cover image — 48
2. The opening shot of *Girls*' first episode — 58
3. Reverse shot of Hannah's parents — 59
4. Charlotte (Kristin Davis) decides to quit her job in *Sex and the City*'s 'Time and Punishment' — 68
5. Hannah (Lena Dunham), centre-framed and smiling in celebration, in 'Iowa' — 72
6. Shirin (Desiree Akhavan) rides the subway in *Appropriate Behaviour*'s opening sequence — 90
7. Shirin and Crystal (Halley Feiffer) ride the subway in the film's closing scene — 91
8. Shirin's moment of equilibrium in the final shot of the film — 91
9. *Broad City*'s Abbi (Abbi Jacobson) wears a strap-on dildo framed from between her legs — 100
10. Fleabag (Phoebe Waller-Bridge) backs away from the camera in the season one finale — 109
11. Fleabag waves goodbye to the camera in the series finale — 110
12. Profile close-up of Marieme (Karidja Touré) during *Girlhood*'s first transition sequence — 159
13. Marieme's fashionable new clothing and hairstyle in *Girlhood*'s first transition sequence — 161
14. Vic's masculine attire in the final act of *Girlhood* — 162
15. June (Elisabeth Moss) leads a group of handmaids in a power walk following a defiant act of suffering agency — 173
16. Profile shot of Marieme crying in the final scene of *Girlhood* — 183
17. Marieme looks determined, after stepping back into the frame — 184
18. Close-up of Laila crying in *Catch Me Daddy*'s closing sequence — 185

19	Tariq (Wasim Zakir) ceases active coercion of Laila and cries	188
20	Tariq forces Laila to drink gin, his body obscuring hers within the frame to communicate his power over her	189
21	Tariq, shouting at Laila	189
22	Close-up of Laila's feet as she stands on a chair with a noose around her neck	189
23	Laila standing, motionless, calling out to her father	190
24	*Catch Me Daddy*'s final image, an extreme close-up of the back of Laila's head	195

Acknowledgements

This book began as a doctoral project at Manchester Metropolitan University, where I was lucky to be part of an exciting research environment and share an office with such a fantastic group of colleagues. Equally, I am grateful to have worked with an exceptional supervisory team. I owe a great deal to Berthold Schoene and Jackie Stacey for their meticulous and challenging criticism and for their continual compassion and support. Many thanks to Andrew Moor for offering thoughtful comments and to my examiners, Fiona Handyside and Emma Liggins, for their insightful and encouraging feedback. I'm grateful to the Arts and Humanities Research Council for their generous three-year doctoral award and to the editors at Bloomsbury for their support with this project. A special thank you goes to my family – Mam, Dad, Sara and Ash – who have always helped and encouraged me. Most of all, I'd like to thank Siân, who makes everything worth it.

Series Editors' Introduction

Postfeminism has had a profound influence on female culture in Westernized contexts, as many of the books in this Library testify. Postfeminism emerged in the 1990s, with the energetic optimism of that time embodied by the Spice Girls. The discourse of empowerment, apparently perfectly mixing feminism with femininity, was a positive message that young women carried with them into the new century. This combination of educational and employment power could be masked by a veneer of femininity that offered fragility and traditionally gendered representation. In *Feel-Bad Postfeminism*, Catherine McDermott explores the concept of postfeminism in contemporary media texts to show how this concept has been adapted by cultural shifts, most notably by the 2008 global financial crisis. The empowerment discourse, with its 'having it all' message, has been less attainable (though evidently no less desirable) in the midst of a post-recession culture characterized by insecurity and reduced opportunities.

What McDermott observes here is that the term 'girl' re-emerged, but unlike its use in 'girl power' in the 1990s, it has come to be linked to texts that deal with less positive messages of postfeminism that are no longer fully legible as feel-good. The former goals of social viability (often through education, career and marriage) and happiness in postfeminist empowerment texts are replaced by a separation of these goals in texts such as *Gone Girl*. The transient nature of the empowerment discourse that McDermott tackles in this book has clear links with Melanie Kennedy's (2019) *Tweenhood: Femininity and Celebrity in Tween Popular Culture*, which unpacks the deification of celebrity and femininity within tween culture, concepts which are central to McDermott's discussion of the way postfeminism came to operate since around 2008. The global financial crash, as McDermott reflects in this book, can be argued to have affected postfeminism in that it removed the certainty and promise of a better life through education, self-maintenance and social viability. The first generation of young women who had seen a degree as a rite of passage rather than the privilege of primarily young men ended up as the graduates who had no clear future, left to work in the unstable world of the gig economy. The resultant lack of certainty leads to what McDermott calls 'messy feminism', which has links with Rosie White's (2018) *Television Comedy and Femininity: Queering Gender*, here applied to texts such as *Girls* and *Fleabag*. It also has links with Barbara Plotz's (2020) *Fat on Film: Gender, Race and Body Size in Contemporary Hollywood Cinema*.

In addition to messy feminism, McDermott also deals with the concept of resilience and how postfeminism has a legacy of agency and empowerment in contemporary coming-of-age texts, such as *The Hunger Games*. In this hypothesis, fragility remains the presumed foundation of femininity; however, women become responsible for the labour of overcoming their perceived gender deficits to find acceptance as viable subjects. Most significantly, this marks a major departure from the norms of postfeminist empowerment discourses that require female subjects to perform and quietly conceal traditional femininity. As McDermott argues, in resilience postfeminist texts, girlhood is imagined as an ongoing struggle to stay alive, and the coming-of-age narrative produces a female subject whose heroism is derived from profound trauma.

This book demonstrates a variety of ways in which postfeminist empowerment discourse has profoundly shaped contemporary fictional genres aimed at women and girls and their expressions of feminine agency and subjectivity. The positive messages of 1990s postfeminist empowerment, McDermott argues, are growing increasingly strained, a feeling which is further aggravated by a post-recession culture of instability and insecurity that poses a significant threat to the postfeminist promise of personal autonomy and liberation. The book illuminates a major cultural turn in which postfeminist empowerment in popular genres has begun to dramatically shift from an affective register of enjoyment, carefree pleasure and fun to one in which postfeminism is articulated as a site of rage, horror and resentment.

This suggests that although postfeminist ideals remain culturally prevalent, there is a profound shift in constructions and perceptions of the capacity for the postfeminist empowerment discourse to deliver a path to fulfilment. As other books in this Library show, the impact of, and legacy of, 1990s postfeminism continues to be seen across popular culture contexts.

Angela Smith and Claire Nally

Introduction

In the best-selling crime thriller *Gone Girl* (Flynn 2012), the protagonist, Amy, has spent her entire life coordinating her personality to match whichever style of femininity is currently in vogue. When we meet her, Amy has been playing the role of easy-going, fun-loving 'Cool Girl', who is always up for anything, whether that might be a threesome or a beer, who swallows her feelings with an adoring smile, and is not only conventionally beautiful but also unconcerned about her appearance (2012: 250). If the Cool Girl sounds too good to be true, the novel suggests, that is because she is. Entirely fabricated and designed to appeal to men, Cool Girl is cool because she excels in both performing and concealing characteristics associated with traditional femininity like passivity and fragility. Published in 2012, *Gone Girl* was at the forefront of an emerging genre which began to express a profound discontent with postfeminist 'happiness scripts' (Ahmed 2010: 59) surrounding romance, marriage and work. Loss, disillusionment, failure and isolation permeate these narratives, typically focusing on women in their late twenties and early thirties whose embodiment of freedom through their spending power, unlimited choice of consumer products and performance of an 'up for it' sexuality (Gill 2007, 2008; McRobbie 2008) has not delivered the anticipated happiness or self-fulfilment.

By contrast, girlhood coming-of-age narratives are increasingly producing femininity within discourses of resilience, envisaging girls as capable of overcoming and adapting to bleak and unforgiving social conditions. *The Hunger Games'* (Collins 2008) sixteen-year-old protagonist, Katniss, is performing too – albeit in her case she must project positivity and resilience in front of the cameras watching her every move in a state-mandated death match with twenty-three other children. There is an acute generational disconnect between the difficulties faced by fictional millennials adjusting to social circumstances radically altered by the 2008 global financial crisis and the apparent successes of contemporary girls in surmounting much harsher obstacles. This book explores what works like *Gone Girl* and *The Hunger Games* can tell us about how it feels to inhabit the world as produced, shaped and informed by the postfeminist empowerment discourses that were especially prevalent in the late 1990s and early 2000s. Part 1 focuses primarily on narratives about women whose coming of age coincided with the height of postfeminist empowerment, and Part 2 explores the continuing postfeminist legacy in girlhood coming-of-age genres.

To understand the relationship between postfeminist empowerment discourses and female subjectivity in contemporary fictional genres aimed at women and girls, I draw on, adapt and develop a number of affective research practices. Although I will give more detail on current debates within affect theory shortly, I will first note that by affect, I mean embodied sensations which include feelings and emotions, but often prefigure them. In broad terms, the book follows Lauren Berlant's (2011) work, which suggests that cultural formations generate subjectivity by mobilizing affects. Kristyn Gorton observes that while it is possible to distinguish between emotion as 'a sociological expression of feelings' (2007: 334) and affect as a physiological response to feelings, it is more widely acknowledged that biology and society cannot be so neatly separated (Goodley, Liddiard and Runswick-Cole 2018; Gorton 2007; Ngai 2005). Although some scholars place more emphasis on affect (Brennan 2004) or on emotion (Ahmed 2004), the two are interwoven and therefore typically used interchangeably, a practice I take up in this book. I am most interested in the role affect plays in constituting subjectivity and, as such, examine the kinds of affects postfeminist discourses mobilize, and their relationship to female subjectivities formulated by media culture.

The legacy of postfeminist empowerment

By postfeminism, I am referring to a contradictory set of discourses which respond to, disavow and individualize feminist politics. It is impossible to discuss postfeminism without reference to its synergies with neoliberalism, as first identified by scholars like Rosalind Gill (2007, 2008) and Angela McRobbie (2008). As the major determining sociocultural discourse of our contemporary moment, neoliberalism is most often defined as the extension of market values and economic practices like free enterprise and competition into social and cultural spheres (Brown 2005; Harvey 2005).[1] Similarly, the genres aimed at women and girls over approximately the last thirty years have been dominated by a postfeminist mode of cultural address. Where the postfeminism of the 1980s was theorized as a 'backlash' against feminist advances made by the women's movements of the 1970s (Faludi 1991), Gill argues that postfeminism in the 1990s and early 2000s 'is at least partly constituted through the pervasiveness of neoliberal ideas' (2007: 164). For Gill, postfeminism cannot be theorized solely as a response to feminism, given that 'the autonomous, calculating, self-regulating subject of neoliberalism bears a strong resemblance to the active, freely choosing, self-reinventing subject of postfeminism' (164). At the same time, it is also important to acknowledge that the ongoing influence of postfeminism coincides with the increased visibility of new contemporary feminisms (Banet-Weiser 2018; Gill 2016; Spiers 2018).

A notoriously complex and contradictory set of discourses, postfeminism is conceived as an epistemology, era, movement, identity and sensibility (Genz and Brabon 2009; Gill 2007, 2008; McRobbie 2008; Projansky 2001). Most recently it has been theorized as both a 'double entanglement' (McRobbie 2008: 6) and a 'distinctive sensibility' (Gill 2007: 147). For Gill, postfeminism is characterized by a number of 'interrelated themes' (2007: 147). These include the depoliticization of feminism, performance of a heightened hypersexuality, the persistent association between femininity and the body and the notion of the self as a never-ending project requiring continual surveillance, maintenance and discipline (2007: 149). This book takes up the themes Gill identifies and considers them as the foundational generic elements of postfeminism expressed across a variety of media. By 'taking feminism into account' (2008: 16), Angela McRobbie argues, popular and political media culture constructs feminism as having completed its duty of securing liberation and equality for women, meaning it is therefore no longer required. Within this framework, feminism is not ignored or entirely disregarded; rather, it becomes legible as a burdensome legacy from which women are now able to gratefully cut loose and subsequently enjoy their newfound freedom to have it all.[2]

Stéphanie Genz and Benjamin Brabon emphasize the multiplicity of meanings postfeminism generates within academia, politics and popular culture, noting that its 'diverse manifestations' (2009: 2) cannot be reduced to a singular, limiting definition. As a case in point, Anthea Taylor and Marg Henderson find that Australian postfeminism advances 'a far more positive relationship between feminism and popular culture' (2019: 1) than is typically found in Anglo-American culture. This gives weight to Genz's argument that the complex mutability of postfeminism offers a constructive 'move away from easy categorizations and binaries, including the dualistic patterns of (male) power and (female) oppression on which much feminist thought and politics are built' (2009: 24). The diverse usage of the term speaks to the range and impact of postfeminism as well as to its elastic capacity to hold meanings that are perhaps more culturally evocative than they are descriptive.

In light of postfeminism's ever-growing cultural ubiquity, a vast archive has amassed investigating and classifying its various manifestations. For instance, Diane Negra and Yvonne Tasker's *Interrogating Postfeminism: Gender and the Politics of Popular Culture* (2007) includes chapters examining the relationship between postfeminist culture and ageing (Wearing 2007: 277–310), masculinity and the makeover genre (Cohan 2007: 176–200) and the racialized implications of postfeminist discourse for African-American women (Springer 2007: 249–76). Joel Gwynne and Nadine Muller's *Postfeminism and Contemporary Hollywood Cinema* (2013) looks at femininities and masculinities in popular film, from discourses of virginity (Farrimond 2013: 44–59) and lesbian sexuality (Bradbury-Rance 2013: 27–43) to fatherhood (Hamad 2013: 99–115) and a history of the 'male singleton' (Brabon 2013: 116–30). However, concurrent with the wide-ranging examinations of postfeminism's cultural operations and manifestations is a growing sense of frustration with its dubious utility and lack of critical specificity.

Indeed, the value of postfeminism as a critical term has itself been subject to interrogation by scholars who either proclaim their 'frustration … boredom and ennui' (Whelehan 2010: 159) or, alternately, claim that postfeminism is 'potentially redundant' (Retallack, Ringrose and Lawrence 2016: 88) as a new fourth wave of feminism has since displaced it. Although the characteristics of the fourth wave are hotly debated, digital technology is widely agreed to be one of the defining features of the movement (Blevins 2018; Boyle 2019; Chamberlain 2017; Cochrane 2013; Kurian 2017; Macón 2021; Munro 2013; Parry, Johnson and Wagler 2019; Rivers 2017; Smith 2015; Tazi and Oumlil 2020). Moreover, in contrast to the depoliticization of feminism Gill (2007) identifies as a central tenet of postfeminism, the fourth wave is also characterized by a surge in political activism (Blevins 2018; Chamberlain 2017; Cochrane 2013).

Katie Blevins (2018) attributes a renewed interest in feminist politics to the democratizing effects of digital technology, noting that the internet has made the feminist movement more accessible, particularly to young people. Parry, Johnson and Wagler (2019) find similarly that 'the fourth wave of feminism is an everyday feminism' (3). Their phrasing echoes that of the Everyday Sexism Project, a website founded by Laura Bates in 2012, aiming to document the daily instances of sexism women experienced around the world, and which Blevins (2018) cites as a key example of fourth-wave feminist activism. Other online campaigns demonstrating the scope of fourth-wave digital activism include #MeToo (initiated by activist Tarana Burke in 2006 and popularized by American actress Alyssa Milano in 2017), 'No More

Page 3', a campaign founded by Lucy-Anne Holmes in the UK, and #YesAllWomen (Soraya Chemaly, 2014).

Accounts of fourth-wave feminism are dominated by Western perspectives, although the term itself has global traction. For Alka Kurian (2017), the 2012 anti-rape movement marked a major advancement of feminist activism in India that might potentially ignite a fourth wave of feminism. In Latin America, Cecilia Macón (2021) argues that fourth-wave feminism is partially driven by an affective link between contemporary activist campaigns such as #QueSeaLey (#MakeItLaw), which fought to legalize abortion, and the recent history of Argentina's military dictatorship (1976–83). Maha Tazi and Kenza Oumlil (2020) contextualize the fourth wave in the Middle East and North Africa in relation to the Arab Spring uprisings in 2011, which they describe as a 'historical turn' that enabled Arab women's activism to gain momentum (45). While it is vital to acknowledge emergent feminist activism, the potential redundancy of postfeminist scholarship per se remains easily refuted, for, as Gill (2016) points out, the existence of feminist politics has never precluded the ongoing proliferation of anti- or postfeminist ideas and modes of cultural production. Indeed, Sarah Banet-Weiser argues that postfeminism 'is not displaced by popular feminism but rather bolstered by it' (2018: 20), pointing to the continued complications within and convergences between multiple competing discourses.

However, Imelda Whelehan's complaint that 'postfeminism can be boring and frustrating to analyze because its message requires little unpacking and lies prominently on the surface of these narratives' (2010: 159) rings true and proves much more difficult to dismiss. Jessalynn Keller and Maureen Ryan argue similarly that postfeminist analysis 'falls short' and cannot account for the 'complicated politics' (2014: n.p.) of our contemporary moment. Of course, given the numerous ways postfeminism is deployed, this certainly is not true of every case. On the one hand, as Fiona Handyside and Kate Taylor-Jones point out, Gill's (2007) article 'Postfeminist Media Culture: Elements of a Sensibility' led to a style of feminist media studies analysis that tended towards adopting 'a tautological approach' (2016: 5–6) in selecting texts primarily based on the degree to which they were seen to conform to aspects of Gill's definition of postfeminist sensibility. Indeed, Gill's article has turned out to be extremely influential and shaped the way feminist scholars understand and approach postfeminism. On the other hand, a growing number of researchers are eschewing the tautological approach, finding, as I do, that this style of analysis can be limiting and often produces predetermined results (Colling 2017; Kanai 2019; Taylor and Henderson 2019). My aim is not to repudiate the concept of postfeminism, nor its necessity as a focus of critical scholarship, but to contribute to the literature on postfeminism by exploring its affective enactments.

The postfeminist discourses that prevailed in the 1990s and early 2000s construct subjects as requiring strict surveillance and self-discipline to maintain their femininity, at the same time as emphasizing their increased freedom, choice and independence. Women's individual empowerment is especially glorified (Negra and Tasker 2005: 107), which leads me to use the term 'postfeminist empowerment' to define this period. I do so with a view to historicizing this era both in cultural and academic discourse. This project, however, is ultimately interested in charting an account of what happened *after* the prevalence of 1990s and 2000s postfeminism. Although the period 'after' this configuration of postfeminism cannot be linked to a precise date, it has a rough synchronicity with the 2008 economic crisis and subsequent recession (Genz 2017; Negra and Tasker 2014), following which the aspirational postfeminist myth of 'having it all' becomes all the more strikingly untenable. As Genz argues, the profound transformation of our cultural and economic landscape has demanded a reassessment of postfeminism. Although the empowerment era of postfeminism 'was marked by optimism, entitlement and the opportunity of prosperity', the escalating precarity of the post-recession era casts doubt on such 'celebratory' notions of female autonomy (2017: 18).

My approach aligns with Taylor and Henderson's understanding of postfeminism as 'a *historical descriptor*' (2019: 2, original italics), by which they mean that the term 'describes the culture that emerges after second wave feminism, thus opening up the term to resignification and localization, and giving second wave feminism its rightful place as a major cultural force' (3). This allows for a more expansive definition of postfeminism, on the one hand, which takes second-wave feminism as a springboard. On the other hand, it also enables productive analytic specificities – like Taylor and Henderson's locally specific interest in Australian postfeminism. Equally, I find it constructive to specify my own take and distinguish the 1990s–2000s era as one typified by postfeminist empowerment. Doing so enables me to map the reverberations and cultural legacies of this late-twentieth-century configuration of postfeminism.

Impasse

The growing frustration with the limitations of postfeminist analysis is indicative of what Berlant in *Cruel Optimism* (2011) labels 'impasse', described as a 'cul-de-sac' in which 'one keeps moving, but one moves paradoxically, *in the same space*' (2011: 199, original italics). There is a sense from prominent feminist scholars that although analyses of postfeminist culture continue to proliferate, the debates themselves have stalled, continually circling the same critical terrain. It is from this understanding that this book endeavours, not to find a 'way out', so to speak, but to instead discover new ways to inhabit and move around in this 'same space' while developing alternative approaches to thinking through the pervasive legacies of postfeminist culture.

For although I agree with Tisha Dejmanee's argument that simply 'declaring a theoretical fatigue with postfeminism does not erase its dominant presence in popular culture' (2016: 131), I would contest her claim that 'a generation or more of women have now grown up not knowing anything but postfeminism' (131). While it remains culturally ubiquitous, postfeminism is not a totalizing or panoptic ideological trap from which there is no escape. Postfeminism is certainly not the only discourse in circulation, as scholars like Retallack, Ringrose and Lawrence (2016) point out. Having said that, postfeminism undoubtedly dominates the media archives available to women and girls over approximately the last thirty years. Scholarship tends to classify popular texts addressing women from the mid-1990s to early 2000s as postfeminist (Genz and Brabon 2009; Gill 2008; McRobbie 2008; Negra and Tasker 2007; Projansky 2001). The expansive cultural scope and influence of these works, such as the popular television series *Sex and the City* (Star 1998–2004)[3] and the film *Bridget Jones' Diary* (Maguire 2001),[4] has been widely noted, though they are rarely criticized outright for their postfeminist attributes (Adriaens and Van Bauwel 2011; Gerhard 2005).

Postfeminist media scholarship is invaluable when it comes to understanding the cultural climate and historical moment which produced postfeminist empowerment discourse. However, these debates are less conducive in making sense of the contradictions and ambivalences inherent to women's and girls' complex relationships to postfeminist culture in a post-2008 world. In view of this, and the dissatisfaction expressed by prominent media scholars, I argue that it is essential to supplement and extend existing analyses of postfeminist culture to better understand the way it 'increasingly operates in and through the emotions' (Gill 2017: 609). This book therefore aims to demonstrate that affective approaches facilitate a multifaceted perspective on the complex and often-contradictory ways cultural producers respond to postfeminist norms.

Defending the still-urgent need for postfeminist scholarship, Gill writes that 'it should not be the only term in our critical lexicon, but it does still have something to offer' (2016: 612). For me, that something crystallizes when using affect theory to explore the legacies of postfeminism. At the vanguard of postfeminist media studies, Gill's understanding of empowerment as an individualized feeling of emancipation sets a clear precedent for articulating and comprehending postfeminism on an affective level. See, for instance, Gill's observation that popular media often puts on display the 'empowered female subject', women who are 'simply following their own desires to "feel good"'

(2007: 153–4). My interest, therefore, is not in identifying whether and in what ways a cultural work can be labelled postfeminist but rather in asking what such works communicate about *how postfeminism feels*. As the book aims to demonstrate, affective approaches are especially important in understanding works that might otherwise be simply categorized as postfeminist based on the presence of the associated generic elements outlined above. Since postfeminist media studies as a field typically focuses on the ideological implications of cultural works (Colling 2017), there is a consequent dearth of attention to the aesthetic dimensions of postfeminist culture, which is a gap this book proposes to fill.

Affect, genre and aesthetics

Affect has become a key mode of enquiry across feminist cultural studies and queer theory in recent years (Clough 2007), marking a multidisciplinary shift towards exploring emotions, moods and feelings. To explore how postfeminism feels in our contemporary moment, I draw on and adapt several affective approaches, most central being Berlant's work, particularly her concept of 'cruel optimism' (2011: 1). A relation that emerges when our desires for particular kinds of lives (and our efforts to secure those lives) become destructive, cruel optimism instigates a stubborn belief that detrimental and harmful ways of living will eventually provide the fulfilment we seek.[5]

As I explain in Chapter 2, Berlant's project, in part, is to engage with affect, aesthetics and attachment in order to assess the effects that an increasingly insecure public sphere has had on subjectivity. For Berlant, attachment is a messy, complex set of processes in which we pin our hopes to ideals, objects and institutions that sustain our sense of 'what it means to keep on living on and to look forward to being in the world' (2011: 24). Our attachments often sustain us at the same time as they exhaust our capacity to organize our lives in ways that might be more rewarding. We endeavour to align ourselves with social convention and expectation (marriage, work, etc.) in the hope of ensuring success, love, financial security or the 'good life' (Berlant 2012: 2), even when our efforts are quite unlikely to pay off. The question of why we remain committed to fantasies of the good life, even after enduring recurrent disappointment, is what motivates *Cruel Optimism*. The very term fantasy, with its roots in Freudian psychoanalytic wish fulfilment, suggests an inherent tension between desire and the reality of our lives. Fantasies, on the one hand, by their very definition, hold little hope or promise of their eventual realization. On the other hand, Berlant points out, fantasies of how our lives might eventually unfold constitute our sense of self-continuity, that ourselves and our world 'add up to something' (2) we can navigate and comprehend. Fantasy, then, is what mediates the tension of an external world continually out of joint with our internal hopes and desires.

The concept of cruel optimism enables me to argue that postfeminist culture promises a gendered formulation of the good life to women and girls, while acting as an impediment to the realization of that very same fantasy. Following Berlant, I regard postfeminism partially as an enduring set of fantasies, ideals and affects circulating around femininity that, although often detrimental, also remain frustratingly prevalent within feminine culture. Similarly, Negra (2008) explains how postfeminist fantasies allow certain kinds of selfhood to seem possible, offering the allure of a feminine subjectivity unencumbered by the historical weight of complicated gender politics and bolstered by the seemingly more straightforward pleasures of domesticity, conventional romance and sentimentality.

Affect theories are especially useful when it comes to examining the relationship between individuals and publics as well as helping us to understand the complex and amorphous structures like capitalism or postfeminism which order our lives. Exploring the cultural role of happiness, Sara Ahmed takes a phenomenological approach to affect. In *The Promise of Happiness* (2010), a book that is both influenced by and intersects with Berlant's work, Ahmed argues that institutions like monogamy, marriage, family and gender each offers particular kinds of happiness to those who comply with their set of privileged norms and behaviours. Ahmed's work connects with a subdivision of affect theory interested in the production of negative or unpleasant affects such as 'ugly feelings' (Ngai 2005), failure (Halberstam 2011), shame (Munt 2007), depression (Cvetkovich 2012) or the painful negotiations of queerness in Western culture (Love 2007). Focusing on the ever-growing gap between the promise of happiness and its absent reality, Ahmed notes that 'the promise of happiness takes this form: if you have this or have that, or if you do this or do that, then happiness is what follows' (2010: 29), thus drawing attention to the continual deferral of happiness, always implicitly sited around some distant corner.

Similarly informed by Berlant, in this case by the notion of impasse, Ann Cvetkovich challenges prevailing narratives of depression as an individual affect caused by either unfortunate genetics or traumatic childhoods, instead reframing depression as a socially produced phenomenon or 'public feeling' (2012) induced by capitalist structures of living. In his work on public moods, Eric Ringmar finds similarly that moods are 'a process whereby a certain way we feel comes to be synchronized with the feeling of the situation in which we find ourselves' (2017: 5), suggesting that as individuals, our feelings tend to coordinate with our social others and our environment. Also relevant here is Arlie Hochschild's (1979) concept of 'feeling rules', which 'govern how people try or try not to feel in ways "appropriate to the situation"' (553). Akane Kanai argues that gendered feeling rules have become 'part of intensifying expectations of young women to seamlessly thrive in a post-Fordist economies' (2019: 7). For Kanai, affect 'centres the social patterns through which it appears and is negotiated, as opposed to feelings as purely individually experienced things' (13). The recognition that individual feelings are connected and negotiated through social patterns, and arise as responses to our wider social environment, is key to the concept of affective or cognitive mapping.

Cultural mapping is a common feature of theoretical work attempting to understand the complexity and disorderliness of contemporary capitalism. Cvetkovich's primary interest, for example, is in developing an account of what it feels like to live under twenty-first-century capitalism, an aim shared with Steven Shaviro, who, following Gilles Deleuze (1994) and Fredric Jameson (1990), conducts an 'affective mapping' (2010: 5) of twenty-first-century film and media texts in which capitalism and the visual image have become entwined. Arguing that the evolution of digital modes of production is directly linked to neoliberal financialization, Shaviro's formal analysis of what he labels 'post-cinematic' (1) media texts detects a constitutive, expressive and participatory relationship between cultural production and complex social processes like neoliberalism. Albeit preoccupied with very different strategies and intentions, Cvetkovich's and Shaviro's work strongly resonates with my own mapping of the enduring vestiges of postfeminist discourses of choice and empowerment.

Similarly, Berlant reads cultural texts for 'patterns of adjustment in specific aesthetic and social contexts to derive what's collective about specific modes of sensual activity toward and beyond survival' (2011: 9). Any impasse or loss of fantasy will involve particular methods of adapting or attempting to form new attachments, as Chapters 1 and 2 will explore. Nick Srnicek notes that neoliberal capitalism cannot be perceived directly as it is a 'non-object' (2012: 10); it therefore requires methods that allow the unrepresentable to be affectively perceived instead. Both Srnicek and Shaviro (2010) take up Jameson's concept of 'cognitive mapping' (1990: 54) as a way of comprehending our global world systems. Accordingly, for Shaviro, media and cultural texts are in themselves 'affective maps, which do not just passively trace or represent, but actively construct and perform, the social relations, flows and feelings they are ostensibly "about"' (2010: 6). Aesthetics, then, becomes the key to making complex structures like capitalism or postfeminism legible.

The book overall, and Chapters 2 and 3 especially, works in line with Berlant's understanding of genre as an evolutionary multiplicity (2008). In *The Female Complaint* (2008), Berlant argues that genres are conceptual and structural conventions that evolve and mutate in relation to changing social and historical conditions. Seeking to understand the genres that emerge in our contemporary present under an oppressive neoliberal social imaginary, Berlant describes genre as 'a loose affectively-invested zone of expectations about the narrative shape a situation will take' (2011: 2). Our relationship to genre, therefore, is what determines our expectations and experiences when watching an event unfold, whether in fictional narrative or in the immediacy of our own lived realities. We are heavily invested in our expectations, both in fiction and in our lives. Nancy Thumim describes fictional genres as maintaining a 'tacit understanding between producer and audience' (2012: 163). Berlant's and Thumim's ideas enable me to consider 'genres of living' (Duschinsky and Wilson 2015: 180), a concept that implies an especially fluid contract or relation. Within this paradigm, it matters who or what produces such a genre and who is the presumed audience for its implicit advice on how to live. How and between whom are the terms and conditions of such a contract drawn up? In other words, where do our ideas about how to live our lives come from?

For Berlant, genre is crucial in orienting subjects towards (or away from) particular kinds of lives. In this book, I consider postfeminism generically, as 'an aesthetic structure of affective expectation' (2008: 4). As a genre, then, postfeminism generates affective expectations of happiness, fulfilment and self-realization.[6] Gill describes postfeminism as a 'patterned yet contradictory sensibility' that is 'connected to other dominant ideologies (such as individualism and neoliberalism)' (2007: 621). In their review of the postfeminist sensibility and its uptake in recent scholarship, Sarah Riley et al. (2017) note that Gill's definition suggests postfeminism operates as or is comparable to an ideology. As they point out, the term 'sensibility' underscores the affective characteristics of postfeminism, though this remains a relatively underexplored area.

Understanding postfeminism as a genre is useful precisely because it enables me to explore the affective qualities of postfeminism. Berlant suggests that to call something a genre 'is to think about it as something repeated, detailed, and stretched while retaining its intelligibility, its capacity to remain readable or audible across the field of all its variations'

(2008: 4). Rather than (only) a sensibility or ideology, I use Berlant's work on genre to consider postfeminism as an aesthetic structure with recurrent conventions that produce gendered expectations. Using genre as a framework, postfeminism becomes legible as a set of mutating socially agreed-upon conventions that offer women and girls conceptual structuring principles for how to live, think and feel. Genre also emphasizes the way that such conventions develop over time; they remain intelligible as part of the same cultural formation yet retain an elasticity that permits their ongoing evolution. The book therefore explores the affective contract, or promise of a feminine good life, that is generated by the recurrent generic conventions of empowerment postfeminism.

Girls

Each of the primary texts I analyse either engages with or else is organized by some notion of girlhood. Since the 1990s, girls have become central figures within media culture, where they play an especially key role in postfeminist genres (Aapola, Gonick and Harris 2005; Driscoll 2002; Gonick 2006; Handyside 2015; Harris 2004; Kearney 2009; Negra and Tasker 2007; Projansky 2014). Academic focus on girls and girlhood has, in turn, grown exponentially. Taking a feminist approach to critical youth studies, girl studies explore 'what it means to be a girl' (Aapola, Gonick and Harris 2005: 1). Girl studies emerged in a sociocultural context in which girls enjoyed increased purchasing power in the marketplace (Kearney 2009), were often paradoxically imagined as either 'at risk' and vulnerable (Pipher 1994: 43) or as empowered 'can-do' girls (Harris 2004: 13) and were taking media production into their own hands through zine culture, riot grrrl and hip-hop (Kearney 2006, 2009). Efforts to define, study and understand the girl are legion, with particular focus on the girl as always in 'the process of developing a self' (Driscoll 2002: 6), embodying hypersexuality (Renold and Ringrose 2013), subject at once to internal self-monitoring (Banet-Weiser 2014) and external media surveillance (Hasinoff 2012).

The significance of the girl within postfeminist culture complicates and compounds historical oppositions between the subject position of the girl and the adult woman. Women's rights movements, Mary Celeste Kearney observes, have typically 'constructed women in opposition to youth', partially 'in order to demonstrate that women were like men and thus deserved the same rights' (2009: 8). Equally, Kearney describes how since the 1990s, 'female youth have reclaimed the term "girl" as a positive label for members of their demographic group, thus demonstrating their resistance to being homogenized under "women"' (2009: 15). Evidently, both girls and women as groups have made efforts to establish themselves as independent from one another, suggesting that the relationship between girlhood and womanhood is subject to complex fluctuation.

As Sarah Projansky suggests, within a postfeminist cultural formation, femininity is often deeply connected to the performance of 'girlness' (2007: 45). Following Projansky, Handyside considers 'the girl coming of age' to be 'a representative figure of postfeminist values and their impact upon the individual female identified subject more generally' (2015: 4). Similarly, as Catherine Grant and Lori Waxman put it, 'girlhood is not meant simply as an age but as an allegorical state' (2011: 2). Evidently, the concept of girlhood has become applicable to all female subjects regardless of age. Catherine Driscoll (2002) proposes that the girl cannot be defined as a demographic or category of identity. In line with Driscoll, I consider the girl as a conceptual figure, often produced as being in process or undergoing a significant transition (2002: 6), and who typically functions as an idealized embodiment of femininity.

Resilience

Where Part 1 concentrates on postfeminist impasse in works about women in their twenties and thirties whose coming of age coincided with the height of empowerment postfeminism, Part 2 primarily (though not exclusively) focuses on narratives about girlhood. Here, the legacy of postfeminist empowerment registers as an imperative towards resilience in a post-2008 media landscape which increasingly suggests that girls (and women) possess a particular aptitude for resilience (Gill and Orgad 2018; McRobbie 2020). Just as Gill (2008) proposes that women are the ideal subjects of neoliberalism, the flexible endurance of resilience appears to sit more closely with conventional conceptions of femininity than masculinity.

In *Future Girl: Young Women in the Twenty-First Century* (2004), Anita Harris finds that young women have a 'special role' and 'have become a focus for the construction of an ideal late modern subject who is self-making, resilient, and flexible' (2004: 6). Accordingly, girls' rapidly increased access to education and employment coincided with the political and social conditions of globalization, producing the idealized figure of the 'future girl' (Harris 2004: 1), who emerges from this specific set of historical circumstances. Within this framework, the future girl 'is imagined, and sometimes imagines herself, as best able to handle today's socioeconomic order' (2). Social and cultural narratives produce the girl as an 'ideal' subject, since adolescent femininity is envisaged to be the only gender identity *not* in crisis under neoliberalism. Desirable qualities like flexibility, self-reliance and self-correction are therefore imagined to be abilities that girls can access and cultivate more easily than boys. Resilience discourse is part of this same cultural context in which the self-making future girl operates. For Harris, resilience is one of many idealized traits the future girl must develop in order to succeed (i.e. become a socially viable subject) within a neoliberal model.

Gill and Shani Orgad foreground the connections between resilience and neoliberalism by analysing magazines, self-help books and smartphone apps addressing primarily middle-class women with tips for managing their (negative) emotions and how to reframe adversity as opportunities for growth. Women are encouraged to 'bounce back' from difficulties, learn confidence techniques and use self-management tools to help them navigate economic insecurity. Both Gill and Orgad (2018) and McRobbie (2020) observe that these kinds of resilience tools have become increasingly targeted towards women in the years following the 2008 financial crisis. As McRobbie puts it, 'Resilience is therefore associated with the way that austerity economics were presented to the public by government as the only viable pathway to avoid further recession' (2020: 61). McRobbie also situates resilience tools in relation to the 'challenge posed by a new age of feminism' (43). As documented by Banet-Weiser, the increased visibility and popularity of feminism has brought equally increased visibility to new forms of popular misogyny (2018). In addition to this new form of backlash, McRobbie argues that what she terms 'perfect-imperfect-resilience' emerges as a method of managing feminism by making it more palatable:

> The 'perfect', which appertains to lifestyle and the terrain of the feminine 'good life'; the 'imperfect', which offers some scope (but within carefully demarcated boundaries) for criticism of and divergence from these ideals; and finally 'resilience', which becomes the favoured tool and therapeutic instrument for recovery and repair. (42)

Women must strive for perfection and succeed in an ostensibly meritocratic neoliberal marketplace (Littler 2013) and are subsequently encouraged to 'own' any imperfections, flaws or failures to succeed. The imperfect therefore functions as a way of absorbing the 'unviability' of such success, while resilient bouncing back is the method for recovering from failure (44).

In McRobbie's understanding, resilience as 'part of our everyday common sense' operates

> as a pro-capitalist therapeutic device attending to, while nevertheless reproducing, the ills wrought upon women as a consequence of prevailing gender inequalities, and also deriving from the specific constellation of contemporary life as a time of risk, uncertainty and precarity. (63)

By this definition, resilience has become a relation of cruel optimism – something we require to overcome the insecurities and hardships that living under twenty-first-century neoliberal austerity entails, yet at the same time reproduces the very same system which perpetrated the harm.

In this book, I primarily work from Robin James's model of resilience, in which overcoming identity-based oppression '*in socially profitable ways*' (2015: 15)[7] offers subjects inclusion within neoliberalized systems of social and political power, thereby updating traditional hierarchies of identity-based oppression.[8] Working from a Marxist perspective, James examines manifestations of resilience discourse in contemporary pop music aesthetics, and how these are connected to neoliberal capitalism. Here, resilience is not characterized by one's capacity to survive adversity but by the ability to overcome trauma or suffering by converting it into surplus value. Kanai similarly observes that 'girls and women must confess weaknesses but only in order to overcome them. For example, emotional hardship may be useful if it can be rewired into endurance and resilience' (2019: 11). Because resilience has become one of the key markers for creating social value, certain forms of trauma and suffering are thereby naturalized (Gill and Orgad 2018; James 2015; Kanai 2019; McRobbie 2020). James similarly connects resilience to gender, noting that where traditional normative femininity was overtly centred on fragility and passivity, in our contemporary moment social viability is predicated on 'visibly overcoming the negative effects of feminization' (2015: 82). In this paradigm, fragility remains the presumed foundation of femininity; however, women become responsible for the labour of overcoming their perceived gender deficits in order to find acceptance as viable subjects.

Postfeminism *is* the system

Just as girlhood is considered central to postfeminist culture, so postfeminism appears to explain everything about Western girlhood and has thus dominated theoretical work undertaken in this area over the last decade (Negra and Tasker 2005; Projansky 2007). However, a shift towards new parameters is clearly under way, as postfeminism is once again associated with a representational style of analysis that prioritizes 'decoding and deciphering images in terms of their normative and ideological baggage' (Gottschall et al. 2013: 1) and must therefore be avoided. In sociological studies of girlhood, affective methodologies have instead begun to take precedence. Emphasizing embodiment and materiality, scholarship in this area explores 'girlhood becomings' (Gottschall et al. 2013: 1), girls' experiences of their bodies and emotions in connection with media imagery (Jackson, S. 2016), 'the sexual politics of schooling' (Ringrose 2013: 1), subject formation in adolescence (Jackson, A. Y. 2010) and also includes a heightened focus on girls' digital networks and peer relations on social media (Retallack, Ringrose and Lawrence 2016; Ringrose 2011; Ringrose and Harvey 2015; Ringrose et al. 2012). What this demonstrates is a clear precedent for understanding girlhood through an affective lens. However, instead of turning away from postfeminism and towards affect, this book brings the two together to produce new understandings of how girlhood and female subjectivities are narratively and generically formulated in fictional media.

Inevitably, as I have suggested, if searching for the signs and symptoms of postfeminism, one will surely find them. There appears to be growing consensus across postfeminist media studies and girl studies alike that identifying and criticizing those symptoms is unlikely to contribute much to – let alone productively intervene in – the current academic debates surrounding culture produced by and/ or about women and girls. Samantha Colling, for instance, provides a corrective to the scholarly tradition of 'reclaiming specified pleasures as ideologically resistant, empowering or conversely oppressive' (2017: 11). Such an approach either reads against the grain to recoup a politically progressive meaning or else condemns works for their moments of conformity. Sidestepping this, Colling acknowledges that the 'girl teen films' she analyses do indeed conform to neoliberal and postfeminist values in a number of ways, yet she finds it much more productive to examine how films such as *Mean Girls* (Waters 2004) are designed aesthetically and affectively to produce a particular version of girlhood as pleasurable.

Several of the works I analyse have been accused of capitulating to the patriarchal status quo or conforming to postfeminist convention.[9] Much like Colling, I recognize that each of the works I have chosen is, in different ways and to varying degrees, shaped and generated by postfeminist culture. However, that isn't to say that they must therefore have entirely capitulated to or be endorsing postfeminist ways of thinking. In Mitchum Huehls's (2016) work on twenty-first-century fiction in a neoliberal age, he declares an interest in literature that 'inhabit[s] the world neoliberalism has produced' (2016: xii). Rather than overtly opposing neoliberal principles, Huehls argues, contemporary fiction has instead begun to explore what it means and how it feels to live in the market-driven, cost/benefit society neoliberal ideology has generated.

Just as Huehls suggests that 'neoliberalism as a way of thinking about the world [has become] a way of being in the world' (2016: 3), so too – in my view – has postfeminism. With its generic principles already thoroughly installed, we cannot simply wipe culture clean of postfeminism's influence and reboot. Similarly, postfeminism cannot be equated to a pernicious strain of malware infecting an otherwise flawlessly operational system. Postfeminism *is* the system – at least to some extent, if not universally. Berthold Schoene interprets Berlant's concept of impasse as something that 'cannot be worked through or overcome', suggesting that perhaps 'the only viable option is to embrace and adapt to it as our new way of life' (2017: 96). I argue this is precisely what the texts I analyse in this book try to do: adjust, accept and adapt to the ways in which postfeminist ideas about how to live our lives have irrevocably altered not only the cultural landscape but also feminine subjectivity. For as Berlant suggests, recognition that one's investments in structures like postfeminism are unworkable, ultimately not paying off or producing the anticipated results, is unlikely to eclipse their capacity to provide a sense of self, world and stability.

Postfeminist cultural analysis remains vitally important, yet this book argues there is much more to consider, in addition to examining the ideological implications of girls' and women's culture. The affective approaches I've outlined enable me to sidestep the problematic of whether cultural works conform to or resist postfeminist convention and to concentrate instead on what they articulate about how postfeminism feels. Seeking to capture a watershed moment in the aftermath of postfeminist empowerment culture, the book explores what it might feel like for women and girls to inhabit the world as produced, shaped and informed by postfeminism.

Structure of the book

The book is structured into two parts, with the first focusing on impasse and the second on resilience. The chapters can be approached as three pairs in dialogue with each other, though each works equally as a stand-alone. I explore feel-bad aesthetics throughout the book; however, this mode of cultural production is most prominent in Chapters 1 and 6. Where the first chapter examines postfeminist discourse itself as a feel-bad genre, the final chapter explores the frustration of female agency and resilience as a mode of feel-bad femininity. Chapters 2 and 3 explore our relationship to genre, be it in terms of a cruelly optimistic investment or in terms of isolation from and rejection of normative genres. Finally, Chapters 4 and 5 map out different modes of resilience in girlhood coming-of-age narratives. This secondary structure draws a thread between the opening and close of the book by returning to and developing the framework introduced in the first chapter, as well as tracking the resonances between the concerns of Parts 1 and 2.

Although the book structurally distinguishes between empowerment and resilience as culturally specific modes of postfeminism, this division is nevertheless a conceptual conceit, designed to differentiate between modes of social viability that may yet turn out to be entwined even while manifesting distinctively from one another. In other words, young women coming of age during the height of resilience discourse are by no means immune to the social expectations of postfeminist empowerment discourse that Gill outlines, and vice versa. Each works conceptually as a culturally and historically specific formulation that mobilizes particular affective frequencies. Throughout the book I also highlight further examples of texts operating within the discourses outlined here, finding points of convergence and productive conflict between and within genres.

I've suggested that postfeminism is a dominant set of conventions and fantasies about femininity. The term 'feel-bad postfeminism' therefore describes how those fantasies which once appeared capable of delivering on their feel-good promise of happiness are now increasingly generating negative feelings. Chapter 1 opens with the argument that postfeminist empowerment is no longer entirely legible as a feel-good genre and, as such, has begun to palpably disintegrate. To understand this feel-bad turn and detail the failures of the postfeminist fantasy, I analyse Gillian Flynn's novel *Gone Girl*. The novel is an exemplar study in how postfeminist culture generates desires for particular types of feminine fulfilment but subsequently does not produce the satisfaction that it promises. I argue that postfeminism has begun to be envisaged within our collective cultural imagination as a feel-bad genre (Lübecker 2015) reneging on its promises of satisfaction for those female subjects who comply with its norms and conventions.

By analysing the culturally resonant figure of the 'Cool Girl', this chapter highlights the ways postfeminist empowerment discourse demands that women at once perform and conceal characteristics of traditional femininity. Coming of age within this paradigm leads to subject dissolution, an exhaustion of 'girl' as a category. This exhaustion is crucial to the articulation of postfeminism as a feel-bad genre. The postfeminist expectation of endless flexibility and continual playful transformation of identity does not deliver growth or change; rather, it simply returns the protagonist to the unhappy place where the novel began.

In Chapter 2, I argue that one of the major ways postfeminism operates in media culture is as a relation of cruel optimism. Using Lena Dunham's television series *Girls* (2012–17), I examine how cruel optimism manifests at the level of narrative structure as a continual looping process of renouncing and then returning to postfeminist convention. Following Berlant, I characterize this dynamic as indicative of postfeminist impasse, produced by the disparity between the aspirational promise of personal and professional fulfilment and its disappointing lived reality. *Gone Girl*'s intertextual underpinnings drawn from crime, gothic and horror genres enable Flynn to exaggerate and amplify the ways that traditional femininity is concealed by the Cool Girl persona, which itself is revealed as inauthentic (Marston 2018). *Girls*, however, produces this impasse as a continual loop of aspiration, frustration and recurrence. It is at the points of aspiration and compliance with convention that the series' protagonist is envisaged at her most socially acceptable (both in the narrative world and in critical reception of the series), that is, the points at which her successful coming of age might finally be achieved. However, *Girls* veers between socially acceptable and socially undesirable forms of subjectivity in a way that emphasizes the dynamic of cruel optimism while highlighting social inclusion as the main reason why we might aspire towards convention in the first place.

Where Chapter 2 explores the difficulty in cutting loose from harmful genres, Chapter 3 complicates the analysis of cruel optimism. Although superficially similar to *Girls*, which proves almost pathological in its efforts to work through women's relationships to postfeminist ways of living, I argue that *Appropriate Behaviour* (Akhavan 2014) is not preoccupied by the same concerns and cannot be so straightforwardly linked to a genre like postfeminism or a relation of cruel optimism. This poses the question of why exactly postfeminist empowerment discourse is so troubling for some female subjects, while others in equivalent circumstances appear relatively unscathed. Therefore, while the primary focus is *Appropriate Behaviour*, this chapter also considers the degree to which postfeminist empowerment discourse extends to the female-led series *Broad City* (Glazer and Jacobson 2014–19) and *Fleabag* (Waller-Bridge 2016–19).

Where the first three chapters investigate the failure of postfeminist empowerment discourse to produce the kinds of happiness and fulfilment it promised, Part 2 explores various ways that the postfeminist legacy of agency and empowerment manifests in contemporary girlhood coming-of-age genres. Chapter 4's principal argument is that resilience has become a key feature of contemporary femininity. Drawing on and extending James's (2015) work, I explore the intersections between femininity and contemporary resilience discourse, examining the narrative structure of resilience and the creation of narrative space in which feminine subjectivity is produced through overcoming profound trauma. I examine the young adult film adaptation *The Hate U Give* (Tillman Jr 2018)[10] to highlight and question the Whiteness[11] of the resilience produced by *The Hunger Games*. Both works are structurally dependent on a trajectory of continually intensified trauma and heightened states of emotion, however; while *The Hate U Give* centres the formation of Black female subjectivity, *The Hunger Games* produces the resilience and narrative agency of its White protagonist at the expense of Black femininity.

Building on the framework established in Chapter 4, the fifth chapter identifies two further modes of resilience – transformative and relational – through analysis of *Bande de Filles/Girlhood* (Sciamma 2014), a film structured around self-reinvention that offers temporary access to different ways of living and forms of social inclusion. Transformative resilience is produced in the service of dominant hierarchies of power, such as patriarchy, whereas relational resilience affirms girlhood social bonds. Relational resilience is characterized by our connections with others, manifesting in circumstances in which we derive the capacity to overcome (or at the very least withstand) trauma through our relational ties. By contrast, transformative resilience is defined as a capacity for change that enables one to overcome adversity in socially valuable ways. Transformation is a concept central to the postfeminist paradigm in both its empowerment and resilience modes, and a key convention within coming-of-age narratives, often imagined as the means to emancipation or the foundation of identity formation. This chapter provides important insight into the complex ways resilience discourse operates culturally. At first, transformative and relational resilience appear pitted against one another, with the former seemingly complicit with postfeminist conventions of self-improvement and flexibility and the latter a liberatory framework constitutive of girls' social ties. Yet the two modes are in fact thoroughly imbricated, suggesting that we must move beyond a model of critique based in uncovering the symptoms of either emancipatory politics or complicity with dominant social hierarchies.

Having established the contours of contemporary feminine resilience discourse and explored examples of its aesthetic modes within popular literature and art house cinema, Chapter 6 develops these concepts in further depth and circles back to revisit the first chapter's feel-bad paradigm. Using Lübecker's (2015) work, I establish the concept of feel-bad femininity to analyse how the film *Catch Me Daddy* (Wolfe 2014) produces desires for resilient agency and then blocks their satisfaction through the denial of narrative closure. James explains how the resilience model encourages us to *use* our negative feelings to generate surplus value that benefits neoliberalized systems of power and that we must do so especially in relation to traditional gender conventions. Meanwhile, Lübecker explains how the feel-bad film produces negative emotion and refuses to generate a positive or cathartic outcome. This chapter also draws on the mythic quest narrative analysed by Teresa de Lauretis (1984), linking it to the coming-of-age-narrative, both of which are organized around overcoming obstacles and adversity in a way that resonates with the structure of resilience discourse. If feminine social viability is, as this book argues, predicated on overcoming perceived gender deficits, the obstacle that must be defeated within resilience narratives is therefore conventionalized femininity itself. Chapter 6 also raises questions about the stakes of social viability. Through analysis of how *Catch Me Daddy* accrues an excess of traditionally feminine affect that threatens the fantasy of a coherent and self-determining subjectivity, I explore the assumption within the so-called anti-relational strand of queer theory (Bersani 1995; Edelman 2004) that any challenge to such a fantasy is of indisputable value. I argue that feel-bad genres provide opportunities to question the complexity of our fantasies surrounding the embodiment of agency and resilience, opening up forms of refusal to participate in social and cultural norms and expectation, while at the same time interrogating the subjective risks in doing so.

To conclude this introductory chapter, I want to briefly comment on the link between the empowerment mode of postfeminist social viability and the contemporary resilience model. *Gone Girl* and *Catch Me Daddy* may not initially appear to have much in common with regard to either genre or narrative; however, they are united in the way they navigate a loss of social inclusion: *Gone Girl* in response to postfeminist empowerment discourse and *Catch Me Daddy* in response to postfeminist resilience discourse. As I later discuss, within a resilience paradigm, the primary route to become a socially acceptable feminine subject is to overcome perceived gender deficits and capitalize on them. By contrast, *Gone Girl* demonstrates how postfeminist empowerment discourse encourages women to conceal their enactment of traditional femininity by performing it as socially desirable agency.

As Meredith Nash and Ruby Grant observe, 'Postfeminism is positioned as part of a contemporary neoliberal refashioning of femininity in which women escape traditional boundaries of femininity through a continual reworking of subjectivity as subjects and objects of commodification and consumerism' (2015: 981). Both the empowerment and resilience modes of postfeminism are therefore predicated on overcoming femininity through processes of transformation. Whereas postfeminist empowerment genres are typically concerned with transformation as private and concealed, newly conventionalized genres of resilience are interested in exposing the transformation process. In both cases, the transformation and the reworking are key to 'escaping' traditional femininity and thus aligning with and adhering to dominant social norms. My aim is to explore methods of relating to and navigating the ways in which women and girls are culturally encouraged to produce them/ourselves as feminine subjects. Tracing the cultural shift whereby postfeminist ideas and ways of living first begin to register as feel-bad, before they then become entrenched as resilience discourse within our imagination of girlhood, each chapter maps complex, contradictory and incomplete ways of being in our contemporary world.

Part One

Impasse

1

Feel-bad postfeminism in *Gone Girl*

There have always been efforts to contradict, oppose and undermine the relative cultural dominance of postfeminist femininity. Gillian Flynn's crime thriller *Gone Girl* is especially notable because it introduces a mainstream audience to the idea that postfeminist norms and ideals might be potentially damaging to women's sense of self and subjectivity. Here, I examine how the novel dismantles two defining features of postfeminist culture – an insistence on limitless choice and the capacity for self-transformation – and exposes these ideas as perniciously harmful illusions. Gill observes that 'the notion that all our practices are freely chosen is central to postfeminist discourses which present women as autonomous agents no longer constrained by any inequalities' (2007: 153). In this vein, postfeminist culture offers a catalogue of what Gill and Christina Scharff call 'new femininities' (2011: 8) for women to adopt. *Gone Girl* articulates these femininities through its 'types' of girl, with its protagonist, Amy, reeling off an inventory of endlessly recyclable identities available to perform and discard at will: 'Amazing Amy. Preppy '80s Girl. Ultimate-Frisbee Granola and Blushing Ingenue and Witty Hepburnian Sophisticate. Brainy Ironic Girl and Boho Babe (the latest version of Frisbee Granola)' (Flynn 2012: 266). We can therefore situate the novel within a cultural period in which narratives and images of girls have become 'hypervisible' (Gonick et al. 2009: 1; Handyside and Taylor-Jones 2016: 1). According to Amy Shields Dobson, this postfeminist cultural period tends to 'construct and address girls and young women as strong, confident, capable, and fun-loving subjects in contrast to earlier models of weak femininity' (2015: 29). Later in this chapter I will discuss the central 'Cool Girl' figure, who embodies precisely these highly desirable attributes and, as such, is the primary identity through which the protagonist achieves her social status.

The figure of the girl has special resonance within postfeminist culture. As Sarah Projansky puts it:

> Girlness – particularly adolescent girlness – epitomises postfeminism. If the postfeminist woman is always in process, always using the freedom and equality handed to her by feminism in pursuit of having it all (including discovering her sexuality) but never quite managing to attain full adulthood, to fully have it all, one can say that the postfeminist woman is quintessentially adolescent … no matter what her age. (2007: 45)

A 'quintessentially adolescent' postfeminist womanhood is neatly captured by *Gone Girl*'s 38-year-old female protagonist who, despite having long reached the age of majority, must enact various types of girlness to attain viability as a feminine subject. What drives Amy's characterization throughout the novel is the unbounded belief in the power of self-transformation – the ability to rewrite one's own story, thus changing one's generic outcomes in the process. *Gone Girl* explores the destructive impact of the postfeminist mode of address. The novel therefore provides an entryway to the impasse of postfeminism, as well as playing a key role in a significant cultural turn wherein postfeminism begins to be imagined as a feel-bad genre that does not produce the satisfaction it promises.

While such a turn cannot be dated precisely, it occurs in rough alignment with the 2008 financial crisis and subsequent global economic downturn. As Tasker and Negra note, postfeminism 'reads differently now that the economic bubble has burst' (2014: 6–7). Indeed, the postfeminist aspiration to 'have it all' feels especially unattainable (though evidently no less desirable) during a post-recession era characterized by precarity and insecurity. A slew of films such as *Girl Most Likely* (Springer Berman and Pulcini 2012), *Bridesmaids* (Feig 2011), *Bachelorette* (Headland 2012), *Young Adult* (Reitman 2011) and

Trainwreck (Apatow 2015) began to find that despite their investments in postfeminist promises of fulfilment, the protagonists found themselves mired in an unhealthy – even toxic – relationship with postfeminist aspiration. *Bachelorette* makes an interesting intertextual reference point for *Gone Girl*. Whereas *Gone Girl* explores the destructiveness of postfeminist femininities through a single protagonist, *Bachelorette* does so through distinctive 'types' as embodied by the film's four thirty-something protagonists, all of whom have been profoundly damaged by their deeply internalized investment in postfeminist culture. Regan's character sums up the shattered postfeminist promise thusly: 'You know what I keep thinking? I did everything right. I went to college. I exercise. I eat like a normal person. I've got a boyfriend in med school. And nothing is happening to me' (2012). Despite following the 'rules' and getting a good degree from a good school, finding herself a good boyfriend and a good job, Regan isn't just unhappy with her life – she's stuck. The film stresses the gap between ambition and reality, and how ill-equipped otherwise privileged young women are to adjust to lowered social and professional expectations. McRobbie (2008) argues that postfeminism promises elevated status and upward mobility in exchange for meeting the punishing demands of heteronormative femininity. Regan is the very embodiment of the postfeminist aspiration of having it all; she has regimented her mind, body and life trajectory, yet in the end, everything she has amounts to little of substance.

Capturing the mood of a post-2008 generation,[1] *Gone Girl* is primarily concerned with the effects of the recession on the privileged, White middle classes. Flynn's dual protagonists, Nick and Amy, are formerly successful writers in New York 'cut loose' (2012: 5) from their careers, their job losses wrought by the declining economy and advent of internet media. Driven to surrender their wealthy upper-middle-class lifestyle, the couple relocate to Nick's midwestern hometown. Envisioned as 'a miniature ghost town of bank-owned, recession-busted, price-reduced mansions, a neighbourhood that closed before it ever opened' (2012: 4), the Missouri setting evokes the omnipresence of loss, debt and dispossession structuring the contemporary American psyche. Likewise, while it is the driving force of *Gone Girl*'s narrative, the desire to maintain social viability within a postfeminist paradigm proves devastating to its protagonist. The novel acknowledges the feel-good power of the postfeminist 'promise of happiness' (Ahmed 2010), while ultimately formulating postfeminist ways of living as incapable of producing happy or fulfilled female subjects. Kendra Marston similarly reads *Gone Girl* as a novel about dissatisfaction with the postfeminist promise of fulfilment, though her interest lies in analysing melancholic White femininity, making the argument that *Gone Girl*, along with films like *Blue Jasmine* (Allen 2013) and *The Virgin Suicides* (Coppola 1999), deploys melancholia 'as a tool through which to distance female protagonists from white patriarchal power structures' and therefore 'position the heroines' race privilege and affluence as disabling sicknesses of the contemporary political and cultural moment' (2018: 4). Postfeminist self-fulfilment remains aspirational in *Gone Girl* but is demonstrably unattainable without incurring great personal cost. In a post-recession landscape, the price of postfeminism has finally begun to register within mainstream media culture. My primary aim, therefore, is to examine the notion that postfeminist empowerment discourse is no longer fully legible as a feel-good genre and detail the ways in which it has begun to collapse from within.

Gone Girl distinguishes itself from the typically homogenous psychological thriller through its formulation and critique of a culturally celebrated style of femininity: the figure of the Cool Girl (Petersen 2014). The Cool Girl is the primary method by which the novel presents postfeminist tropes and ways of living within a feel-bad mode of address. Opening on the morning of their fifth anniversary, present-day scenes told from Nick's perspective as he realizes his wife his missing are alternated with Amy's diary entries dating back to their first meeting seven years earlier. The first half of the novel uses these alternating perspectives to paint a contradictory picture of their marriage: whereas Amy's diary suggests Nick is lazy, aggressive and potentially violent, Nick's narration portrays Amy as irrationally perfectionist, obsessive and highly strung. The second half of the novel further unravels the conflicting narrative perspectives by revealing that Amy is alive, in hiding and, having successfully faked her death, is now working to frame Nick for her murder. The diary chapters, which create a seamless version of postfeminist femininity, are shown to be entirely fabricated to incriminate Nick. Through the much-quoted Cool Girl monologue, the novel exposes this fun-loving and easy-going type of girlhood as an artificial construction:

> Men always say that as the defining compliment, don't they? She's a cool girl. Being the Cool Girl means I am a hot, brilliant, funny woman who adores football, poker, dirty jokes, and burping, who plays video games, drinks cheap beer, loves threesomes and anal sex, and jams hot dogs and hamburgers into her mouth like she's hosting the world's biggest culinary gang bang while somehow maintaining a size 2, because Cool Girls are above all hot. Hot and understanding. Cool Girls never get angry; they only smile in a chagrined, loving manner and let their men do whatever they want. Go ahead, shit on me, I don't mind, I'm the Cool Girl. (2012: 250–1)[2]

Just as Amy assures Nick that she is a 'cool girl' (2012: 250), the diary entries work to deceive both the reader and the fictional police detectives that Amy is simply a loving wife trapped in a failing marriage and afraid for her life. The fundamental artifice at the core of postfeminist femininity is deeply woven into both narrative content and structure.

Reiterative and defiant agency

Postfeminist empowerment genres are those in which compliance with postfeminist norms and ways of living (such as those outlined by Gill) ultimately leads to happiness and fulfilment. This sense of fulfilment is often achieved by linking narrative closure to traditionally postfeminist objects of desire like heterosexual romance, marriage and motherhood. As Ahmed explains, 'Happiness functions as a promise that directs you toward certain objects, as if they provide you with the necessary ingredient for the good life' (2010: 54). Monogamy, marriage, family and gender compliance are prime examples of socially privileged ways of living, with happiness promised to those who align themselves with these normative institutions (Ahmed 2010). For example, the final episode of television series *Sex and the City* delivers closure through the reconciliation between protagonist Carrie Bradshaw and her emotionally unavailable love interest 'Mr Big'. This is especially notable because, as Emily Nussbaum notes in her *New Yorker* article, in most of the series 'Big wasn't there to rescue Carrie; instead, his "great love" was a slow poisoning' and their relationship provoked 'as much anxiety as relief' (2013). *Sex and the City* had therefore successfully demonstrated that the affections of a prototypical leading man are not only unsatisfying for women but also actively harmful. In light of this, the final episode feels regressive, a turning back to romantic comedy tropes the series had previously sought to undermine, or at the very least interrogate. By producing traditional romance as the primary object through which narrative closure is achieved, the series assures its audience that dominant gender norms remain intact. Moreover, despite its compounding and contravening of the romantic comedy genre, *Sex and the City* ultimately produces postfeminist ways of living as capable of delivering satisfaction for feminine subjects.

In blunt contrast, *Gone Girl* reminds us that postfeminist scripts of romance and marriage might very well produce a subject in alignment with societal norms, yet they also prove overwhelmingly incapable of producing this subject as happy or fulfilled. Whereas the goals of social viability and happiness were seamlessly united in postfeminist empowerment texts, *Gone Girl* marks a fundamental separation between the two. Ahmed argues that gendered 'happiness scripts' provide 'a set of instructions for what women and men must do in order to be happy' (59). The concept of gendered happiness scripts is particularly apt in relation to the novel, as one of its chief preoccupations is with social roles, scripts and performances. Flynn's dual protagonists are painfully aware of social and generic convention, and both feel subsequently worn down by the cultural expectations they have absorbed. With postfeminist femininity as its chief focus, the novel is alert to the significance of narrative genres to the formation of subjectivity, as well as recognizing the freedom afforded to those with the capacity to shape their own narratives.

Gone Girl's anxieties regarding endlessly reiterative social conventions resonate with Judith Butler's formulation of agency, which is predicated on the repetition and subversion of established norms. In *Bodies That Matter: On the Discursive Limits of 'Sex'* (1993), Butler describes performativity as 'that reiterative power of discourse to produce the phenomena that it regulates and constrains' ([1993] 2011: xii). What this means in terms of gender, for example, is that 'feminine' is not a fixed definitive category but rather something that is actively being (re)produced through repetition. Butler's central claim is that ' "agency," then, is to be located within the possibility of a variation on that repetition' ([1990] 2010: 198). In other words, we repeat, but with a difference, and thereby gradually alter the norms of signification. For Butler, there is no agency to be found 'outside' or beyond culturally constructed identities ([1990] 2010). Accordingly, the 'critical task for feminism is ... to locate strategies of subversive repetition enabled by those constructions' (Butler [1990] 2010: 201). Mari Ruti has recently taken issue with Butler's model, deploring that it 'remains remarkably respectful of hegemonic power' and therefore limits our full potential and capacity for agency (2017: 40). As Ruti explains, for Butler 'everything, including resistance, must be done *in relation to* power rather than direct opposition to it' (40, original italics). Ruti's argument draws out the distinction between a complicit negotiation with power and our capacity to categorically oppose it.

Ruti is deeply critical of Butler's assertion that the only way to create 'new social possibilities' is 'through a collaborative relation with power' (Butler, Laclau and Žižek 2000: 4). Of course, Ruti is not the first to point out that 'every attempt to subvert norms presupposes the very norms it seeks to undermine' (2017: 41). Accordingly, 'every reiteration of femininity on some level falls back on stereotypical notions of femininity' (2017: 41).³ Nonetheless, for Ruti this presupposition 'is why the Butlerian performative subject is caught up in an endless loop of collaborating with power' (2017: 41). Rather than dismiss Butler's model entirely, Ruti acknowledges that performativity 'can be a genuinely rebellious practice' and might well be 'all we are capable of' (2017: 41). However, she offers another reading of Butler by comparing performativity to a 'related ideal of queer mobility' (2017: 41), stressing that both hew a little too closely to the norms of consumer capitalism and the neoliberal imperative towards self-reinvention. This, Ruti goes on to argue, is one of the reasons why contemporary queer theory has taken an increasing interest in 'acts of defiance that undermine the entire worldview that hegemonic power – now often explicitly named as neoliberal capitalism – represents' (2017: 42).

To establish a model of defiant agency, then, Ruti turns to Lacan and Žižek. Ruti's stance on 'the radical potential of Lacanian ethics' (2017: 8) is set in motion as she generates a fruitful dialogue between Lacan and Butler. Ruti makes a convincing case for the need of a defiant queer subject whose agency is forged in the act of risking her social viability by saying 'No!' (Žižek 2005: 140)⁴ to hegemonic expectations.⁵ Key to this formulation of agency is the idea that we can free ourselves (never entirely, but perhaps enough) from hegemonic capitalism if we can learn to separate its desires from our own. A model of defiant agency articulates the ways that ideological interpellation will always fail to entirely capture us. As Butler notes in *Gender Trouble*, 'The injunction to be a given gender produces necessary failures, a variety of incoherent configurations that in their multiplicity exceed and defy the injunction by which they are generated' ([1990] 2010: 199). In other words, although normative ideology is powerfully reiterated and thus reinforced, there will always remain instances of collapse that might at least potentially enable defiance.

Butler's argument about the repetition and subversion of norms remains convincing and the most realistic option for most subjects. However, Ruti rightly argues that this is not enough, and that those points at which dominant ideologies fail to fully capture us are significant as they offer us an important opportunity to defy what is socially expected of us. Ruti's frustration with the performative model, this 'too humble' relation to power, asks us to truly consider the question 'Is that all there is?' when it comes to our alleged entrapment within normative ideology. The concept of defiant agency therefore presents a compelling alternative that operates in complementation rather than substitution of the performative model.

Both models of agency play an important role in *Gone Girl*'s examination of postfeminist normativity. There is sense within the novel that generic conventions, rather than providing a set of useful guidelines, have instead exhausted their potential, as 'we know the words to say' in any given situation and 'are all working from the same dog-eared script' (Flynn 2012: 81). These lines speak a weariness with repetition – of feeling trapped by an understanding of the world in which all subjectivities, scripts and roles are readily available, and all we are capable of is deviating within pre-existing norms and boundaries. While *Gone Girl* is clearly disillusioned with reiterative agency, it also highlights the difficulties of enacting agency through a defiance of social norms. Expressed most clearly through the Cool Girl monologue, there is an evident desire to refuse postfeminist convention – yet at the same time, *Gone Girl* articulates the near-impossibility of truly doing so.

The novel stages several key moments in which Amy attempts to say 'No!', all of which are presented as ultimately in alignment with postfeminist convention. According to Ruti's model, any act of defiance that relies upon adhering to social expectation will eventually fail. This is precisely what happens: Amy is searching for a decisive act of defiance – against Nick and against the hegemonic postfeminist norms she has conformed to her entire life. Yet the allure of social inclusion and alignment proves too powerful to resist. While Amy's character risks her life, her marriage and her autonomy, she never truly risks her social viability in the way Ruti demands. This is important to bear in mind, as the novel is both speaking to disillusionment with a Butlerian model of subjectivity and at the same time sounding a warning about the dangers of pursuing social viability at the expense of one's own desires. Indeed, *Gone Girl*'s protagonist is presented as almost entirely incapable of conceiving her own desires beyond socially acceptable feminine norms.

In *Gone Girl*, the act of concealing one's 'inner directive' (Ruti 2017: 45) and choosing to follow normative paths has a profoundly damaging impact on subjectivity. There are crucial points at which the novel seems to acknowledge other paths that Amy might take; however, for a subject caught up entirely in a quest for social viability, such alternatives are not an option. The novel is not, therefore, simply a quest for happiness, fulfilment or even social belonging; rather, I read *Gone Girl* as a novel about maintaining feminine social viability in a postfeminist culture.

Cool Girl postfeminism

The tropes and fantasies formulated by postfeminist empowerment genres crystallize in the figure of the Cool Girl, who is 'cool' (or socially viable) because she retains elements of traditional feminine passivity whilst being careful to conceal them – for example, by anticipating others' desires in advance and presenting them as her own. Performing and concealing traditional femininity is one of the primary demands postfeminist empowerment discourse places on women. For a contemporary female subject, the outward appearance of traditionally feminine attributes such as passivity or fragility is wholly undesirable. Similarly, *Gone Girl* recognizes overt preoccupation with marriage and conventional beauty standards (exemplified also by *Bridget Jones' Diary*) as something women must disavow. By contrast, the Cool Girl articulates a form of socially desirable femininity. Amy's now-infamous Cool Girl diatribe (already quoted previously) immediately follows the revelation that Amy has faked her death (and framed Nick for murder) and is presented (both by the character and to some extent the narrative) as justification for her actions:

Men always say that as the defining compliment, don't they? She's a cool girl. Being the Cool Girl means I am a hot, brilliant, funny woman who adores football, poker, dirty jokes, and burping, who plays video games, drinks cheap beer, loves threesomes and anal sex, and jams hot dogs and hamburgers into her mouth like she's hosting the world's biggest culinary gang bang while somehow maintaining a size 2: because Cool Girls are above all hot. Hot and understanding. Cool Girls never get angry; they only smile in a chagrined, loving manner and let their men do whatever they want. Go ahead, shit on me, I don't mind, I'm the Cool Girl. (2012: 250-1)

This passage outlines the requirements for women to be deemed socially desirable subjects. Writing about the distinctive features of contemporary postfeminist culture, Gill – drawing on the work on Jean Kilbourne (1999) – notes that 'being "confident", "carefree" and "unconcerned about one's appearance" are now central aspects of femininity in their own right – even as they sit alongside injunctions to meet standards of physical beauty that "only a mannequin could achieve"' (2008: 441). Gill's definition of postfeminist femininity resonates with the Cool Girl, who must conform to conventionalized beauty norms, while appearing indifferent to her weight, and enjoy being 'one of the guys' rather than share her messy, feminine feelings. Cool Girl updates the Bridget Jones style of femininity: whereas Bridget is overtly fashioned as what McRobbie terms a 'self-monitoring subject' (2008: 20) who diarizes her obsession with weight loss and finding the right man, Cool Girl must aspire to these same goals, albeit in secret. The transformation of passivity into agency and enjoyment is key to this iteration of postfeminist femininity. If Cool Girl were simply to acquiesce to her boyfriend's wishes, it would render her too passive, too traditionally feminine. Instead, Cool Girl must work to anticipate her male partner's desires, and in doing so, present her love of video games, threesomes and hamburgers as entirely authentic, that is, as her own choice and agency. Unfortunately, the Cool Girl monologue is easy to read as an indictment of women who simply enjoy stereotypically masculine activities like playing football or drinking beer, as some critics have done (Moss 2014: n.p.). However, the narrative makes it clear that the 'problem' with the Cool Girl is that 'they're not even pretending to be the woman they want to be, they're pretending to be the woman a man wants them to be' (2012: 251). Masculinist norms continue to set the terms of socially acceptable femininity to which women must adapt, all the while concealing the performative inauthenticity and artifice of their conformity.

Echoing the familiar neoliberal assumption that anyone not thriving under its regime simply isn't trying hard enough, *Gone Girl* emphasizes how all-encompassing the norms of Cool Girl femininity are: 'Every girl was supposed to be this girl, and if you weren't, then there was something wrong with *you*' (252, original italics). By stressing that 'there are variations to the window dressing' – for example, a Cool Girl who 'loves seitan and is great with dogs' (251) to attract her vegetarian boyfriend – the novel demonstrates that it is the performative nature of the persona that is truly important. Specificities are negligible; what matters is that Cool Girl is classified as someone who 'likes every fucking thing he likes and doesn't ever complain' (251). The uncomplaining Cool Girl has some ties to what Caitlin Yuneun Lewis identifies as an 'idealized classic white femininity', defined by 'emotional restraint, demureness, and ethereality' (2011: 191). However, she also diverges in some significant ways. Classic White femininity resonates with the trope of the 'cool blonde' (Mulvey 2006: 97), characterized by her aloof and withholding nature in films like *The Birds* (Hitchcock 1963) and *Marnie* (Hitchcock 1964). According to Molly Haskell, Hitchcock's blondes are not punished for their bad behaviour but instead because they withhold 'love, sex, trust' from the male characters (1974: 349). As Haskell writes, 'The plot itself becomes a mechanism for destroying their icy self-possession, their emotional detachment' (349). By subjecting the icy blonde to 'excruciating ordeals, long trips through terror in which they may be raped, violated by birds, killed', the narrative is structured to punish attractive yet unavailable women. In contrast to the icy blonde, the brunette character in Hitchcock's films is 'down to earth, unaffected, adoring, willing to swallow her pride', although her flaws include a tendency 'to be possessive and … too available' (349). It is especially significant here that Lewis identifies emotional restraint as an idealized feminine quality, while Haskell notes that Hitchcock's 'good' women are characterized by their accessibility to the male protagonist. The tension and contradiction between restraint and accessibility is vital to Cool Girl femininity, which prizes restraint when it comes to women's own desires, yet at the same time encourages women to be emotionally available in accommodating male desire. Cool Girl therefore updates classic White femininity by embodying the contradiction: she is conventionally attractive and emotionally restrained, down to earth and accommodating, without ever crossing the line into possessive behaviour that would make her undesirable to men.

Another way of thinking about Cool Girl is in relation to Ahmed's figure of the 'feminist killjoy' (2010: 50–87). According to Ahmed, those figures who do not easily fit into normative institutions that promise happiness become 'affect aliens' (42), including the 'melancholic migrant' (121–59) who refuses the fantasy of a post-racial society or the feminist killjoy who continues to raise the subject of institutionalized sexism. Because they cannot or will not find happiness in the 'right' places, Ahmed's affect aliens are by definition socially undesirable subjects. As Ahmed argues, 'Feminists might kill joy simply by not finding the objects that promise happiness to be quite so promising … they disturb the very fantasy that happiness can be found in certain places' (2010: 65–6). Comparing the feminist killjoy to the Cool Girl allows us to see more clearly the ways in which performing Cool Girl femininity sustains that same good life fantasy. We can even trace Cool Girl's ancestry through Betty Friedan's figure of the happy American housewife in *The Feminine Mystique* (1963).[6] Ahmed situates the feminist killjoy in relation to the fantasy of the happy housewife, the socially desirable figure of the 1950s and 1960s for (some) women to embody and measure themselves against.[7] This particular fantasy is founded upon concealing 'the signs of domestic labor under the sign of happiness' (2010: 50). Whereas the feminist killjoy exposes the unhappiness of dominant social scripts and objects, the happy housewife upholds them with 'a beaming smile' (2010: 50). Postfeminist empowerment discourse is similarly predicated upon the concealment of traditional femininity to preserve its harmful fantasy.[8] Because she conceals the labour of traditional femininity with a performance of agency and empowerment, the Cool Girl therefore operates quite ironically as an update to the happy housewife.

The imperative to perform yet conceal traditional femininity brings us back to the relationship between agency, desire and social expectation. Ruti explains that Lacan sets the inner directive of desire against 'the morality of power, of the service of goods' (Lacan 1959–60: 315 in Ruti 2017: 45), describing a clash between what is socially expected of us and our own aspirations. Lacan goes on to say that hegemonic expectation dictates that 'as far as desires are concerned, come back later. Make them wait' (1959–60: 315). We can now see how this translates to the postfeminist paradigm, which asks women not just to put their desires on hold but also to indefinitely mask the very existence of such desires. Immediately following the Cool Girl monologue, *Gone Girl* suggests perhaps some women would not be opposed to holding their desire, if only the gesture were to be acknowledged and returned in kind:

> I waited patiently – *years* – for the pendulum to swing the other way, for men to start reading Jane Austen, learn how to knit, pretend to love cosmos, organise scrapbook parties, and make out with each other while we leer and then we'd say, *Yeah, he's a Cool Guy*. (2012: 251, original italics)

Amy's narration implies that there is a willingness to perform to a certain degree; however, there is an expectation of reciprocity that goes unfulfilled. Significantly, by the end of the novel, at the same time as highlighting the damaging effects of self-transformation and concealment on female subjectivity, *Gone Girl* also acknowledges similar effects on masculine subjectivity. Nick is characterized as newly terrified of his wife, 'the fun, beautiful murderess' (2012: 452):

> Me, Nick Dunne, the man who used to forget so many details, is now the guy who replays conversations to make sure I didn't offend,

to make sure I never hurt her feelings … I am a great husband because I am very afraid she may kill me. (2012: 452)

This suggests that although the roles have, to a degree, switched – now Nick is the one who must convincingly conceal his desires – the territory itself remains bleakly unchanged (de Lauretis 1984). Moreover, the switch only further emphasizes the lack of reciprocity. After all, Amy must take drastic measures to enforce Nick's compliance with the perfect husband role, and even then, Nick has no qualms about exposing the illusion of his devotion and the artifice of their happy family. Narrated from Amy's perspective, the final scene shows that while she and Nick are following their predetermined scripts, Nick deviates from what he is 'supposed to say' (2012: 463), informing Amy that his ostensive devotion is derived from pity, 'because every morning you have to wake up and be you' (2012: 463). Finally, it must also be noted that Nick's partial performance is motivated by saving his own life and protecting their future child; crucially, his viability as a masculine subject is not at stake.

Aspirational postfeminist fantasies of marriage and motherhood are produced as affectively feel-bad for both characters (as accentuated by Amy's response to Nick: 'I really, truly wish he hadn't said that. I keep thinking about it. I can't stop') (2012: 463). Cool Girl femininity is a trap, one which leads to an unhappy marriage and a child who bears the signifiers of deception and despair rather than domestic happiness and futurity. By undermining postfeminist expectations of domestic fulfilment, the novel emphasizes the negative and undesirable feelings generated by postfeminist empowerment. In short, Cool Girl femininity produces feelings of discontent that work to expose the fraudulence of the postfeminist promise.

The dead girl's suicidal viability

An enduring cultural figure across both fictional and lived genres, the dead girl embodies a complex relationship between femininity, perfection, agency and social viability. *Gone Girl* invokes the dead girl trope as a dark mirror of the Cool Girl persona and the damage it inflicts on women's subjectivity. The novel first introduces the dead girl as a method Amy intends to use to 'destroy Nick' by engineering 'a story that would restore my perfection. It would make me the hero, flawless and adored. Because everyone loves the Dead Girl' (2012: 263). Despite the fatal conclusion of her narrative arc, the conventions of the dead girl's story are considered preferable to those of the 'Dumb Average Woman' (2012: 263) with a cheating husband – a persona Amy is desperate to avoid. Once again, social status is what's at stake: Amy is interested in destroying Nick's at the same time as regaining her own. Identifying that the most effective way to achieve both ends is through Amy's (carefully staged) death, *Gone Girl* demonstrates that the pursuit of postfeminist happiness scripts does not lead to self-fulfilment as promised but rather to a position in which suicide is considered the best option for retaining maximum social viability. The novel therefore presents a paradox in which opting out of the social world through self-annihilation becomes, in effect, a method of increasing one's viability as a social subject.[9]

Amy's narration explains how, in her quest to maintain her viability as a feminine subject, she performs socially acceptable White upper-class femininity by taking part in masculinized activities, cultivating an accommodating persona and epitomizing what Gill calls 'the sexually autonomous heterosexual young woman who plays with her sexual power and is forever "up for it"' (2007: 151). The novel draws attention to an implicit social contract in which fulfilling the norms of postfeminist femininity provides the reward of a conventional (heterosexual) romantic relationship.

While the relationship itself is the object at stake, the fantasy behind the aspiration is one of achieving self-coherence as a subject within the dominant social order through alignment with heterosexual romantic norms. The novel turns on the violation of this contract, as Amy's character discovers that Nick's affair has forced her to adopt 'a new persona, not of my choosing' and subsequently refuses to play the part of 'Dumb Average Woman Married to Average Shitty Man' (2012: 263). Amy is characterized as acutely aware that if this story becomes attributed to her, she will join the ranks of 'women with the endless stories that make people nod sympathetically and think: *Poor dumb bitch*' (263, original italics). *Gone Girl* captures here the gendering of social viability and transgression. Nick's cheating is not a threat to his own social position; instead, his transgression reflects unfavourably on Amy, who as a result stands to lose her social status.

The dead girl trope encapsulates the relationship between the spectacle of public fascination and the ostensibly flawless beauty that only death can confer. Chronicling the disquieting union between femininity and death, Elisabeth Bronfen argues that 'the feminine corpse becomes a trope for that immaculate wholeness impossible in life' (1992: 129). For instance, Alice Bolin analyses television series *Twin Peaks* (Frost and Lynch 1990–1) as an exemplar of how death, beauty and perfection become entwined in the cultural imagination. The series' central mystery revolves around the murder of teenager Laura Palmer; as Bolin observes, 'Palmer's corpse is *Twin Peaks*' truly memorable image' (2014: n.p.). In his review of the series, Greil Marcus similarly describes the 'unforgettable' image of Palmer's 'lifeless face' as 'pristine, unmarked, untroubled, gray-blue from its hours in the river, with dots of water clinging to the skin like beads' (2006: n.p.). The indelible image of the beautiful dead girl plays a crucial role in Amy's revenge scheme. Marcus's romanticized language corresponds to the fantasy of Amy's 'slim, naked, pale body, floating just beneath the current, a colony of snails attached to one bare leg. My hair trailing like seaweed' (2012: 276). Flynn's vision of a beautiful drowned woman is reminiscent of the historical dead girls of Renaissance and Pre-Raphaelite art, such as John Everett Millais's influential painting *Ophelia* (*c.*1851–2),[10] and of a contemporary publishing trend featuring dead girls on the covers of young adult novels. The cover art for Alyxandra Harvey's novel *Haunting Violet* (2011), for example, demonstrates the continuing resonance of the dead girl as a figure of cultural fascination

Figure 1 Young adult novel *Haunting Violet* (Harvey 2011), featuring a beautiful dead girl as its cover image. *Haunting Violet* cover designed by Fernanda Brussi Goncalves © Bloomsbury Publishing Plc.

(Figure 1).[11] The endurance of romanticized dead girl imagery supports the novel's assertion that suicide offers Amy a more preferable narrative outcome in which an illusive memory of her deathly beauty and perfection survives.

While underscoring the dead girl as a continuing and fundamental signifier of feminine perfection, the novel is also in dialogue with media in which death affords women a measure of narrative agency. Katherine Farrimond (2017) analyses the figure of the dead femme fatale in retro noir films such as *Shutter Island* (Scorsese 2010) and *Mulholland Falls* (Tamahori 1996) 'where the dead woman becomes more dangerous from beyond the grave' (2017: 40).[12] Farrimond complicates the notion of the female corpse as a wholly passive object, noting that the dead femme fatale expresses a 'deadly threat to the male protagonist' (2017: 41). Flynn's dead girl is a similarly complex figure, retaining the associations with 'passivity and the loss of selfhood' (2017: 40) Farrimond identifies, yet is also envisaged as potentially capable of exerting influence after death, as one of Amy's key objectives is to frame Nick for her murder, thus condemning him to the death penalty. *Gone Girl* is therefore operating intertextually with stories in which women have more influence over the narrative in death than in life. However, as Bolin observes, 'the Dead Girl is not a "character" in the show, but rather, the memory of her is' (2014). The dead girl might indeed be a socially desirable figure, yet her narrative agency remains limited; in essence, she cannot lay claim to the personhood and interiority afforded to other characters, instead becoming a repository for their memories of her.

It is also worth briefly considering the extent to which the dead girl is imagined as a figure of escape, an immutable tactic to evade the pressures of conventional femininity. As Lewis identifies in her analysis of Sofia Coppola's films *The Virgin Suicides* (1999) and *Marie Antoinette* (2006), 'the traditional roles Coppola depicts (wife, mother, daughter, object of male lust) can be stultifying, suffocating, and perhaps only escapable through death' (2011: 190). In *Gone Girl*, the romantic figure of the dead girl is yet another fantasy of wholeness and coherence; she appears to offer a way out of the social order while simultaneously securing the social acceptance that remains out of reach to the living. The allure of the dead girl lies in her facility to opt out of the pressures to either conform to or rebel against social convention, while still managing to hold onto some semblance of agency and selfhood. Although the novel makes a convincing case for suicide as a vehicle for attaining social viability, this trope is quickly rejected. As Amy's narration complains: 'It's not fair that I have to die. Not really die. I don't want to. I'm not the one who did anything wrong' (2012: 314–15). Here, self-striking is ultimately a capitulation, rather than a Lacanian rejection of the status quo.

Genre flailing

By consistently associating postfeminist happiness scripts and tropes with emptiness, blankness and lack, *Gone Girl* unravels their aspirational influence and exposes the damage they cause to female subjectivity and the coming-of-age process. However, with nothing new, let alone redemptive or cathartic, assuming shape in the wake of the postfeminist genre's undoing, Amy's fate is to return to live among the remnants of postfeminism. After all, this is not a coming-of-age narrative in which identity formation is what's at stake; rather, it is a story about the aftermath of being produced as a feminine subject in the postfeminist framework. When a genre's ways of living are culturally imagined as the cause of frustration and disappointment, we can begin to comprehend it as a genre in crisis. The crisis of postfeminism manifests in its scripts, roles and categories, all of which overwhelmingly produce unhappy subjects. *Gone Girl* makes it unequivocally clear that Amy's performance of the Cool Girl persona only brings her unhappiness. Amy therefore finds herself in a predicament: the genre she believed would offer her a positive (i.e. a world- and self-defining) outcome has failed. As Berlant explains, such failure is inclined to result in a serious crisis of 'genre flailing':

> In a crisis we engage in genre flailing so that we don't fall through the cracks of knowledge and noise into suicide or psychosis. In a crisis we improvise like crazy, where 'like crazy' is a little too non-metaphorical. (2017: n.p.)

For obvious reasons, suicide and psychosis are undesirable outcomes. We therefore learn to extemporize, or 'flail', when trying to prevent these kinds of outcomes that begin to seem if not inevitable, then perhaps a little too plausible. *Gone Girl* posits these untenable options in the wake of Amy's postfeminist crisis through the dead girl, as well as the 'psycho bitch' (Flynn 2012: 441) figure,[13] neither of which offers a narratively or socially viable form of generic closure. Having said that, while Amy's character might understandably be unsatisfied with being written off as a psycho bitch, Marston points out that for the reader, generic pleasures are generated precisely through 'the representation of female melancholia as potentially harbouring the capacity for a violent psychological break' (2018: 119). As well as resonating with the feminine tropes *Gone Girl* mobilizes in response to the collapse of postfeminism, Berlant's observation also speaks to the novel's structure and its use of outlandish thriller conventions. For instance, the novel's structure veers wildly between unpicking crime genre conventions including the missing wife trope, the romantic comedy 'meet cute' and the femme fatale, to name a few. In doing so, *Gone Girl* grasps at various overlapping articulations of femininity, casting its net as widely as possible in its dissection of culturally resonant feminine subject positions.

Rather than spinning out into limitless subjectivities, Amy exhausts her options: by the end of the novel there is nobody left for her to become. The use of first-person narration offers readers a kind of access to Amy's interior world. Yet most of all, the novel is dominated by a sense of what or who Amy is not, rather than who she is or could be. Amy's characterization hinges on 'pretending to have a personality' (2012: 250), with lines like 'What persona feels good, what's coveted, what's *au courant*?' (250, original italics) articulating a self-transformative style of femininity that is dictated by normative social desirability. The novel informs us that a 'Real Amy' exists, 'and she was so much better, more interesting and complicated and challenging, than Cool Amy' (2012: 254). Yet this 'Real Amy' is nowhere to be found in the text itself, suggesting that while her character might possess some slim self-awareness that her own desires exist, her sense of self is overwhelmed by normative fantasies of who she should be.

There is a sense that the prescriptiveness of gender normativity is not the only problem; rather, the very processes of repetition and variation are what feel limited in scope. Amy's repetitions of social norms have led not to a subversion of those norms but to an exhaustion of her selfhood. Butler argues, quite rightly, that there is 'not a transcendental subject' and 'no self that is prior to the convergence or who maintains "integrity" prior to its entrance into this conflicted cultural field' ([1990] 2010: 199). The way the novel insists upon (yet does not manage to articulate) the existence of a 'Real Amy' directs us to this desire for a transcendental subject, a desire to locate a coherent sense of self beyond or somehow outside the postfeminist paradigm, its performances, tropes and scripts, not to mention the cultural weight they carry. The fact that this prior external self is a fantasy does not impede the search, nor extinguish the desire.

Genre flailing is especially legible in *Gone Girl*'s use of preposterous thriller conventions; for example, the revenge scheme relies on intensified violence and high-stakes manipulation that include Amy reporting two false rape accusations, framing her husband for murder, covertly inseminating herself to trap him in their marriage and slitting her ex-boyfriend's throat. These examples are a large part of why *Gone Girl* has been criticized for trading in misogyny. As many critics have argued, they read uncomfortably as a greatest hits compilation of pervasive misogynist myths about female behaviour (Hess 2014; Morris 2014; Saner 2014). Indeed, part of what contributes to the reading of Amy as a 'psycho bitch' (Flynn 2012: 441) is that she is characterized not only by her terrible deeds but also by the fact that these are terrible deeds that only women perpetrate. Amy's violence and manipulation are acutely feminized. She is not merely a villain; rather, she is a uniquely female villain. However, Amy's exploits are also examples of genre flailing, responding to her character's confinement in gender scripts as she attempts to leave the postfeminist Cool Girl behind and forge a new story for herself. To this end, the novel unfolds a series of potential escapes, each of which leads to another unforeseen trap. Initially escaping the parental pressure to be perfect, Amy is confined by the Cool Girl persona she eventually rejects. After framing her husband for murder, Amy rejects the escape route offered by the dead girl trope, retreating to a cabin in the woods where she is robbed and forced to seek refuge with an ex-boyfriend, Desi, whose offer of food and shelter comes at the price of Amy's material freedom.

Gone Girl draws a comparison between Nick and Desi: Nick wants an uncomplaining wife who will not challenge his irresponsible behaviour (following his redundancy) or his choices (to move to his hometown). By contrast, Desi wants something altogether more sinister, namely, to recreate the high-school version of Amy he once knew by encouraging her to change her appearance, controlling her weight and threatening to notify the police if she leaves his gated mansion. Here, the novel acknowledges that the postfeminist happiness trap, while damaging to Amy's psyche, is (marginally) preferable to being trapped by a man who practices 'control in the guise of caring' (390). There now remain two selves for Amy to choose between, both of which require a turning back rather than a moving forward: she can return to being Desi's old girlfriend again, or she can escape and return to the remnants of her marriage with Nick. If Desi represents a more tangible assertion of power and control, Nick stands for the altogether more slippery power and lure of normative ideology. The cycle of escape and confinement demonstrates the difficulty of rewriting one's own story according to generic conventions dictating social desirability. It also introduces freedom, in addition to social viability, as the driving force of the narrative, making it clear that Amy is not willing to settle for suicidal viability; she demands the freedom to live. However, it is telling that Amy's final options are represented by two male characters, and that her attempt to strike out on her own has failed – just as there is no Real Amy, there is also no real freedom to be found.

Instead of selfhood and subjectivity taking shape through the coming-of-age process, *Gone Girl* suggests that postfeminism is producing subjects characterized by their ability to conceal their 'true' selves (if such a thing exists). That Amy's character appears to be devoid of authenticity steers towards women's association with lack or blank subjectivity, a long-held idea in Western culture (Mulvey 1975). In her analysis of Sofia Coppola's filmmaking, Lewis links the concept of blankness to postfeminism, positing that 'lack is a defining feature of Coppola's female protagonists' (2011: 190). Lewis goes on to explain that this lack is derived from their construction as idealized White subjects in addition to 'the limits of their roles' (2011: 190) under postfeminism. Similarly, if contemporary women are 'blank' or 'lacking', *Gone Girl* advises, it is because postfeminism made them this way. Accordingly, I argue that the way *Gone Girl* formulates, recycles and discards all the different femininities, subject positions and personae offered by postfeminism points to an exhaustion of 'girl' as a category, a path towards subject-dissolution, rather than subject-formation. Postfeminism is therefore produced as a set of scripts, ideals and objects that are more likely to impede coming-of-age success than deliver it, thus emphasizing that the dominant frameworks through which women are socialized and encouraged to conform are producing profoundly unhappy subjects.[14]

The concept of genre flailing can help us to understand how the novel produces postfeminism as affectively feel-bad. The final chapters stage Amy's return to Nick as equivalent to a resumption of postfeminist ways of living as a safeguard against falling through the cracks of genre into socially undesirable territory. In the final scene, Nick and Amy appear reconciled as Amy explains that the following day is both her pregnancy due date and their anniversary, thus connecting motherhood and marriage as the two sustaining forces of their unhappy partnership. Here, *Gone Girl* resorts to the traditional signifiers of feminine narrative closure. However, these signifiers appear in a severely corrupted format as Amy returns to her cheating husband, uses his frozen sperm to inseminate herself and continues to 'pretend together that we are happy and carefree and in love' (2012: 457) as they await the birth of their child. Marriage and motherhood are not reproduced here as narratively satisfying outcomes; instead, they are refigured to produce not only dissatisfaction but also genuine horror. By seeing Amy off in her final vision as a wife and mother, Flynn produces a narrative in which a woman who strives to be socially desirable above all else can only turn back on herself. Even though the protagonist has come to realize the futility of her masquerade, the end of the novel finds her enacting yet another script: 'We are on the eve of becoming the world's best, brightest nuclear family' (462). Amy's transformations, her identity shifts, together with the extreme measures she has taken to destroy her marriage, have all led her back to the normative model that instigated her revenge schemes in the first place. The final scene thereby exposes the crisis of postfeminism, wherein its ways of living are produced not within the affective structure of the happily ever after but as part of a feel-bad formula. The inevitably feel-bad outcome of the female quest for social viability within a postfeminist paradigm suggests that the ideal of postfeminist perfection is not worth striving for. When our quest for social viability is undertaken at the expense of our own desires, *Gone Girl* advises, we are likely only to harm ourselves in the process. Consequently, there remains a continual friction between our desire to be socially viable subjects and our willingness, when necessary, to relinquish any protection afforded to us by our alignment with the social order.

2

Postfeminist impasse and cruel optimism in *Girls*

In this chapter, I argue that postfeminism operates as a relation of 'cruel optimism' (2011: 1), Berlant's term for the enduring bonds we form to objects, relationships, fantasies and ways of living that harm us. Analysing the television series *Girls* through the lens of cruel optimism reveals a shifting and contradictory dynamic that characterizes women's investments in postfeminist culture. Whereas the previous chapter examined *Gone Girl* as a somewhat hyperbolic response to the imperative to comply with postfeminist norms, here I look to *Girls* as an illustrative example of a more everyday context for exploring the same kinds of postfeminist fantasies centring on love, sex, work and friendship. Crucially, this chapter builds on the analysis of *Gone Girl*'s return to postfeminist convention by examining how *Girls* intensifies and protracts this same dynamic through its strategies of reiteration. While *Gone Girl* contravenes expectations that its protagonist's transgressions and transformations will result in narrative progression, through its episodic medium *Girls* explores the shape of a recursive impasse in which commitments and investments in normative ways of living are continually formed, renounced and revisited.

Following Berlant's methodology, I examine *Girls* as a project expressing a particular femininity born of a particular cultural moment. Specifically, I argue that *Girls* belongs to an emerging genre navigating the contradictions and complexities that coming of age in a primarily postfeminist media era entails. To illustrate this, I analyse three examples of how feminine subjectivity is primed and oriented towards ways of living marked by the generic conventions of postfeminism. I am especially interested in the series' interpretation of postfeminist tropes of work, marriage and romance. My primary example is the 'rom-com run' convention found typically in the romantic comedy genre, in which one member of the central couple makes a grand gesture by racing (usually to the airport or across New York City streets) to declare their love for their partner.[1] I read the series' restaging of the rom-com run trope as a form of investment in postfeminist culture that drives the narrative at the same time as inhibiting its progress. By analysing scenes that emphasize marriage as a method or signifier of self-transformation and narrative resolution, I examine how *Girls* produces postfeminism as an impasse characterized by the return to failed fantasies of fulfilment. Prior to this, I compare key scenes from *Girls* and the quintessential postfeminist series *Sex and the City*. In doing so, I demonstrate how the economic and sociocultural context by which each series is informed manifests not only in the narrative storylines but also in their structure, overall indicating a significant shift in cultural imaginaries of girlhood, femininity and female professional success. In summary, this chapter argues that *Girls* illustrates how maintaining faith in a postfeminist promise of fulfilment develops into a relation of cruelty. According to *Girls*, our investment in postfeminist ways of living is likely to thwart the fulfilment we desire and set out to achieve.

One of the chapter's central aims is to examine the relationship between postfeminist generic expectation and the coming-of-age trajectory in order to explore how the recursive nature of cruel optimism manifests at the level of narrative structure. I discuss *Girls* in relation to one of Gill's key elements of postfeminism – namely, a culture of self-maintenance and the notion of the self as a never-ending project requiring continual work (2007: 149). As a generic element of postfeminist culture, self-maintenance resonates deeply with the coming-of-age genre in which the most crucial element is an achievement of growth or change. Protagonists must undergo psychological and moral transformation, striving for happiness and satisfaction, at which point personal and narrative resolution is reached.

Following four central characters – Hannah, Marnie, Jessa and Shoshanna – as they navigate their mid-twenties in New York, *Girls* plays precisely on this sense of generic potential through its premise and title. For as Katherine Bell (2013) notes, a narrative in which four young women make the move to the city in order to expand the scope of their selves and their worlds is enough to instil genre expectations of a certain kind of story. In this story, a girl becomes a woman, and gradually, through 'one mistake at a time' (as promised by the first season's promotional tagline),[2] growth or maturation will take shape. As Colling observes, 'In the neo-liberal context, transformation is sold as self-empowerment' (2017: 29). In this respect, *Girls* continually frustrates its audience and critics by continually taking a regressive 'one step forwards, two steps back' approach to the progression of both character and narrative development. It is this frustration of expectation that I will pay particular attention to going forward.

The first episode of *Girls* introduces its central protagonist Hannah off-centre, occupying the far right of the frame, eyes cast downward in concentration on a mouthful of spaghetti threatening its escape (Figure 2).[3] Significantly, nutritional sustenance is not the only thing escaping Hannah. What follows is a conversation in which Hannah's

Figure 2 The opening shot of *Girls*' first episode (Dunham 2012: 1.1). *Girls* © Apatow Productions/Home Box Office (HBO) 2012–17.

parents inform her that their post-college financial support, which she has taken for granted for two years, is next in line to be withdrawn. Her parents will no longer fund her life in the city. *Girls'* opening image makes for a somewhat unconventional introduction to a protagonist. For instance, the way Hannah looks down towards the corner of the frame is not so unusual a composition as to become stylistically distracting but just enough to suggest a self-involved and self-limiting perspective. Within the context of the whole series, this initial shot is indicative of the way *Girls* often situates Hannah in isolation from other characters, thereby foretelling her self-absorption and lack of interest in the lives and interiority of others. By positioning Hannah's face at the 'wrong' edge of the frame *Girls* also inverts the classic shot-reverse-shot set up popularized by Hollywood filmmaking, thus forgoing eyeline matching with the more traditional reverse shot of Hannah's parents that follows. This suggests a relational discrepancy in recognition and expectation between Hannah and her parents, as is confirmed by their conversation, which sets the tone and central dilemma for the series (Figure 3).

As well as establishing the central conflict of the series as Hannah's struggle to 'become who I am' (1.1), this scene also effectively

Figure 3 Reverse shot of Hannah's parents (Dunham 2012: 1.1). *Girls* © Apatow Productions/Home Box Office (HBO) 2012–17.

communicates the disparity between the life Hannah inhabits and the one she desires and feels entitled to. The life Hannah anticipates is what Berlant terms 'the good life' (2011: 2). To capture and define the contemporary neoliberal condition, Berlant explains that subjects form optimistic attachments to ideals, objects, ideologies and political or social promises believed to enable the good life to materialize. The origin of such optimism is an anachronistic social imaginary invested in the hope that the fantasies we construct about our lives and the world will eventually 'add up to something' tangible (2011: 2). Berlant's use of the term 'fantasy' points to the vivid imaginaries individuals often construct about how their lives may unfold, the unconscious lure of attachments and their increasing unsustainability. A small-scale example is the belief that conventional living (a steady job, a traditional family) confers rewards such as access to basic requirements like food and shelter as well as more abstract rewards like happiness and fulfilment (Ahmed 2010).

In the United States, conventional ways of living are inseparable from the pervasive fantasy of the American Dream of opportunity and prosperity for all, which remains an alluring mythological narrative of progress, despite mounting evidence to the contrary (Chafe 2012; Lewis 2012). The conventional American fantasies outlined by Berlant include the promise that meritocracy, upward mobility and democratic equality will allow us to obtain and maintain a good life (2011: 3). These good life ideals are bound up in the family, the state and public social institutions. Such fantasies, Berlant details, have begun to wear out under the ascension of neoliberalism[4] in the United States and Europe. The good life that once seemed achievable if one adhered to conventional forms of living is now manifestly out of reach for increasing numbers of people, in large part due to the destructive effects of neoliberalism.

The withdrawal of financial support in *Girls*' opening scene disrupts Hannah's previously secure expectations of living and marks the first tacit reference to the effects of neoliberalism on a once-protected middle-class population. Mark Fisher (2014) describes *Girls* as one of the first television series to centre on 'graduates without a future', a term used by journalist Paul Mason in reference to a generation of young, highly educated people 'who can expect to grow up poorer than their parents' (2012: n.p.). Indeed, the series proposes that Hannah's social class, secure American upbringing and her parents' stable middle-class income are the main factors structuring the life she expects to lead. Hannah's relatively privileged subject position is entwined with an implicit generational contract of progress. An unspoken cultural narrative of continual progress promises each generation an improvement in their living conditions as compared to their parents. By opening the series in an upscale restaurant, scored by tastefully bland piano tones, *Girls* immediately communicates a sense of the comfortable, cataclysm-proof middle-class lifestyle to which Hannah's parents are accustomed, and which Hannah expects to inherit. The scene also works to suggest that the abrupt withdrawal of funds may not be entirely devastating to someone in Hannah's position. However, it indicates a breach of contract and introduces Hannah's first significant barrier to achieving a life similar to or better than the one enjoyed by her parents. Until the fracturing moment of parental withdrawal, Hannah's social circumstances had implicitly promised her immunity from the semi-precarious life she goes on to inhabit throughout the series.

Girls explores the impact of a recalcitrant entry into the middle-class precariat, a subject many critics have written on, noting for instance Hannah's 'entitled' response to her new-found precarity, and that her situation is more stable than that of many people worldwide (Rowles 2012; Shepherd 2012; Suebsaeng 2012). Although I remain sympathetic to this critique, I also consider Berlant's (2011: 20) insight that

> people's styles of response to crisis are powerfully related to the expectations of the world they had to reconfigure in the face of tattering formal and informal norms of social and institutional reciprocity.

As I noted, the set design in the opening scene produces an anticipation of enduring middle-class comfort and security. Considering this in tandem with Berlant's observation, we can begin to understand how *Girls* communicates both its protagonist's expectations and the way that those expectations dictate her style of response in this scene, and throughout the series. The pilot episode establishes her family's withdrawal of reciprocity as a defining moment for Hannah, as she realizes that the normative presumptions underpinning her social contract have been shattered. The prior security of Hannah's social position is fundamental to her character's acute sense that any protection from precarity has now been revoked, and with it her anticipation of a good life.

Berlant's central thesis is that 'a relation of cruel optimism exists when something you desire is actually an obstacle to your flourishing' (2011: 1). Cruel optimism is therefore an affective state in which the desired object can appear to bring the individual closer to fulfilment or happiness, yet also obstructs the realization of that fantasy (2011). Of course, a desire for enduring and mutually supportive relations with institutions or political systems is not inherently cruel. Our optimism becomes cruel, according to Berlant, when the workings of an institution or political system inhibit such a relationship from forming. In essence, our optimism keeps us pointed in the direction of a promised good life designed to remain out of reach.

If fantasies of the good life contribute to our sense of self-continuity (Berlant 2011), subjectivity is often organized around and in relation to such fantasies as a method of preserving deeply held beliefs about ourselves and our ways of being in the world. *Girls'* vision of an extended contemporary American girlhood initially appears to portray a traditional version of the self, one defined by autonomy and individualism (Sandywell 1999; Weedon 1987), and with a trajectory culminating in fulfilment or completion. Yet it becomes apparent that *Girls* does not take place in relation to such a mythic arc, but in a neoliberalized world in which the terms and conditions of reciprocity have shifted. In this world, Hannah's subjectivity is exposed to a refusal of completion, closely connected to the problem of self-actualization, which has begun to supplant more traditional notions of self-fulfilment. Self-actualization is becoming a key term in discussions of contemporary postfeminist subjectivities and is associated with neoliberal individualism (Genz and Brabon 2009), self-entrepreneurship (Chen 2010; Cronin 2000), consumerism (Cronin 2000; Fradley 2013), authenticity (Dejmanee 2016) and what Joel Gwynne terms postfeminist '(self)objectification' (2013: 79). What this scholarship suggests is that self-understanding and self-definition through processes of actualization marks a key shift in conceptions of selfhood, yet so far this dynamic has not been explored in detail. A subject seeking self-actualization must make her self real/ity. Whereas traditional self-fulfilment is conceived as an attainable fixed state of being in the world, self-actualization is a never-ending process of iterative actions undertaken to establish and maintain selfhood (Cronin 2000). Such actions can appear and feel like fulfilment. *Girls* presents the search for self-actualization as a continual process of self-preparation and engagement in life-building activities. While the search for self-fulfilment is geared towards eventual completion, a quest to self-actualize will always reach an impasse as its processes are interminable and inconclusive, engaging in a lifetime of work on the self that forecloses arrival.

Although the concept of the good life does not look or feel the same for every individual, at its core exists a belief that compliance with normative imperatives will secure certain rewards. Berlant describes this relation as 'a cluster of promises we want someone or something to make to us and make possible for us' (2011: 23). *Girls* characterizes Hannah as deeply affected by the withdrawal of a good life she feels was promised to her. It also produces her character as a specifically feminine subject who is hailed by a gendered promise of a good life, instilled with postfeminist assurances of fulfilment for (some) women who follow its catalogue of conventions.

Negotiating a postfeminist legacy

The idea of gendered promises returns us to questions of genre; in particular, Berlant's understanding of genre as 'a loose affectively-invested zone of expectations about the narrative shape a situation will take' (2011: 2). Our investments in particular genres are crucial in fashioning our expectations of what might unfold, either within narrative fiction or within our own lives. Joshua Adam Anderson writes that 'genre primes us and orients us toward a mode of apprehending things according to its own determinations. We don't know what to make of something that hasn't come with the metadata of genre affiliations; often we don't even know what to desire' (2015: n.p.). Genres, then, can orient us towards desiring particular kinds of lives; in fact, without the guidance of genre, we have little concept of how to build our lives at all (Anderson 2015; Berlant 2011). If genres provide us with conceptual structuring principles for how our lives are most likely to unfold, we can begin to understand how a character like Hannah comes to assume that an imprecise yet affectively intelligible promise of a good life has been made to her. It is through genre, then, that complex affective structures like postfeminism offer subjects ways of living in which they are invited to invest their subjectivity.

In the introduction I discussed some of the ways postfeminism has been theorized, most recently as a distinctly feminine manifestation of the neoliberal zeitgeist (Gill 2007, 2008; Gill and Scharff 2011; Harris 2004; McRobbie 2008). I also noted that while postfeminism is culturally ubiquitous and undoubtedly dominates the media archives available to women and girls over the past twenty-five years, it is certainly not the only women's discourse in cultural circulation (Retallack, Ringrose and Lawrence 2016). In the broadest critical terms, a postfeminist text embodies and/or advocates the view that because the crucial but arduous labour of feminism is completed, women can now concentrate their efforts on enjoying themselves and 'having it all' (should they so choose). The only drawback is of course that the terms of enjoyment remain defined and limited by patriarchal perspectives on feminine desirability. The impact of postfeminism as a culturally dominant discourse is only now beginning to crystallize, coinciding with a media resurgence of multiple new strands of feminism, as well as what Negra and Tasker term the 'recession-era' (2013: 344) in the aftermath of the 2008 financial crisis.

Fictional and lived genres are intricately interwoven, each informing and maintaining the production of the other. As Tania Modleski argues, 'In our culture *all* women imbibe romance fantasies from a variety of sources' (1999: 48, original italics). Such fantasies are the staple of the romantic comedy, a genre promoting a particular variant on how to live a good life – not just any good life but a uniquely gendered promise extended exclusively to feminine subjects. This promise is organized around resolutions to questions relating to the quest for 'the one', often combined in contemporary romantic comedies with the perennial feminine conundrum of how to have it all. *Sex and the City* promises to deliver a pithy and sexually explicit exploration of these questions, by producing an aspirational feel-good experience of postfeminism in which agency, sexual autonomy and empowerment via consumerism are unproblematically endorsed, valorized and, most importantly, enjoyed (Adriaens 2009; Arthurs 2003; Gerhard 2005).

The series is now widely agreed to have been instrumental in defining the genre expectations of postfeminism that weigh heavily on the contemporary feminine condition explored in *Girls*.[5] Those expectations range from the accessibility of material pleasure found in designer clothing, cocktails and stilettos to the anticipation of a fulfilling sex life and glamourous professional career. Yet although comparisons to *Sex and the City* are as inevitable as they are ubiquitous, what *Girls* in fact exposes is how much has changed in our cultural imaginary of women's lives in New York. *Sex and the City*'s dazzling vision is worlds apart from the ever-changing landscape of recession and underemployment that *Girls* negotiates. Fisher observes that '*Girls* retrospectively reveals that the key fantasy that structured *Sex and the City* had nothing to do with sex (or, for that matter, consumerism)'. Rather, he suggests, 'Work was the central absence in the series; something that the characters were rarely seen doing, the silent background to their pleasures and misadventures' (2014: n.p.). By contrast, a conspicuous absence of any professional career at all is explored to great effect in the early seasons of *Girls*, where unpaid internships, low-paid service industry jobs and stretches of unemployment are the norm in an increasingly neoliberalized economy.

While *Sex and the City* may not have narratively foregrounded the labour involved in their jobs (Lotz 2006: 96), the series nonetheless features four female characters (Carrie, Charlotte, Miranda and Samantha) whose identity and concept of success are predicated largely on their hugely successful professional careers. *Girls'* first season emphasizes that the professional ambitions of *Sex and the City*'s successful protagonists are initially shared by the current generation, especially in relation to creative work. A writing career is Hannah's core ambition, while Marnie initially has a job as an art gallery assistant. However, compared to their function in *Sex and the City*, these careers play very different narrative and structural roles. A defining feature of *Sex and the City* is that each episode is structured by Carrie's voice-over detailing her research on the sexual mores of Manhattan for her newspaper column. This recurring convention lends the series a sense of stability and structural cohesion. Just as Carrie can infamously rely on her job to fund an endless supply of haute couture, so too can the audience rely on the consistency of *Sex and the City*'s episodic structure and sitcom genre conventions to introduce and resolve narrative conflict. These conventions allow the concept of 'work' to fade into the background, as Fisher (2014) suggests, despite the central role of Carrie's voiceovers. Carrie's writing also plays a specific formal role in guiding the audience through each episode's central thematic debates, with the four characters each representing a conflicting perspective or stance on the issue at hand (Nelson 2007: 90–1). By contrast, Maša Grdešić argues that *Girls* uses Hannah's writing (in the form of tweets, essays and her diary) as a metafictional device that 'is more actional than thematic' (2013: 357–8). In the fourth episode of season one, for example, the diary 'primarily advances the action: it plays a crucial role in Marnie and Charlie's breakup, and passages from it become lyrics to "Hannah's Diary," a song performed by Charlie's band' (2013: 357). Evidently, writing does not provide the same kind of structural underpinning in *Girls*. There are long stretches of the narrative which sideline a writing career altogether, most notably during season five in which Hannah teaches high school English. The irregularity of Hannah's writing provides *Girls* the means to explore the challenges of making a living as a writer at the same time as structurally performing the inherent instability of finding creative work in a post-recession economy. Just as Hannah cannot rely on her creative talents to provide opportunities for meaningful work, the audience cannot depend on *Girls*' structure or format to provide a permanent secure foothold. As I discuss later, *Girls*' atypical structure is key to the way it communicates a sense of the fractured instability intrinsic to living in a post-crash landscape.

Girls foregrounds a similar attachment to the idea of creative work with a storyline in which Marnie is 'let go' from her job as an art gallery assistant. Marnie's aspirations clearly correspond with those of *Sex and the City*'s Charlotte, whose character effortlessly achieves her ambition to manage a successful art gallery, before choosing to quit her job in anticipation of motherhood in the episode 'Time and Punishment' (4.7). Where *Sex and the City* stages conflict around the postfeminist dilemma of work versus motherhood, *Girls* highlights the effects of austerity on professional aspirations and realities. In 'Time and Punishment', Charlotte's decision is met with negative responses from the other characters. Beth Montemurro argues that 'aspirations toward domesticity are clearly viewed as the "wrong" way of doing things or the wrong goals, and Charlotte herself is well aware of this' (2004: n.p.), noting that the episode rejects Charlotte's position as the 'traditional feminine voice' and instead foregrounds the 'voices of the career-focused workers-not-wives' (n.p.). It is true that Charlotte's ambivalence is woven into the fabric of the episode, surfacing particularly in a scene where Charlotte demands that Miranda validate her choice, going as far as to argue that her decision stems from the gains of 'the women's movement' (4.7). However, the episode neatly wraps up the dilemma by presenting Charlotte's decision as ultimately optimistic, thereby carefully reconciling any tensions created by the conflict between the 'traditional feminine voice' and 'the career-focused workers-not-wives'. Astrid Henry argues that the episode offers an implicit critique of 'Charlotte's "easy" choice-based definition of feminism' (2004: 72), yet although the series briefly questions the traditional choice to stop working and raise a family, it ultimately validates it on a formal and narrative level.

Narrative validation is achieved through dialogue when Charlotte's replacement reassures her that she wishes her own mother had been at home more often. Here, the camera holds on Charlotte's bright smiling face – an indicator of her satisfaction at finally obtaining the external endorsement she had sought from her friends. Upbeat jazz kicks in as she exits the gallery, smiling contentedly at a passing mother and baby (both visually coded in red and pink clothing), before striding towards the bright light in the background of the shot (Figure 4). These formal markers of Charlotte's satisfaction with her decision thus work to ameliorate any prior friction, cementing the notion that individual freedom of choice is paramount to *Sex and the City*'s style of femininity. Henry's argument that 'ultimately, the episode revolves

Figure 4 Charlotte (Kristin Davis) decides to quit her job in *Sex and the City*'s 'Time and Punishment' (Star 2001: 4.7). *Sex and the City* © Darren Star Productions/Home Box Office (HBO) 1998–2004.

around Charlotte's ambivalence' (2004: 72), albeit accurate in some respects, overlooks the way that the series' grounding in the comedy genre and strict sitcom format works to contain both the ambivalence and any implicit criticism that arises from it by producing the decision as ultimately satisfying at a narrative level.

Unlike *Sex and the City*, which stages and contains conflict between the traditionally feminine 'choice' to leave the workforce and the legacy of second-wave feminist politics through Charlotte's decision to quit her job, *Girls* centres on the fractured conditions for creative work in an austerity economy. Broadcast in 2001, *Sex and the City* presents a scenario in which a 22-year-old woman steps eagerly into Charlotte's role as director of a prestigious art gallery. A decade later, *Girls* features a character of the same age who cannot even hold on to an assistant job at a much smaller gallery. Whereas Charlotte is imagined as successfully fulfilling her ambition and ultimately happy with her decision to quit, Marnie's unemployment is unforeseen and entirely beyond her control, giving further evidence of a shattered generational contract. As Fisher suggests, 'The four women might be privileged, but they are no longer privileged enough to get the work they thought was destined for them, which is now reserved for those who are even more comfortably off' (2014: n.p.). It is important to note that Marnie's character is not fired or deemed unsuitable for her job, as demonstrated by her former manager's insistence that she is merely 'downsizing', because 'I run a fucking art gallery, Marnie. I can't afford two employees' (2.1). Within the contemporary televisual imagination, jobs like Charlotte's are no longer presented as coveted competitive positions which one can work harder to achieve. Rather, they have simply disappeared.

In *Sex and the City*, the enclosed space of the gallery gives way to an expansive, brightly lit urban space. The lighting and framing suggest potential and new possibilities, inviting questions as to what lies ahead for Charlotte's character as well as hinting that perhaps Charlotte's commitment to her work limited rather than fostered her full potential. In coupling this scenario with episodic closure, the series announces Charlotte's resignation as a narrative event and as a moment of positive character development. By contrast, the 'letting go' scene in *Girls* is much briefer, taking place early in the second season opening episode as part of a 'catch-up' sequence reintroducing the characters. Its structural position suggests that unlike the weight given to Charlotte's predicament in *Sex and the City*, this does not rank as a significant narrative event in quite the same way. Similarly, when Marnie's manager attempts to smooth things over with the dialogue 'you're gorgeous and totally bright. You'll land on your feet' (2.1), this is contradicted by the awkwardly closed frame constraining Marnie and expressing the withdrawal of her access to New York's once-endless opportunities. *Girls* therefore significantly complicates the notion that the world of postfeminist pleasures experienced by Carrie and her friends is attainable by today's generation of young women (Grant and Nash 2017). Of course, at the same time, the narrative preoccupation with such pleasures demonstrates women's immeasurable investments in postfeminism as a source of fulfilment.

The unreliability of postfeminist markers of fulfilment in *Girls* is evidenced by ambivalence towards them as well as other varying states of attachment. The narrative situations that unfold during *Girls* (particularly those concerning the relations between sex, love and romance) suggest that to renounce such postfeminist genres might be beneficial, as their conditions undermine whatever potential for fulfilment remains. Considering postfeminism as a relation of cruel optimism highlights *Girls*' exploration of ambivalent attachments to a style of femininity that has failed to provide fulfilment. According to Berlant (2011), once such an attachment is formed to a promise of fulfilment, relinquishing it comes close to losing the anchor for living itself. When stuck in impasse, Berlant argues that irrespective of how we might proceed, 'massive loss is inevitable' (2012: 1). Remaining wedded to postfeminism may be the source of their unhappiness, but without its promises Hannah and her friends stand to lose the very possibility of feminine fulfilment itself.

Girls illuminates what it feels like to live the contradictions of the postfeminist promise. Dunham's generation retains the influence of second-wave feminism, has grown up in a postfeminist media age and is currently living through a resurgence of updated feminist politics. Above all, *Girls* details what it feels like to be stuck between these genres of living, unable to conceive of new attachments or genres that might actually satisfy. As old genres prove unreliable and in the absence of new ones that could viably guide the way, subjectivity is unable to ground itself. It is this disparity between the postfeminist promise of personal and professional fulfilment and its lived reality that elicits what Berlant terms 'impasse' (2011: 4–5). Impasse is a 'cul-de-sac' in which 'one keeps moving, but one moves paradoxically, in the *same space*' (2011: 199, original italics). This definition opens up the spatial implications of our attachments to good life promises. Impasse for Berlant is not a static subject position but a state of momentum with confined spatial boundaries. When we reach impasse, we keep moving, but there are limits to where or how far we can go.

Postfeminist impasse

There are two primary ways *Girls* expresses an acute sense of postfeminist impasse. First, by restaging aspirational postfeminist conventions, for example, through the rom-com run trope. Second, the series exploits the coming-of-age genre by establishing an expectation of growth and transformation that is continually denied both narratively and structurally. *Girls* uses stylistic and narrative reiteration techniques to create a recursive storytelling structure that runs counter to traditional narrative convention. The circularity of the series contravenes the most fundamental (Western) narrative arc – the three-act structure that traces a path from initial problem to climax before eventual resolution – thereby producing the coming-of-age trajectory as a state of perpetual delay and regression.

A sense that transformation does not necessarily lead to progress is created through the stylistic repetition of opening scenes across the series. The initial scene of the family dinner with Hannah and her parents is followed by an intimate shot panning across Hannah and Marnie's legs as they wake up together entangled. Aside from conveying their close friendship, this brief shot gains significance from its replication in the first episodes of seasons two (2.1) and three (3.1 'Females Only'), and the season six finale episode (6.10 'Latching'), all of which open with a near-identical sequence in which the only alteration is Hannah's sleeping partner. Narratively, this communicates the central relationship of each season, tracking Hannah's intimate relationships with Marnie, her ex-boyfriend Elijah, and boyfriend Adam, before circling back to Marnie in the final season. More importantly, the repetition structurally signals that *Girls* begins, once again, where it has begun once before. Relationships may shift and change; however, any kind of narrative growth that may occur does not provide the kind of development or progression we expect from coming-of-age genres. Season four (4.1 'Iowa') disrupts the pattern and creates another, echoing the pilot episode's family dinner. This time, Hannah is centre framed (Figure 5) in a much more traditional composition as compared to the series' opening episode, a formal indicator of change that suggests a kind of emotional stability absent from the pilot (Figure 2). Hannah raises a glass to celebrate her acceptance at a prestigious graduate

Figure 5 Hannah (Lena Dunham), centre-framed and smiling in celebration, in 'Iowa' (Dunham 2015: 4.1). *Girls* © Apatow Productions/Home Box Office (HBO) 2012–17.

school – an achievement that appears to bring her closer than ever to the good life imagined at the beginning of the series. Comparison of these scenes further illuminates *Girls*' model of narrative regression. Through its formal repetition, the scene foregrounds growth and transformation at the beginning of season four, yet this is reversed by narrative events occurring only four episodes later as Hannah returns to New York, having intentionally alienated her graduate student cohort and subsequently abandoned the programme. Stylistic reiteration of the opening sequences therefore creates a cyclical structure in which character and narrative development is severely obstructed, projecting a trajectory of fulfilment and forward momentum that never quite materializes.

Girls' atypical structure is essential to its interrogation of the concept of transformation as key to unlocking personal fulfilment. In this case, reiteration is used to produce idealized feminine milestones as moments of frustration rather than resolution. In his examination of normative family discourses in television, Gary Needham observes that sitcoms typically correlate narrative closure to a sense of 'upbeat family togetherness' so that consequently 'happy families and happy endings are one and the same thing' (2009: 148). Comparably, postfeminist media culture draws together milestones of idealized femininity such as heterosexual romance and traditional marriage in such a way that the happy couple becomes synonymous with the happy ending. Yet *Girls*' reiteration of the failed marriage trope both signifies and subsequently inhibits the concept of self-transformative coming of age. The series features two wedding sequences, the first of which takes place during the season one finale (1.10 'She Did'). This placement might typically suggest the aforementioned happy resolution; however, the wedding in question is that of Hannah's impulsive friend Jessa to a boorish financier she has known for only two weeks, and which ends in divorce four episodes later (2.4 'It's a Shame about Ray'). Having successfully skewered any sense that marriage might equate to the pinnacle of feminine satisfaction and accomplishment, the season five opener features a second example of ill-advised matrimony, this time used as a device to suggest a fresh start for Marnie's character (5.1 'Wedding Day'). As Pilot Viruet observes of the episode's conclusion, 'it's a nice, optimistic ending – even if we know *Girls* will never let this last' (2016: n.p.). This comment suggests that an audience now attuned to *Girls*' modus operandi might be able to predict the ambivalent, essentially unstable outcome. Indeed, far from a fresh start, another divorce looms only six episodes later.

Since marriage remains a key signifier of both idealized femininity and conventionalized adulthood, to achieve this milestone would be a clear indicator of the passage from girlhood to womanhood. The way *Girls* presents marriage as a milestone of feminine coming of age that is evidently desirable yet patently unattainable indicates a continued investment in (at least) the fantasy of conventional marriage, if not perhaps the reality. Here, the concept of 'double coding' (Colling 2017: 8) is useful in considering how *Girls* produces postfeminist impasse. Colling explains that double coding is a form of irony that revisits the 'already said' (Krutnik 1998: 28 in Colling 2017: 8). She cites Umberto Eco's description of it as the result of a specifically postmodern quandary:

> I think of the postmodern attitude as that of a man who loves a very cultivated woman and knows that he cannot say to her 'I love you madly', because he knows that she knows (and that she knows he knows) that these words have already been written by Barbara Cartland. Still there is a solution. He can say 'As Barbara Cartland would put it, I love you madly'. At this point, having avoided false innocence, having said clearly it is no longer possible to talk innocently, he will nevertheless say what he wanted to say to the woman: that he loves her in an age of lost innocence. (Eco 1992: 227 in Colling 2017: 8)

Colling goes on to argue that girl teen films which use fairy-tale realism in contemporary settings, such as *Freaky Friday* (Waters 2003) or *A Cinderella Story* (Rosman 2004), 'use cinematic markers of enchantment' which work as 'invitations to enjoy another world that will end "happily ever after"' but that also 'cannot be delivered earnestly in the twenty first century context' (2017: 26). Double coding techniques, according to Colling, are essential to this genre 'because where Eco's lover cannot say "I love you," girl teen films equally cannot outright say "happily ever after"' (27). By double coding their use of fairy-tale conventions through self-conscious irony, girl teen films can evoke the pleasures of particular tropes at the same time as disavowing them.

Double coding, then, is what allows *Girls* to produce the affective pleasures of the wedding ceremony (particularly through costuming and set design) even as it satirizes and undercuts those same pleasures. Reiterating failed marriage indicates postfeminist impasse as the narrative begins to take place 'paradoxically, in the *same space*' (Berlant 2011: 199, original italics). Scenarios, images and tropes of growth and self-transformation accumulate, yet the narrative does not progress. Regardless of the 'content' of these images – that is, irrespective of whether the series appears to support or undermine marriage itself – their reiteration creates a sense of narrative recursion by returning to the same trope, the same institution, the very same fantasy that *Girls* has already informed us is 'not working' (Berlant 2011: 263).

The rom-com run

The rom-com run trope is a crucial sequence in which the male lead rushes across city streets (typically New York, the quintessential romantic comedy locale) to demonstrate his love for the female lead and prove himself worthy of hers. In films like *When Harry Met Sally* (Reiner 1989), the run is the decisive act, a visual manifestation of resolution that signals narrative conclusion and promises closure. Here, the happy couple and the happy ending are indeed 'one and the same' (2009: 148), as Needham suggests.

While seemingly aspiring to this kind of neat emotional resolution, *Girls*' updated version of the rom-com run (in the final episode of season two, 2.10 'Together') includes narrative indicators that serve to undermine such a happy reading. The sequence begins with Adam, Hannah's on-again-off-again boyfriend, alone in his apartment, demonstrating his inclination towards anger and destruction as he tears down the construction project he has been working on. Adam's actions are in response to something that happened in the previous episode (2.9 'On All Fours'), which sparked a divisive debate among commentators as to whether a scene between Adam and his then-girlfriend Natalia depicted rape or was merely an example of unpleasant sexual conduct (Becker Stevens 2013; Hess 2013; Lyons 2013). Rather than stake a claim in this debate and attempt to deliver a verdict myself, I read this scene instead as an indicator that *Girls* is by no means staging the typical context or catalyst for a romantic reconciliation. Although the romantic comedy structure hinges upon a hitch or obstacle that threatens to thwart the burgeoning romance of its protagonists, this typically takes the form of a miscommunication between the two, or a failure of the leading man to fully commit (Abbott and Jermyn 2009; Deleyto 2009). Unlike these examples, which are usually played for comedic effect, Adam's character is presented as aggressive, destructive and potentially violent. From the outset, the series jeopardizes the very notion of his viability as a leading man.

Equally, season two's emphasis on Hannah's fear that she is 'unravelling' (2.10) sets her apart from the prototypical romantic comedy heroine. As the scene continues, Adam answers a video call from a distraught Hannah who cannot, or perhaps is opting not to, conceal the physical symptoms of her rapidly deteriorating mental health. Commenting on the return of Hannah's obsessive-compulsive disorder in 'It's Back' (2.8), Erica Lies observes that 'Hannah's symptoms aren't sitcom-cute' (2013: n.p.). As Stayci Taylor notes, there is a tendency within romantic comedies to characterize female protagonists who are otherwise 'perfect' as having one flaw (typically clumsiness) designed to create 'audience appeal' and enhance 'likeability' (2015: 65). It is therefore significant that *Girls* presents Hannah's mental illness as a genuine anxiety disorder rather than a quirky or reassuring flaw (Jacey 2010; Taylor 2015).[6] Having established that neither character is especially compatible with typical romantic comedy conventions, *Girls* then stages the rom-com run with an apparent sincerity that disturbs the established rhythm of *Girls*' cynically pragmatic sexual politics.

As Adam sprints shirtless across New York streets, the mawkish instrumental soundtrack works hard to elicit the requisite emotional response, conjuring a sense of enduring romance. The final vision of the season is Adam tearing down Hannah's door, the camera following him into her bedroom as the music slows and he lifts Hannah from beneath her covers. They kiss as the camera retreats and the screen fades to black. The staging presents Adam as the figurative knight in shining armour, thereby appearing to cast Hannah as the archetypal damsel awaiting his entrance. Therefore, although Adam's character may not physically or emotionally resemble his romantic predecessors, he nonetheless becomes affectively linked with them in undertaking this heroic journey. Here, the concept of double coding works slightly differently than the examples Colling provides. In girl teen films, 'happily ever after' must be coded as ironic or tongue-in-cheek. By contrast, *Girls*' rom-com run is shot and scored to evoke the earnest pleasure of the happily ever after trope, with the dark streets, rapid cuts and directional right framing closely emulating the lighting, editing and framing choices at work in the corresponding scene in *When Harry Met Sally*. When viewed in relation to the recursive model I have outlined, it becomes clear that the rom-com run trope appears to resolve the season narrative in *Girls* while simultaneously restaging the rom-com genre.

However, Adam's grand heroic gesture simply returns both characters to where they have already been, thus emphasizing the futility of the postfeminist fantasy. The dynamic on-screen spectacle of the run itself appears to signal a forward momentum by presenting Hannah with a viable romantic partner and the audience with a satisfying conclusion to a season of television. The rom-com run is double coded here as a form of pastiche. Richard Dyer's understanding of pastiche is that it 'imitates formal means that are themselves ways of evoking, moulding and eliciting feelings, and thus in the process is able to mobilize feelings even while signalling that it is doing so' (2007: 180). *Girls* signals its attachment to fantasies of postfeminist romance, just as it has done with marriage and work, by activating their affective pleasures at the same time as constructing those fantasies as festering from within. This is no conventional happy ending, merely another cyclical lurch of the impasse. The romantic comedy model teaches us to accept the run as signifying both happiness and resolution, neither of which is present in *Girls*. Expectations remain unsatisfied and fulfilment out of reach. Moreover, viewers are very well aware that as one season ends, another commences. Instead of finite closure, the loop begins anew. There is no ending, no climax, only momentary respite. Where the romantic comedy film concludes, *Girls* exploits its televisual medium by allowing the narrative to circle back into the incessant processes of self-actualization.

If impasse is indeed 'a space of time lived without a narrative genre' (Berlant 2011: 199), then this implies an unmooring from the anchors of living that genre provides us with. Impasse is therefore a space in which we learn to adjust to the loss of a fantasy (2011: 11). *Girls* explores this loss at a narrative level by producing the rom-com run as an impasse, an indicator of Hannah's return to the promise of a romance she already knows isn't working. A crucial aspect of a relation of cruel optimism is a lack of alternatives, for if there were other viable options, it would perhaps not be so difficult to let go of idealized fantasies of what our lives should be like. A similar shortage of options is created by gradually estranging Hannah's character from her friends, family and even her infatuated neighbour. The close relationships between Hannah and her friends that were a staple of the first season have begun to fray. In episodes eight ('It's Back') and nine ('On All Fours') of season two especially, the series emphasizes Hannah's atomization by focusing on other character arcs, shifting Hannah to the margins and foregrounding her seclusion as her anxiety heightens.

In this moment, Hannah's vision of her awaited good life seems further than ever from her lived reality. Adam's arrival, therefore, represents to Hannah, and crucially, to the audience, the very possibility of happiness itself, despite her (and our) knowledge that their previous attempts at a relationship were not fulfilling. Another role played by genre is that it guides us towards an expected conclusion. To live without a genre means living without a clear idea of how a situation is likely to unfold and, importantly, end. Typically, the decisive act that signals a clear outcome of narrative and character completion (i.e. in *Girls*, the run), instead of heralding the resolution anticipated by the viewer, exposes impasse. A closer look at the actual state of play reveals narrative stagnation. Nothing *happens* in season two (which is a widespread critique of *Girls* in general). There is turmoil and insecurity. There are shifts and adaptations, yet no discernible progress is ever being made.

Girls displays an increasing awareness that postfeminist genres do not deliver on their promises, that following their lines will not map a path towards fulfilment. However, the rom-com run also reflects that although *Girls* does not entirely believe in the prospect of finding fulfilment in such worn-out generic promises, the longing for them to succeed persists. Adjustment for Hannah equals further entrenchment of her commitment to a promise she knows is false. Meanwhile, adjustment for the series per se resides in the creation of a new genre of impasse that articulates the inherent difficulties of detaching from the postfeminist promise. The postfeminist genre, much like Adam, runs its course; it even arrives. Ultimately, however, the postfeminist romantic fantasy finds no foothold in *Girls*, as it is usurped by the new contemporary genre of impasse, which finds it cannot accommodate the happy couple.

Inconvenient conventions

Berlant argues that the function of cultural and societal conventions can be reduced to disciplinary measures seemingly intended to direct a populace towards cruelly optimistic genres of living. On-screen, the repeated mediation of such conventions often manifests as a simplistic or derivative cliché. Yet Berlant also accounts for the appeal of norms, and our fascination with convention as being a kind of 'aspirational anchor' (2012: 3), a way of tethering ourselves to the world. Read like this, the rom-com run can at once retain its outdated gender politics and function as an aspirational image of femininity that points in the direction of familiarity, stability and flourishing (2011: 3). Subjects can desire postfeminist normativity, even as it inflicts suffering upon the desiring subject. Or, as Berlant attests, 'it is awkward and it is threatening to detach from what is already not working' (2011: 263). I would add that falling for a false promise is not only inconvenient but also embarrassing. To acknowledge that we have misplaced our optimism feels less like a failure of genre to live up to and fulfil our expectations than our own failure to reap the rewards it promised. Perhaps the promise was never valid or viable in the first place. Still, losing hold of the fantasy that fulfilment resides in postfeminist genres has the capacity to devastate the sense of self-continuity that is derived from our attachments to genre (24). *Girls* shows us that the rom-com run doesn't lead to the happy ending hoped for, yet it reproduces it all the same.

The rom-com run, then, expresses a complicated and contradictory set of genre pleasures. Aesthetics, according to Berlant, 'is one of the few places we learn to recognize our emotions as trained and not natural' (2013: n.p.). Personally speaking, upon viewing the scene for the first time, I found myself in the uneasy position of recognizing that I am aesthetically trained to find relief in the powerful image of a woman saved by a man, even though I believe myself to be firmly aligned with a feminism profoundly critical of both the desire and the image. *Girls*' repetition of the romantic comedy staple establishes a sense of self-continuity that imparts an assuring recognition of femininity while placing postfeminist pleasure in immediate conflict with feminist critique. While it would be easy to dismiss this tension, a more nuanced understanding can be derived from the insight that in repeating postfeminist tropes, *Girls* does not 'become' a romantic comedy. Rather, *Girls* deploys and subsumes the romantic comedy into its own uncomfortably stretched-out genre of impasse, painfully detailing the present condition of femininity.

Like Berlant, *Girls* tracks an extended 'crisis ordinariness' (2011: 10) or an unremarkable, ongoing absorption of catastrophe into the everyday. There is a pervasive sense in *Girls* that something unintelligible has gone terribly wrong. That something, which remains imperceptible to the characters, is expressed affectively to the spectator through the televisual mediation of the overwhelming impact of postfeminist genres on Hannah and her peers. The rom-com run is no longer a singular, exceptional event that ruptures the ordinary, or a symbol of ultimate romantic love, as *Girls* distends the ostensible moment of completion into an unconsummated stretched-out shape of the 'usual' (Berlant 2011: 58).

Articulating the ways that specific tropes deviate from precedents that work within a particular tradition or genre enables us to be, as Berlant puts it, 'reflexive about contemporary historicity as one lives it' (2011: 5). Jackie Stacey interprets contemporary historicity as a feeling that occurs when subjects are unable to respond to an event using 'existing affective genres' (2015: 252). The present, according to Stacey, 'becomes most visible when it fails to live up to its promises (in which we had invested so much, psychically and economically)' (2015: 252). I argued at the beginning of this chapter that *Girls* is produced in relation to and as a response to the dominance of postfeminist cultural discourses. Rather than dismiss such normative investments as simply 'bad objects', my consideration of postfeminism as a relation of cruel optimism proves a fruitful method for engaging with the hopeful pleasures, ambivalent desires and conflicts arising from our fascination with and aspirations towards convention. *Girls*' meticulous enactment and unravelling of conventional postfeminist fantasies offers an important cultural understanding of the cruel hopes that direct feminine desires towards patently false promises. When *Girls* finds that femininity is no longer entirely intelligible through the lens of the romantic comedy, it is compelled to find new methods of sense-making. The calculated rearticulation of the rom-com run functions to unfold the boundaries of the romantic comedy genre, thereby creating its own entirely new genre, which assumes shape through its deviations from the normative model. In turn, the creation of the new genre expands the potential of the old. As *Girls* repeats and exposes its genre mechanics, it begins to dawn on us that the romantic comedy as a dominant postfeminist narrative masks the impasse at its core.

This chapter illuminates a particular resonance between *Girls'* reiterations of postfeminist tropes and fantasies and Berlant's concept of cruel optimism. Which is not to say that *Girls* simply confirms what Berlant has already told us. For what *Girls* does, first, is explore cruel optimism in the context of postfeminist media culture. The series produces a historically and culturally specific feminine condition, detailing the effects of postfeminism as a dominant cultural discourse. In essence, what *Girls* produces is a distinctively feminine form of impasse, thus shading in the details of Berlant's concept. Second, *Girls* expands on the definitions of impasse offered by Berlant. In the series, postfeminist impasse is expressed through recursion, a continual turning away from and return to normative convention. The structural rhythms of the series, centred on the reiterative anticipation and denial of growth or catharsis, do not make for traditionally 'satisfying' viewing. *Girls* therefore provides a dynamic of impasse not described or explored by Berlant. For this reason, it is vital to bring the two into conversation with one another. Whereas Berlant provides the vocabulary for the feeling or relation of remaining committed to harmful conventions, *Girls* gives us the shape of a culturally specific response to postfeminist normativity. Although *Girls* cannot possibly encompass a universal perspective on postfeminism, its significance lies in the way it formulates a complicated and conflicted relationship to hegemonic feminine conventions.

3

Searching for belonging in *Appropriate Behaviour*

Where Chapter 2 explored the difficulty in cutting loose from harmful genres, this chapter complicates the analysis of cruel optimism and operates somewhat atypically compared to the others, in that it does not directly address the postfeminist problematic. As Chapters 1 and 2 have illustrated, the demands of generic convention and the social pressure to live certain kinds of lives can be constricting. However, Desiree Akhavan's film *Appropriate Behaviour* shows that the lack of genre to guide the way can be equally devastating. If this book is overall concerned with what happens *after* the height of postfeminist empowerment, this chapter abandons the frame of postfeminism almost entirely to demonstrate that sometimes the impact of a culturally dominant discourse is in fact barely perceptible compared to other more pressing anxieties that arise in the search for social belonging.

A cursory glance finds comparable premises underpinning *Girls* and *Appropriate Behaviour*: they are set in New York, explore extended girlhoods and are directed by and star their creators.[1] However, while it may be superficially similar to *Girls*, I argue that *Appropriate Behaviour* is not preoccupied by the same concerns and cannot be so straightforwardly linked to a genre like postfeminism or a relation of cruel optimism. Likewise, while *Broad City* and *Fleabag* are also indebted to *Girls* and share many of its narrative characteristics and concerns, the former's exuberantly surreal affective register is worlds apart from the quiet devastation in *Girls*, and the latter offers a complex reflection on our investments in romantic narrative closure.

Primarily a character study, *Appropriate Behaviour* follows a single protagonist, Shirin, in the aftermath of a breakup with her girlfriend, Maxine. Although Shirin's romantic life is the focus, this is framed by her family, social and professional relationships, situating the central relationship within a wider context. Interestingly, the film does make brief reference to aspects of postfeminist culture by casually affiliating Shirin with *Sex and the City* and the fantasy series *Twilight* (Meyer 2005–8). As I discuss later, rather than signalling a deep-rooted connection to postfeminist genres, these moments are designed principally to highlight Shirin's incompatibility with Maxine, who eschews normative feminine culture. These references are nonchalant, suggesting that while postfeminism is tangibly present as one of the genres structuring Shirin's life, it is far from the primary or most pressing one. The question of how postfeminism feels does not therefore appear to be wholly irrelevant to *Appropriate Behaviour*'s concerns; however, the film suggests that neither is it especially urgent. Instead, it expresses the difficulties in negotiating one's own subjectivity in relation to disparate social groups, exploring how living without a convention or a cliché can fuel isolation from communities to which one ostensibly belongs.

The story of Shirin and Maxine's relationship is told in a series of non-chronological flashbacks. The film's structure diverges into dual narratives: flashback sequences allow the viewer to piece together the fragments of Shirin's relationship, whereas the present-day narrative follows Shirin in its aftermath. Whitney Monaghan (2016) reads the film's parallel narratives as an example of queer temporality or a formal refusal of normative time. Monaghan links the film's structure to its narrative questioning of the traditional milestones of linear progression – what Jack Halberstam terms 'those paradigmatic markers of life experience – namely birth, marriage, reproduction, and death' (2005: 2), suggesting that the 'dual narratives seem to obscure teleological progression in favour of awkwardly flowing along in their own time' (2016: 156). The awkward narrative flow Monaghan identifies works in opposition to what Elizabeth Freeman terms 'chrononormativity', defined as the way time is used to 'organize individual human bodies toward maximum productivity' (2010: 3). Her explanation provides an understanding of how our lives tend to unfold according to a particular timeline, dictated and reinforced by institutional and cultural expectations of when certain events are supposed to occur. In a society structured by chrononormativity, Freeman argues, 'the state and other institutions, including representational apparatuses, link properly temporalized bodies to narratives of movement and change' (4). 'Properly temporalized' individuals are those who achieve their milestones and meet their targets on time. The legibility of individuals' lives therefore depends upon their adherence to temporal normalcy. In other words, for an individual's life trajectory to make sense, it must fit within the ideological framework structuring their broader society. Equally, in narrative terms, those stories that conform to traditional storytelling structures of movement, change and closure are those that culturally 'make sense'.

In *Appropriate Behaviour*, chrononormativity comes into play in two ways: first, at the narrative level, as Shirin's life unfolds at a pace that makes her unintelligible to her family. She does not make sense to them, as she is uninterested in or incapable of living her life according to the traditional milestones of adult femininity. Second, at a structural level, Monaghan notes that while for her, Akhavan's dual narratives are a point of interest, many critics feel differently. For instance, Stephen Holden of the *New York Times* criticizes *Appropriate Behaviour*'s 'lack of an ending or even a sense of direction' (2015: n.p.). Similarly, the choice of descriptors, from 'haphazard' (Merry 2015) to 'unambitious' (Rooney 2014), suggests that evidently, critics are unappreciative of *Appropriate Behaviour*'s asynchronous and deliberately directionless structure. Just as Shirin becomes illegible to her family, so too does the film to some commentators, unaccustomed perhaps to the way that queer narratives tend to favour 'extremes of temporal experience: asynchrony, discontinuity, belatedness, arrest, coincidence, time wasting, reversal, time travel, the palimpsest, boredom and ennui' (Needham 2009: 153), and therefore do not fit so neatly into traditional storytelling structures.

Living without genre

In Chapter 2, I noted that to live without genre would entail living without knowledge of how a situation might develop or reach completion. Of course, nobody's life unfolds outside culture, and therefore nobody truly lives without genre – how could that be possible? What the film expresses so acutely, however, is a sense of feeling isolated from genre, the uncertainty caused by operating without a guide or generic path to follow. *Appropriate Behaviour* does offer two generic paths Shirin could take: Iranian-American conventionality (as epitomized by Shirin's brother, Ali, and his fiancée Layli) and the politicized queer sexuality that her ex-girlfriend Maxine embodies. Layli's character seems to represent all Shirin is not. She is polished, polite and professional, with an appropriately middle-class career as a surgeon – unlike Shirin, who lacks a steady job and is uninterested in finding a respectable middle-class boyfriend to marry. Importantly, the film steers clear from suggesting that Shirin's bisexuality is the reason she doesn't quite fit into her family's ideal ways of living. Rather, she simply doesn't, and the film (wisely) does not offer an explanation as to precisely why this might be the case. Although being bisexual does play a role, it is evident that Shirin's queerness extends beyond her sexuality. Indeed, there is a sense that Shirin does not belong to the two primary genres that structure her life – not because they are in opposition to one another but because she cannot find a place within either.

The notion that genre provides a framework for how a situation may develop is conveyed by Akhavan in a press interview, where she says that her filmmaking is informed by growing up without a sense of what her future would look like:

> When I came out to my family, none of us had ever met an Iranian gay person that we knew of ... it was unspoken completely, so we were all in shock and nobody knew what the future would look like for me. (Kermode 2015)

Akhavan's words resonate with those of Ahmed, who writes that 'the more people travel upon a path, the clearer the path becomes' (2017: 46). Because Akhavan did not know anyone who had travelled upon her particular path (or even one like it), the route towards her future was unclear. Needham suggests similarly that 'queers themselves can be conceived of as existing outside the logic of linear time, as having no future, as being written out of history' (2009: 153). The markers of life progression that might typically structure one's future are disrupted, as though prior to coming out, Akhavan's future was foreseeable. If queerness is 'unspoken completely', there is no history and no pre-established generic guide to draw upon. It is worth noting that Akhavan does still anticipate a future of some description; shock and uncertainty do not scrub out all future hope. Rather, once Akhavan speaks of her own queerness, her projected linear progression towards a knowable future becomes, if not lost entirely, then certainly indeterminate.

In a similar fashion, the film tracks Shirin's search for a genre to help her make sense of what her life *could* look life. This search is of course also characterized by a desire for the good life Berlant identifies. However, that life is far less informed by the dominant norms of postfeminist femininity than in a series like *Girls*. As noted, in certain respects *Girls* and *Appropriate Behaviour* engage with similar subject matter. Their protagonists struggle with dating and relationships, where to live and how to find meaningful work in a post-recession era in which financial difficulties are a matter of course for even the once-protected middle classes, living spaces are often shared by necessity rather than choice and work is irregular and precarious. They therefore have similar material problems and drives, but their methods for coping diverge. If one of the primary ways *Girls* makes sense of Hannah's life is through the postfeminist genres she grew up on and cannot detach from, *Appropriate Behaviour* is structured by a desire for genre itself, as expressed through the film's tagline: 'Being without a cliché to hold onto can be a lonely experience.' There is sharp recognition here that the desire for generic convention is important precisely because it is how we make sense of our lives (Berlant 2011; Kristeva 1969; Marks 1979).[2]

Appropriate Behaviour, of course, does not operate in a vacuum; however, unlike *Girls*' intertextual relationship to *Sex and the City*, it does not immediately appear to be informed by the same recognizable 'anxiety of influence'. The film's most obvious interlocutor (aside from *Girls*), identified by Akhavan as a primary influence, is Woody Allen's *Annie Hall* (1977), which deviates from the well-established romantic comedy convention of 'happily ever after', as the central couple part ways for good rather than reasserting their relationship. By focusing on the breakdown of a relationship rather than a reconciliation, *Appropriate Behaviour* similarly refuses to smooth over or disavow something that is no longer working, instead lingering over and scrutinizing the wreckage. Because the film is neither emulating nor deliberately opposing a specific generic lineage in quite the same way as a series like *Girls*, its sense of loss or disappointment is much more difficult to pin down to an attachment to an affective structure like postfeminism. *Appropriate Behaviour* is not led by genre, and it is not working through desires and attachments for false postfeminist fantasies. In other words, an affective relation of cruel optimism is not at stake here.

Instead, the film reflects on how we are to build lives without knowledge of what those lives might look or feel like. To return to Anderson's observation quoted in the previous chapter, 'we don't know what to make of something that has not come with the metadata of its genre affiliations' (2015). We do not know what to make of an object, a text, a person that does not provide information about its genre. Where does it belong? What are its conventions? What should (or could) our expectations be? This speaks to Shirin's character as being someone who does not seem to know how to build a life. There are paths available to follow, yet they do not seem appropriate to her. Without the detailed guidance that genre provides, Shirin does not know what to make of herself. Analysing Virginia Woolf's *Mrs. Dalloway* (1925), Ahmed writes:

> To follow the paths of life (marriage, reproduction) is to feel that what is before you is a kind of solemn progress, as if you are living somebody else's life, simply going the same way others are going.

It is as if you have left the point of life behind you, as if your life is going through motions that were already in motion before you even arrived. (2010: 71)

Were Shirin to follow Layli's more socially normative path or Maxine's political footsteps, the film makes it clear that she would simply be 'living somebody else's life'. Ahmed continues by arguing that although Mrs Dalloway has followed conventional paths that promised her happiness, she feels differently once she has arrived and that 'for Mrs. Dalloway, to reach these points is to disappear' (2010: 71). Just as Amy's character finds in *Gone Girl*, the implication is clear: if we follow a laid-out path simply because it is expected of us, if we live someone else's life, we are likely to lose ourselves in the process. *Appropriate Behaviour* is about a character who expressly does not want to disappear into a reality that is not her own. Yet Shirin is keen to discover her own conventions, a cliché or a path to follow. There exists a tension, then, between seeking the comfort of generic precursors and insisting on embarking upon a path of one's own.

Appropriate Behaviour is characterized by ambivalence and contradiction, its style and asynchronous narrative effectively conveying the shifting dynamic between intimacy and emotional distance, isolation and confinement that recurs throughout the film. Akhavan's visual style at times seems set in deliberate opposition to key compositional elements such as sound or narrative content. The film's opening, for instance, subtly creates a sense that Shirin is isolated from other people as well as confined by her surroundings. Its first scene holds on a close-up of Shirin's face as she travels on a New York subway train, the handheld camera destabilizing the static composition so that Shirin's face is never entirely accommodated by the frame as she instead shifts slightly in and out of shot. Shirin is then awkwardly confined to the right of the frame in a shot overwhelmed with visual information in the mid- and foreground that emphasizes the relationship between Shirin and her surroundings. A group of children visually dominate the shot and their excited chatter fills the aural diegesis. The decision to

Figure 6 Shirin (Desiree Akhavan) rides the subway in *Appropriate Behaviour*'s (Akhavan 2014) opening sequence. *Appropriate Behaviour*, directed by Desiree Akhavan © Parkville Pictures 2014. All Rights Reserved.

include the dark window of the train to Shirin's right, its blurred edges encroaching on Shirin's bodily space, creates a sense of spatial capture. Here, Shirin is trapped, not by the camera or the framing, but by her environment (Figure 6).

The film is careful not to insist that Shirin is completely isolated from others, and nor is she entirely trapped. As this introductory sequence foretells, there are pockets of air, moments that appear to build towards a resolution that never quite arrives. The closing sequence further illustrates a contradictory polysemous aesthetic by reiterating the film's opening, a decision which both invites comparison and signals a change in Shirin's outlook. Shirin is once again travelling on public transport, now accompanied by her best friend Crystal, a character who appears rarely yet does provide a counterpoint to Shirin's isolation. The bleached-out sunlight framing them is in direct contrast to the darker palette of the opening scene, an evident marker of change. They are framed in what appears to be a conventional two shot, excluding the vertical handrail cutting the screen in half and effectively separating them. Although the strong lighting and inclusion of Crystal indicates that the requisite change has occurred, the composition suggests that even when Shirin is in the company of her best friend, she is still alone (Figure 7).

Searching for Belonging in Appropriate Behaviour

Figure 7 Shirin and Crystal (Halley Feiffer) ride the subway in the film's closing scene (Akhavan 2014). *Appropriate Behaviour*, directed by Desiree Akhavan © Parkville Pictures 2014. All Rights Reserved.

Figure 8 Shirin's moment of equilibrium in the final shot of the film (Akhavan 2014). *Appropriate Behaviour*, directed by Desiree Akhavan © Parkville Pictures 2014. All Rights Reserved.

The train slows as Shirin sees Maxine outside on the platform. Shirin is centre framed, which is notable in its rarity, and provides a compositionally balanced shot that contrasts with the cluttered framing of the opening sequence, therefore signalling a moment of emotional equilibrium (Figure 8). They share a stilted wave goodbye, the camera holding a contemplative close-up of Shirin as Electrelane's rhythmic bass and electronic organ overlays and merges with the diegetic soundtrack.

The formal composition up until this point is highly suggestive of a resolution, not only for Shirin herself but also for her relationship with Maxine. The choice of Electrelane's 'To the East' (2007) is noteworthy, as its upbeat melody contrasts with the melancholy lyrics about the speaker's desire to reconcile, most likely with a romantic partner. It also recalls Shirin and Maxine's happiest moment of the film; the flashback sequence in which they fall in love is scored non-diegetically to the Electrelane song 'Oh Sombra!' (2004), another apposition between love and melancholy. The form of both the film and its closing song sits in conflict with our knowledge of their narrative content, complicating a reading of the conclusion as purely indicative of transformation or growth, even though it does not entirely preclude such a reading altogether either. The closing sequence works hard to communicate that something has changed, though it is unclear how or what exactly. In essence, the film is about someone whose circumstances *appear* to change, yet essentially remain the same.

The ambivalent title offers a useful key to the film itself; on the one hand, 'appropriate' can refer to a set of fluctuating norms and expectations, while on the other it describes something belonging to oneself, seizing and appropriating norms and conventions as required. Akhavan portrays Shirin as rarely capable of adapting to or acting according to her different social environments, the role of middle-class Iranian-American daughter seemingly in conflict with that of the ideal 'queer' woman that Maxine's character exemplifies. Shirin's way of living is too aimless, too alien, so much that it frustrates her family, particularly her brother who cannot understand Shirin's divergence from his own normative path. However, Shirin finds Maxine's attempts to 'broaden [her] horizons' by reading queer literature, and her insistence that coming out to her parents is the key to asserting Shirin's queer identity, equally stifling. Maxine's character functions in part as an aspirational figure of ultimate queer perfection or self-actualization. Essentially, Maxine tries to politicize Shirin, implying that Shirin could become more appropriately queer if she read the right books, attended activist meetings and came out to her parents. Shirin is caught between these styles of living: her non-heteronormativity, lack of a steady job and the shared apartment her brother disparages as a 'refugee camp', marking her as too queer for her family to comprehend. Yet there is also the suggestion that Shirin is not nearly queer enough for Maxine; as Shirin quips, she is not quite ready yet for Leslie Feinberg's queer classic *Stone Butch Blues* (1993), having not yet finished the much-derided *Twilight* fantasy series. This is one of two instances where the film intertextually references postfeminist culture in order to demonstrate the cultural and political differences between Maxine's and Shirin's characters. In a later scene, Maxine professes to 'hate' *Sex and the City*, finding it 'boring', whereas Shirin finds it 'pretty fucking entertaining'. While not a huge divide between the characters, the film clearly aligns Shirin with two postfeminist texts that are often perceived as feminine 'guilty pleasures' (Petersen 2012) or criticized for their gender politics and traditional narratives (Merskin 2011; Siegel 2002; Taylor 2011). Shirin is therefore coded as less overtly political, or more casually complicit with normative feminine culture than Maxine, who staunchly disavows it.

Appropriate Behaviour at first seems to be telling a story in which resolution entails Shirin fully committing to either way of living and leaving the other behind. In other words, precisely the dilemma resisted by Feinberg's semi-autobiographical protagonist in *Stone Butch Blues*, who accordingly decides to remain in the sphere of the in-between, rejecting the edicts of hetero- and homonormativity alike. The argument instigating Shirin and Maxine's breakup messily summarizes Shirin's options from Maxine's point of view: either Shirin can continue in a 'creepy codependent relationship' with her parents and settle into the life of a good Iranian daughter or Shirin can come out to them and live the queer life that Maxine's character embodies. Maxine's dialogue here, especially the use of the term 'codependent' to pathologize Shirin's relationship with her family, is typical of the notion Ahmed identifies, that 'custom and culture become things that this brown queer child has to leave behind' and that 'happiness is assumed to require getting out' (2017: 52). As Ahmed continues, 'In the case of a brown migrant family, the family is imagined as a dead weight: there is an expectation that her family will be more oppressive, less tolerant; less supportive of her freedom' (52). Later in the film, Maxine's surprise that Shirin's family is unaware of her bisexuality is met with sarcasm by Shirin:

> I'm sorry, what country is it that you get stoned to death if you're convicted of being gay? Oh, yeah. Wait, I know. It's Iran. The country that my entire family comes from.

This dialogue alludes to the prejudiced perception that immigrant families respond negatively to their children's queerness. Yet the film refutes the notion that Shirin's family is what stands in the way of either her bisexuality or her happiness. Shirin does in fact come out to her family, the ambiguous outcome of the scene not only working against any traditional notions of catharsis but also negating any impression that her family might be intrinsically less tolerant or supportive. As we shall later see, the film sidesteps the issue of choice and in doing so evades the classic narrative of forward momentum and resolution. Instead, *Appropriate Behaviour* illuminates the isolating effect of feeling trapped within and between two ways of living, with the conventions of either Shirin cannot fully comply.

Queerlinearity and conventionality

Appropriate Behaviour advances a queerlinear mode of spectatorship, unfolding a richly complex coexistence of conflicting aesthetics in which Shirin's difficulties cannot be easily essentialized or determined. I use the term queerlinear instead of non-linear, for as Dyi Huijg (2021) points out with her coinage of the term 'curvilinearity' (used to articulate neurodivergent subjectivities and life trajectories), the prefix 'non-' presumes linearity as the norm. Instead, queerlinearity offers a way of imagining queer life trajectories that does not always necessarily set them as deviating from or in opposition to the norm.

Queerlinearity resonates with Freeman's chrononormative model, which demands that our use of time must be productive, in such a way that 'the past seems useless unless it predicts and becomes material for a future' (2010: 5). A presumption of chrononormativity permeates the scene introducing Shirin's family. Establishing a misalignment between their standards of success, Shirin's brother makes a derisive comment that she is doing 'jack shit' with her master's degree in journalism. To Ali, Shirin's education is irrelevant as it resides firmly in the past and has not provided the requisite material for her future in the way his own degree has led to a productive career in medicine. Along similar lines, her mother, Nasrin, attempts to mine Shirin's history for potential, as she proudly recounts Shirin's high school swimming success. Her father, Mehrdad, agrees, saying, 'this body's made for swimming, look at these shoulders', while affectionately touching Shirin's shoulder. As a result, Shirin's prior achievement is mapped onto her present-day body, as though Mehrdad is attempting to bridge the physical divide between father and daughter, as well as the intangible disconnect between Shirin's past ability and her future prospects. In the same way, Shirin's hands inspire Nasrin, who takes hold of them, proposing a career in hand modelling, implying that if the relevant material cannot be extracted from Shirin's past, perhaps she ought to simply make use of whatever is available to her in the here and now.

As well as drawing attention to paths not taken, and pursuits Shirin is capable of, yet evidently not (yet) embarked upon, this scene effectively conveys that the distance between Shirin and her family is not in fact that great a divide. Ali and Layli's cohesive relationship functions narratively not only as a foil to Shirin's lack of professional ambition but also as aspirational image of the connection Shirin seeks throughout the film. However, although Akhavan's audience is likely conversant with the pop culture norms and generic conventions surrounding sibling rivalry and middle-class family aspirations towards professions such as medicine, there is little sense that Nasrin and Mehrdad are disappointed in Shirin or compare her unfavourably to her brother. Interestingly, although her demeanour registers a resigned embarrassment and she is framed as being slightly set apart from the rest of her family, Shirin does not avoid her parents' casual physical affection; however, neither does she return it. All of which suggests that Shirin feels simultaneously detached from as well as trapped within her family structure yet offers no easy explanation as to why this might be. Instead, Shirin's evident detachment is granted uneasy coexistence with her parents' well-intentioned support. Writing about awkwardness in American comedy, Adam Kotsko points out that feelings of discomfort are often generated by 'the fact of being an outsider who is misread as an insider' (2010: 72). Ringmar might also consider Shirin as someone who is 'badly attuned' to her environment, noting that 'there are many ways in which we can fit, or not fit, in' (2017: 5), and that our attunement to particular situations is what generates particular affects. Both Ringmar's and Kotsko's observations lend apt descriptions to *Appropriate Behaviour*. There is a distinct impression that Shirin's family perceive her as someone who ought to fit in with their ways of living, and they consequently cannot fathom why she does not. It is this sense of Shirin's mistaken identity that produces an affective unmooring, for neither her parents nor Shirin herself appear able to access an appropriate frame of reference.

A second family-oriented sequence reiterates Shirin's detachment from her family and compounds her temporal atypicality as regards to conventional milestones. Shirin's relationship to normativity is figured as being misalignment with her family's, as shown in a short scene intercutting between Shirin and Mehrdad, and Ali and Nasrin, each sibling sniping about the other to their parents. Shot for comedic effect, the scene juxtaposes their differences (their attitudes towards marriage and conventionality) and similarities (the way each speaks about the other), deepening our understanding of each sibling's relationship to the family unit and their adherence (or not) to expected social norms. Ali's assertion that Shirin has 'no goals or aspirations, she takes nothing seriously, she's becoming a loser' is visually reinforced as his dialogue overlays two close-up images of a burnt oven tray and a spiral of flypaper. Unlike Mehrdad, who tells Shirin to mind her own business when she feigns concern for Ali's well-being, Nasrin agrees with Ali by saying, 'You don't think I'm doing my best? She's not easy.' Shirin's concerns are summarily dismissed, whereas Ali's are supported by both dialogue and visual imagery. In addition, while Ali and Nasrin are discussing present-day worries (Nasrin: 'I think she has self-esteem issues'), Shirin's dialogue, spoken in a hushed tone as through telling a ghost story, cautions, in the conditional mood, that her brother 'would do anything to please [their parents]' and that 'one day he could pull a gun on his co-workers'. There is no indication that Shirin truly believes any of her assertions, or that they are likely to translate into reality. Mehrdad's reaction is similarly incredulous, and although he does not refute Shirin's claims, this is perhaps because it would be unnecessary to do so. Ali does not require defence here, so when Shirin asserts that she simply doesn't 'want [Ali] to find himself 20 years from now, fat and bald', Mehrdad's only reaction is that 'the men in our family don't go bald', effectively puncturing Shirin's narrative in which her brother becomes imprisoned by normativity.

While evidently uninterested in maligning socially conventional lives, the film does draw attention to the ways in which happiness and the attendant good life are associated with normativity, or as Ahmed puts it, how happiness often 'involves a way of being aligned with others, of facing the right way' (2010: 45). Ahmed suggests that when happiness is linked to normativity, it comes to mean 'living a certain kind of life, one that reaches certain points and which, in reaching these points, creates happiness for others' (2010: 48). From her family's perspective, if Shirin would simply face the 'right way' (presumably by aspiring and working towards conventional life goals), she would be able to fulfil the potential they perceive to be at risk of being wasted. However, not only is Shirin out of sync with her family's way of living but also her misalignment and apparent lack of ambition in reaching those 'certain points' (an appropriate career, a romantic partner) is perceived as a denial of happiness, both Shirin's own and her family's.

Examining the synergies between queerness and 'slow cinema', Karl Schoonover argues that because queerness abides by an atypical temporality, it 'often looks a lot like wasted time, wasted lives, wasted productivity' (2012: 73). Shirin's way of living appears to look much like this to her family, her brother worrying that in not reaching the expected milestones Shirin is wasting her potential. Shirin's queerlinearity renders her illegible to her family, who cannot conceive of a temporal logic beyond the dominant model of 'time-as-productive' (Freeman 2010: 5). Ali's perception is that Shirin is 'perfectly capable of being normal', highlighting Shirin's arguable inability to fulfil expectations of living a successful life. *Appropriate Behaviour* is devoted to Shirin's search for an attachment to hold onto, evoking the reassurance of having a path laid out for one to follow, that no matter how restrictive or problematic the norms of a genre of living might be, at least one knows what to do and how to be. Gestures towards the coming-of-age narrative produce a desire to see Shirin either devise or slot into her own genre, or to find a way of living gracefully among the two she already inhabits. However, the film ultimately suggests that the genres of Iranian-American conventionality and queer sexuality are not in conflict; it is in fact Shirin herself who is at odds with both.

While Shirin struggles to reconcile the two genres she inhabits and her search for a new path, comedy series *Broad City* offers another example of a queerlinear narrative which rejects altogether the heteronormative good life fantasies *Girls* obsesses over and offers chronoqueer notions of success and growing up (Kamińska 2020; Kanai and Dobson 2019). Co-starring its creators as best friends Abbi and Ilana, *Broad City* is about millennial women navigating life in New York – a premise it shares with *Girls* and *Appropriate Behaviour*. However, although each links their characters' arrested development to their socio-economic circumstances (DeCarvalho 2013; Kamińska 2020; Wanzo 2016), Ilana and Abbi enjoy rather than agonize over their extended adolescence. As Aleksandra Kamińska observes, *Broad City* portrays failure as 'an acceptable mode of living' (2020: 1048), offering an alternative way of thinking about (or indeed ignoring altogether) the normative fantasies and coming-of-age milestones the character in *Girls* might also fail to meet, yet remain fixated on.

Broad City's model of failure and enjoyment relies, in part, on the characters' acute 'inability to be recognized as adults' (Kamińska 2020: 1056). This is seen primarily in their refusal to conform to the expected scripts and milestones associated with adulthood, which 'can be also read as an act of queering normative life trajectories' (1060). Similarly, while Kanai and Dobson characterize Abbi and Ilana as high-energy strivers within the context of a gendered neoliberal labour market, they also note that the vast majority of their efforts are either aimless or else otherwise unsuccessful, and that 'the show critically questions the relation of such striving to idealized gendered economic subjectivities and the promise of career and financial success' (2019: 519). With Ilana slacking off at her sales rep job and encouraging Abbi to do the same, the series instead prioritizes what Schoonover identifies as an active waste of time and productivity.

Another notable aspect of the series is its casual and matter-of-fact approach to queer sexuality. Ilana has sexual relationships with men and women, and is openly attracted to Abbi, who at first identifies as straight, and in the final season has a relationship with a woman and comes out as queer. The show also queers normative notions of heterosexuality when in the fourth episode of season two ('Knockoffs'), Abbi hooks up with the neighbour she has been obsessed with for several episodes, who subverts her expectations of the encounter (and ours) by asking her to 'peg' him with a strap-on dildo. Though Abbi is initially intimidated by the prospect, after a phone call with the sex-positive Ilana (who is so excited by the idea that she does a backflip), she steps back into the bedroom with confidence, in a provocative shot of Jeremy framed between Abbi's legs, the green dildo jutting into the top of the frame (Figure 9). This scene above all showcases Abbi and Ilana's open and accepting friendship, disclosing yet more queer connotations. Ilana is delighted to receive the call and also points out when Abbi says she doesn't know what to do: 'Bitch, you know. You wouldn't have called *me* if you didn't' (2.4). The scene therefore hinges not on whether Abbi ought to peg Jeremy but on Ilana equipping her with the knowledge

Figure 9 *Broad City*'s Abbi (Abbi Jacobson) wears a strap-on dildo framed from between her legs (Glazer and Jacobson 2015: 2.4). *Broad City* © 3 Arts Entertainment/Comedy Central 2014–19.

and enthusiasm to try something Abbi admits she hadn't 'envisioned' in her fantasies about him.

A storyline about this kind of non-normative heterosexual sex is rare, for as Caroline Framke notes, 'There just aren't many shows out there that include sex toys beyond quick gross-out jokes. Dildos especially are depicted less as legitimate sex toys than ridiculous novelties on par with those bachelorette party dick straws' (2015: n.p.). In *Broad City*, it is notable that the humour does not stem from a gross-out joke, nor does the series present either the sex toy itself as ridiculous or mock Jeremy's character for his desires. Even later in the episode after Abbi has ruined his customized dildo in the dishwasher and tries to replace it with a sub-par version, humour is derived from Jeremy's exacting standards ('Did you seriously think that you were just gonna stick that inside of me and I wouldn't feel the difference?'), rather than his sexual preferences. Humour is similarly drawn from Ilana's dramatic enthusiasm – for the sexual act itself (noting, for instance, that she kept a strap-on under her pillow for years in the hope of having a similar encounter) – and most of all, for the opportunity to help broaden Abbi's sexual horizons ("This is a dream come true. Thank you for sharing this with me'). Rather than generating pleasure from mocking non-normative sexuality, it is instead presented as a pleasurable act that both Abbi and Jeremy enjoy (in addition to Ilana's vicarious enjoyment).

With its focus on pleasure and friendship over careers and romance, *Broad City*'s rejection of normative markers of adulthood renders Abbi and Ilana illegible as adult subjects, in much the same way Shirin's queerness renders her illegible to her family. However, Abbi and Ilana's orientation towards each other provides a sense of belonging that is absent in both *Girls* and *Appropriate Behaviour*. Because although they may be illegible as 'appropriate' or normative adults, Abbi and Ilana always remain legible to one another, with their friendship underpinning the heart of the show. Since much of Abbi and Ilana's energy is directed towards their friendship with one another, Kanai and Dobson suggest similarly to Kamińska that the show encourages us to 'imagine an alignment of such gendered enthusiasm and passion that is oriented primarily towards important social and collective bonds, and away from capitalist re-attachments' (522). This kind of affective social and collective orientation is something I return to later in Chapter 5's discussion of *Girlhood*, which focuses on the relational bonds between its teenage protagonist and her friends.

Requeering the coming-out narrative

One of the primary tensions driving *Appropriate Behaviour* is that Shirin's family does not know that she is bisexual. Shirin's reluctance to be open with her parents about her sexuality is also one of the key conflicts between her and Maxine. From early scenes in which her parents make assumptions about her presumed heterosexuality by teasing her about boys, it is easy to infer that the distance between Shirin and her family is an effect of her sexuality, either due to her difference from them or Shirin's closeted preservation of sameness. As Margaretta Jolly notes, the concept of coming out continues to hold traction in fictional and autobiographical narratives (2001), typically focusing on self-disclosure as a process of painful yet ultimately uplifting self-discovery or an inspirational story of tolerance and acceptance. Despite the post-closet framework that emerged during the late 1990s, arguing that particularly for Americans, coming out had become normalized and played a less significant role (Seidman, Meeks and Traschen 1999), coming out is still fundamentally linked to the experience of being/becoming gay (Jagose 1996; Meeks 2006). In this model, narrative conflict and momentum is generated via a character's sexuality, and narrative closure is attained through the coming-out process.

Expectation might therefore dictate that coming out would either save the relationship with Maxine and/or resolve the distance between Shirin and her parents. However, as each flashback of Shirin and Maxine's relationship details, Shirin's coming out was far from the only conflict they shared. Similarly, later scenes in which Shirin does come out to Ali and Nasrin do not fully support either reading regarding the distance between them. If coming-out genres demand narrative momentum and transformation through the process of self-disclosure, *Appropriate Behaviour* thoroughly deflates those expectations by refusing to perform coming out as an event that provides either protagonist or audience with a sense of resolution.

This refusal bears some resemblance to Nicholas Holm's interpretation of the deadpan comic mode and Berlant's concept of 'flat affect' (2015: 193). While deadpan is typically understood as an 'emotionless and expressionless presentation of self' (2017: 104), Holm widens this characterization to include any 'lack of aesthetic and affective markers that conventionally help guide audience interpretation – not just facial cues and body movement and comportment but also a wide range of visual, linguistic and even audial markers' (105). One example of this flattened or recessive comic mode, Holm suggests, is the increasing absence of a laugh track to emphasize punchlines, which withholds formal comic markers from the audience, providing them with fewer clues to interpret (106). Holm connects deadpan to flat affect, or what Berlant describes as an 'underperformed emotional style' (2015: 199) in which an individual's presentation cannot be affectively linked to their internal state. Flat affect, most importantly, constitutes a 'recession from melodramatic norms' (193) which demand that emotion be performed with overt intensity. Crucially, flat affect is not characterized as a refusal or withholding of emotion per se; rather, it signals a refusal to perform certain types of emotions demanded by the dominant affective structure (Berlant 2015; Holm 2017). I argue that *Appropriate Behaviour*'s reversal of expectation regarding the dominant norms of self-disclosure registers as precisely this kind of refusal.

Shirin comes out to Ali and Nasrin separately over the course of two scenes, both set during a New Year party at the family home. The setting recalls an earlier flashback sequence in which Shirin introduces Maxine to her parents as a friend rather than a romantic partner. It also associates coming out with the auspices of the New Year, inviting the potential of a fresh start for Shirin. In contrast to the film's heavy use of isolating single reverse shots, Shirin and Ali share the frame when she tells him about her prior relationship with Maxine, though tellingly, each character mostly remains on their own side of the screen, with a dark empty space separating them. While the two shot gives the potential for some form of togetherness, their communication remains one-sided: Shirin directly faces Ali for the duration of the scene, whereas he continually turns away, urging her to join the party with him. Nonetheless, the scene can be read as having a relatively positive outcome as Ali does not say anything overtly disapproving. It can equally be argued that Ali's indifferent response of 'and that's a thing?' in response to Shirin's declaration of her bisexuality, along with his objections to telling their parents, opens up the capacity for a negative reading. What is more significant is that Ali's terse dialogue and casually dismissive tone are both in keeping with his character, as established early in the film. Within the context of the film in its entirety, Ali's reaction is not truly a reaction at all; instead, it constitutes a non-response. Like much of the film, information is received and assimilated, and nothing really changes. Shirin is not suddenly rendered 'appropriate' by her disclosure. The understated rhythm of the scene is particularly relevant in terms of generic conventions that demand coming out to be an event, regardless of the reception. As well, coming out is viewed by Bonnie J. Dow as a 'stock storyline' mainly interested in the effects on personal relationships (with heterosexuals) or narratives of acceptance and tolerance (2003: 261). Here, however, the coming-out scenes are separated by two quick cuts to what almost appear to be filler shots: a waiter hands a drink to a guest, and a couple chat on the busy dance floor. The party continues, unchanged. Altogether, Ali's non-response forecloses a reading of the scene as an event, and their relationship resumes, intact.

Unlike Shirin and Ali's conversation, the second coming-out scene with Nasrin uses a series of isolating reverse shots, though each character once again occupies their own half of the screen. For the duration, Shirin speaks English, and her mother responds in Persian. Crucially, Nasrin's mode of communication does not change in response to Shirin's statement: 'Mom, I'm a little bit gay.' Therefore, while it could be possible to read Nasrin's codeswitching as a method of distancing, her bilingualism is in fact established early and continues throughout the film. Where Ali is exasperated, appearing to interpret Shirin's sexuality as simply one more example in a litany of ways that Shirin refuses to be normal, Nasrin's reaction is a patent denial, simply saying 'No. You're not' and silencing her with a 'Shh'. Her response does not lend itself easily to a positive interpretation; however, the disavowal registers similarly as a non-event where neither the situation nor their relationship is altered.

If we assume that coming out has conventionally been a moment of truth-telling in lesbian and gay cinema (Martin 1998: 281), *Appropriate Behaviour* makes this same connection when Ali cannot see the point in Shirin telling their parents now that her relationship with Maxine has ended. By saying that 'it's a pretty big thing not to be honest about', Shirin counters Ali's conflation of her sexuality with the relationship itself. Not coming out, accordingly, would be to live a lie – as knowledge of the 'real' Shirin depends upon it. As expectations around the coming-out narrative dictate, the audience may be anticipating a cathartic resolution to emerge from the process. Yet the film instead relates the implausibility of catharsis arising from the act of coming out. As Butler asks, 'What or who is it that is "out", made manifest and fully disclosed, when and if I reveal myself as lesbian? What is it that is now known, anything?' (1991: 15). Shirin's honesty is not a revelation or a liberation; she acquires no truth or self-knowledge. It simply happens, and the film moves on to its closing sequence. In this sense, Shirin's sexuality is not incidental, but neither is it a problem to be resolved. The two scenes work somewhat differently, yet both have the same narrative function in deflating any anticipation of growth or change as the expected result of coming out, leaving Shirin's character in much the same position as when the film began. This poses a question of why, exactly, does coming out signal the absence of character development? As with the rest of the film, there are no straightforward answers to be found. One suggestion might be that if coming out typically signifies a rebirth of sorts for the queer character, perhaps *Appropriate Behaviour* is simply reluctant to situate such self-redefinition as a 'prize' one attains by integrating within heteronormative society.

Appropriate Behaviour might not feature a protagonist who undergoes a fundamental transformation; however, the narrative is also not at an impasse in the same way that *Gone Girl* and *Girls* reach a kind of paralysis, caught in the cracks between postfeminist aspiration and reality. Perhaps to an audience trained to perceive forward momentum and transformation as the only acceptable way to deliver narrative satisfaction, the film falls short. However, as Monaghan suggests in her comparison of the opening and closing sequences, *Appropriate Behaviour*'s 'lack of direction does not mean that the film cannot end on a hopeful note' (2016: 157). The film appears to sidestep expectations of transformation and growth, while still managing to deliver a sense of closure for its protagonist. Freeman argues that within chrononormative societies 'having a life entails the ability to narrate it not only in these state-sanctioned terms but also in a novelistic framework: as event-centered, goal-oriented, intentional, and culminating in epiphanies or major transformations' (2010: 5). *Appropriate Behaviour*, however, reminds us that stories do not need to culminate in major epiphanies to be deserving of resolution. Shirin's life might not make normative cultural sense, yet Akhavan ensures that her queerlinear way of living aligns with filmic convention. The film is structured to deliver narrative closure, despite very little (if indeed any) growth or change occurring. Shirin remains awkward, at times inappropriate; her self-disclosure does not radically alter her family dynamics, and she might always feel alone, even with the people she loves. This suggests that for Shirin's story to come to a close, nothing *has* to change. According to Halberstam, 'queer subcultures produce alternative temporalities by allowing their participants to believe that their futures can be imagined according to logics that lie outside of those paradigmatic markers of life experience' (2005: 2). The film offers a vision of a hopeful future independent of normative convention. Queer stories and queer lives might unfold in unexpected rhythms – perhaps not even endeavouring a movement towards typical goals and milestones or including radical shifts and transformations – but they can still achieve moments of satisfaction, fulfilment and hopefulness.

Breaking up with the camera in *Fleabag*

In the British series *Fleabag*, heterosexual romance and self-transformation are decoupled from narrative closure. Created by and starring Phoebe Waller-Bridge, *Fleabag* is a half-hour comedy drama which, over two seasons of six episodes each, follows the thirty-something eponymous protagonist's darkly comic struggles after the death of her best friend. The series' defining stylistic feature is its use of direct address, a device which allows Fleabag to engage with the camera, speaking in comedic asides, or else offering the audience conspiratorial glances and wry smiles. *Fleabag*'s use of direct address recalls *Gone Girl*'s preoccupation with notions of narrative control and agency, deception and concealment. Here, however, Fleabag's need to present herself as in control of her own narrative is precisely because, as the show gradually reveals, she isn't in control at all and is in fact plagued with guilt about cheating on her best friend, Boo, who then accidentally killed herself by stepping out into a bike lane.

Faye Woods argues that Fleabag 'performs social mastery through her direct address', but that the conspiratorial device is also an indicator of her performance of femininity and 'attempts to conceal her own moments of flailing, frustration and fury' (2019: 207–8). While Fleabag's own life is messy, fraught with financial and emotional instability, and lacking in intimacy, her direct address performs the opposite; suddenly, through a sly glance or aside, Fleabag presents herself as in control of her narrative, able to repackage embarrassing situations into witty one-liners, the direct address enabling a closeness of sorts, and one which at first conceals the absence of social connection in her life.

Direct address is not only about control but also, Kathryn VanArendonk notes, functions as an escape from reality. By turning to the camera, Fleabag 'pulls us into her fantastically charming, self-destructive orbit while also stepping out of her own life for a moment' (2019: n.p.). With her witty comic asides, Fleabag confides in us primarily so that she doesn't have to confide in other people. The camera and, by proxy, the audience become an affective outlet for the frustration, resentment and humour that Fleabag cannot or will not express to anyone else. VanArendonk describes the relationship between Fleabag and the camera as one of 'false intimacy', as opposed to the 'real intimacy' shared with a nameless character in the second season known as the 'Priest'.[3] Rather than draw a distinction between true/false or authentic/performative, I would instead argue that all intimacy is to a degree performed, and that this does not preclude it from also carrying authenticity. However, it is clear that the intimacy of Fleabag's direct address is both a substitute for the connection Fleabag once shared with Boo and a method of distancing herself from other characters by creating a 'secret camera friend' (as Waller-Bridge describes it) to talk to instead of her family or sexual partners. In this sense, her disclosures function as authentic acts of intimacy, while also being deeply performative. Authenticity and performance are inextricable, therefore, with neither negating the other's presence.

Narrative control via direct address also serves a wider function, as Orlaith Darling observes, of exposing 'smooth, collected' socially viable neoliberal femininity (as epitomized by Fleabag's sister, Claire) as a performance and suggesting 'that displays of emotion, which are anathema under neoliberalism, are natural' (2020: 13). Throughout the series, Fleabag's character is often imagined as a 'body onto which people project their "failures" and "excesses"'; for example, when Claire suffers a miscarriage in a restaurant bathroom during a family meal and returns to the table in grim denial, it is Fleabag who lies to protect her sister, by telling everyone that it was she who miscarried and thereby taking on Claire's excess of femininity as her own (14). However, in the final episode of the first season, there is a transition comparable to the one in *Appropriate Behaviour*'s final sequence where the absence of change or epiphany is linked to narrative closure. Like Shirin, 'Fleabag has not transformed herself' (14). What happens instead, Darling argues, citing Fleabag's father's affirming dialogue ('I think you know how to love better than any of us. That's why you find it all so painful'), is that Fleabag 'has taught those around her to re-frame "excess" as the ability to love' (2019: 14). Rather than transforming its protagonist, *Fleabag* asserts that she does not need to adhere to neoliberal edicts of self-improvement to become a more socially acceptable subject.

The series finale presents another reflection on transition versus transformation, while also decoupling narrative closure from heterosexual romantic milestones. Having grown closer over the course of season two, Fleabag and the Priest have sex in the penultimate episode, despite his earlier assertion that they could only be friends. Fleabag's attraction to the Priest is significant because he is the only character who observes and comments on Fleabag's acts of direct address, turning towards the camera as she does and asking Fleabag, 'Where did you just go?' (2.3 'Episode 3'). Being seen by the Priest in this moment initially provokes panic and shock but later prompts a genuine intimacy between the two characters during a scene in a church confessional booth. VanArendonk notes that here, Fleabag is 'actually confessing, in a way that she's never been able to do as directly or as honestly when she's speaking to her secret camera friends' (2019: n.p.). We only see what Fleabag presents to us, whereas the Priest notices her in the moment she turns away from her life and towards us. Being perceived in this unexpected way makes Fleabag gradually turn towards the Priest instead of the camera, and notably, in the scene where they have sex, Fleabag pushes the camera away entirely. Her success in not only turning herself away from the camera but also turning the camera itself away from her evokes Fleabag's unsuccessful attempts to do the latter in the season one finale (Figure 10). It is during this episode that Fleabag's narrative control first unravels entirely. Overwhelmed by painful flashbacks to her betrayal of Boo (which she had previously been able to suppress and thereby conceal from the audience), on this occasion, when Fleabag backs away from the camera, it continues to follow her. This progression recalls *Appropriate Behaviour*'s avowal that narrative change can occur without the expected transformation occurring within the protagonist herself. After all, Fleabag has not undergone some grand transformation which allows her to narratively progress; instead, it is the moment of being seen as she truly is – a person in such desperate need of escape that she dissociates from her life – which marks the moment of transition. Once again, Fleabag is not transformed from an inappropriate to an appropriate subject; instead, she is simply accepted.

Figure 10 Fleabag (Phoebe Waller-Bridge) backs away from the camera in the season one finale (*Fleabag*, Waller-Bridge 2016: 1.6). *Fleabag* © Two Brothers Pictures/BBC 2016–19.

The true moment of change comes once again from Fleabag's newfound ability to turn away from the intimacy offered by the camera and turn instead 'toward her own life, her own family, her own relationships with people who can speak back to her' (VanArendonk 2019). This is the final image of the series, following the Priest's gentle rejection (Figure 11). *Fleabag* thereby ends their romance and, then perhaps even more significantly, resolves the series by breaking up with the camera. As with the rom-com run in *Girls*, both generic precedent and years of cultural training govern my own initial desires to see Fleabag and the Priest get their happily ever after. Yet what the series delivers is altogether more satisfying. The end of their relationship signals a decisive break from the dominant cultural idea that the most appropriate or desirable narrative outcome is a romantic one. The series instead invests in Fleabag and her own future instead of in her capacity for self-transformation or to achieve milestones of heterosexual normalcy. Rather than continue to package embarrassing moments, bad sex and uncomfortable feelings as a series of quips and witticisms, *Fleabag* makes the bold choice to have its protagonist step away from the intimacy and scrutiny of the camera's lens.

In this chapter, I've sought to work somewhat against the grain of the previous two, making a departure from the difficulties of shaking loose the firm grip postfeminist genres can claim over feminine

Figure 11 Fleabag waves goodbye to the camera in the series finale (*Fleabag*, Waller-Bridge 2019: 2.6). *Fleabag* © Two Brothers Pictures/BBC 2016–19.

subjectivity and instead exploring the challenges of feeling isolated from popular or normative genres. Where Chapter 2 examined the impact of devastating attachments to postfeminist culture through the frame of cruel optimism, this chapter is concerned with what it might be like to feel detached from normative genres, especially those genres to which we ostensibly belong, and with which our social others appear to seamlessly align. It also offers insight into the pleasures of queer temporalities and the importance of finding different forms of narrative closure that do not rely on traditional happiness scripts. Therefore, while establishing that postfeminism is not the sole defining frame for making sense of girlhood and femininity, this chapter has also emphasized that belonging, isolation and a simultaneous disillusionment with and desire for social and generic convention remain crucial to millennial genres.

Part Two
Resilience

4

Suffering, resilience and defiance in *The Hunger Games*

Part 2 explores how the postfeminist legacy of agency and empowerment manifests in contemporary coming-of-age genres as an imperative towards resilience. In this chapter, I sketch out the intersections between resilience discourse and contemporary girlhood genres, using Suzanne Collins's best-selling trilogy *The Hunger Games* as a primary case study. Chapter 5 extends my examination of resilient femininities by exploring contextually specific modes of transformative and relational resilience in French coming-of-age film *Bande de Filles/Girlhood*. As I discussed in the introduction, our post-recession era has seen an increased focus on resilient femininity in contemporary media (Gill and Orgad 2018; James 2015; McRobbie 2020). The Netflix series *Unbreakable Kimmy Schmidt* (Fey and Carlock 2015–19), for example, uses surreal comedy aesthetics and a heightened sartorial colour palette to construct protagonist Kimmy as upbeat and optimistic as she perseveres in her transition to life in New York after escaping a fifteen-year imprisonment by a doomsday cult leader. Resilience genres typically use these kinds of feel-good aesthetics to offset the disturbing or unpleasant subject matter that shapes their protagonists' subjectivity and traumatic coming-of-age experience. *The Hunger Games* is especially instructive in this regard, as its heroine must practise resilience, not simply to overcome adolescent trauma or to achieve adult accomplishment but to secure her continued survival.

My discussion in this chapter draws on Robin James's (2015) work, which analyses the aesthetics of resilience in contemporary pop music and how these are tied to neoliberal capitalism. While resilience is colloquially understood as the ability to 'bounce back' from adversity, James theorizes resilience as the capacity to overcome trauma or suffering by converting it into surplus value. I adapt this theory slightly, because as I will later clarify, what James terms simply 'resilience' (and sets in opposition to melancholy), I find more useful to call 'suffering resilience'. To illuminate the types of resilience *The Hunger Games* formulates, I use two models of agency. In the first part of this chapter, I develop the idea of suffering resilience by introducing Jane Elliott's concept of 'suffering agency' (2015), which captures a subject's capacity to make choices within extremely restricted circumstances. Then, in the second part, I return to Ruti's model of defiant agency to explore how *The Hunger Games* constructs moments of 'defiant resilience'. The final section examines the narrative structure of resilience, comparing *The Hunger Games* to the film adaptation of *The Hate U Give*.

One of my chief interests in this chapter is the idea that social viability for women and girls increasingly relies upon their capacity to perform resilience. Working from a Marxist standpoint, James argues that overcoming identity-based oppression 'in socially profitable ways' (2015: 15) offers subjects inclusion within neoliberalized systems of social and political power, thereby updating traditional hierarchies of identity-based oppression. As Chapter 1 demonstrated, to attain social viability within discourses of postfeminist empowerment, female subjects must perform and conceal traditional femininity to present their conformity with feminine social norms as freely chosen and agentic. Traditional femininity is figured as 'damage' under this paradigm – something for women to quietly overcome. By contrast, resilience as a newly conventionalized feminine norm requires women and girls to reveal their feminine damage to overcome it (James 2015). As James puts it, 'Women are always-already damaged by patriarchy' (2015: 82). Fragility therefore remains the presumed foundation of femininity, and the negative effects of patriarchy are regarded as the default setting, with women becoming responsible for the labour of overcoming their perceived gender deficits to find acceptance as viable subjects.[1] This marks a major departure from the norms of postfeminist empowerment discourses that require female subjects to perform and quietly conceal traditional femininity.

Within the academy, resilience is 'a complex and contradictory multi-disciplinary concept, with multiple meanings' (Mykhnenko 2016: 191). Broadly speaking, debates about what constitutes resilience straddle two lines of thought. First, there is the notion that resilience means individuals and systems must remain the same in the face of adversity. Andrew Zolli and Ann Marie Healy call this 'the capacity of a system, enterprise, or a person to maintain its core purpose and integrity in the face of dramatically changed circumstances' (2012: 7). The second view entails adapting positively to adversity or undertaking a process of transformation towards a more sustainable and productive path (Martin and Sunley 2015: 13 in Mykhnenko 2016: 191). Personal or systemic adaptability is key to this view of resilience, implying that both internal and external conditions are subject to change. The first strand prioritizes internal coherence, the other transformation. Yet, as Ron Martin and Peter Sunley point out, resilience scholarship 'tends to portray systems as responding dichotomously to shocks, either recovering to original state or pushed to a new state, whereas in reality response is a complex mix of continuity and change' (2015: 8). This means that whether at the individual or systemic level, there are likely to be elements of retaining core stability that work alongside the ability to change and adapt to one's circumstances.

Dating an increased focus on the term 'resilience' to around 2007 when it began to supplant 'security' as the chief focus of governmental social and national strategies,[2] Mark Neocleous observes its increasingly far-reaching scope beyond the academy. Resilience has distinctive currency in social and governmental discourses and practices where it is heralded as the solution to all conceivable problems. Resilience training has been introduced in institutions ranging from British schools to the Comprehensive Soldier and Family Fitness US military programme, which includes modules designed to instil resilience in military employees and their families (Neocleous 2013: n.p.).[3] The very notion of resilience training indicates from the outset that the priority is in encouraging individuals to adjust their attitudes and beliefs, as opposed to working to change structures and social environments (Martin and Sunley 2015).

As a desirable attribute individuals or populations are urged to cultivate, resilience entails a kind of elasticity or ability to endure against all odds. As I noted in the introduction, this kind of resilience is closely linked to traditional notions of femininity. A key way that resilience discourse manifests in pop culture is through narratives of overcoming trauma and adversity, in which female characters are uniquely capable of turning obstacles into opportunities, transforming their damage into strength. Arguing that resilience discourse underpins neoliberal[4] ways of thinking, James explains that individuals and systems are evaluated based on how resilient they are and encouraged to capitalize on any deficits or 'damage' they may endure (2015: 7).[5] In describing resilience as the 'new means of production' (2015: 4), James highlights that overcoming adversity and turning less into more is highly socially valued. Of course, if resilience creates social value, then something is required to be resilient against to produce that value. Consequently, within this model, any trauma, crisis or adversity becomes necessary or even desirable to maintain the means of production. Viability as a social subject depends upon the capacity to convert trauma into a valuable resource, that is, to turn a negative into a positive.[6] This kind of resilience proves key to the success of Katniss, the protagonist of *The Hunger Games*, both within the trilogy's narrative and with respect to its popularity as perhaps the most prominent example of a recent phase in dystopian fiction in which young women are seen to lead the resistance.[7]

Set in a future post-apocalyptic American society, *The Hunger Games* trilogy centres on an annual contest staged by a totalitarian government. In the titular Hunger Games, children of the disenfranchised population are selected by weighted lottery to participate in a televised fight to the death until a sole victor remains.[8] The first novel (*The Hunger Games*, 2008) details how Katniss wins the game and inadvertently sparks the revolution that unfolds over the next two instalments, *Catching Fire*

(2009) and *Mockingjay* (2010). The outlandish dystopian premise of a state-sanctioned death match recalls Berlant's observation in *The Female Complaint* that 'extreme genres' can work as 'forms of realism' to express the materiality of social suffering, particularly when such suffering is historically inherited (2008: ix). The novels resonate with their audience precisely because the suffering they express feels like social realism for a generation who have come of age in a context characterized by rapid technological change, globalization, war and recession (Suderman 2015: n.p.). Similarly, the congruence between the trilogy's construction of entrenched systemic inequalities and the mechanics of resilience discourse suggests that the novels are designed to *feel* like an amplified version of the injustices and inequalities endemic to our own society.

In James's study of the aesthetics of resilience in contemporary pop music, she finds that aural damage is intentionally generated through musical gestures like soars, glitches, stuttered vocals and other discordant noisemaking produced so that a spectacle of restoration and renewal can ensue. These affective musical gestures, James argues, are key to producing resilience as desirable. James looks at the UK number one hit Calvin Harris (ft. Florence Welch) song 'Sweet Nothing' (2012), interpreting the lyrical content about a woman who is 'hollowed out' and 'running on fumes' and who – because all she has got is 'nothing' (2015: 1) – must find a way to capitalize on a void. Through soars, drops and manipulations of speed and pitch, the song '*performs* the process the lyrics merely describe' (1). In essence, the song is 'not so much *about* nothing as *made of and with nothing*' (1). As the character undergoes the process of resiliently creating something from nothing, the listener too experiences that very same process because of the form and structure of the song and its musical gestures (4). Following James, I examine some of the ways resilience-as-suffering is embedded into the world-building of *The Hunger Games* at a fundamental, deep-structural level, before shifting focus to examine the centrality of defiant resilience in its portrayal of young female subjectivity.

Suffering

The type of suffering or damage James refers to, and that I take up in this chapter, derives from long histories of difference-based oppression and ongoing structural inequalities. James's interest in exposing neoliberal instrumentalization of suffering as something that can be put to 'work' intersects with Ruti's critique of systemically induced suffering. Ruti intervenes into the debate between Berlant and Lee Edelman in *Sex, or the Unbearable* (2014) centring on the role of queer negativity, non-sovereignty and optimism. Although both, according to Ruti, 'endorse notions of queer negativity' (125) to varying degrees, their approaches diverge; Edelman remains steadfastly wedded to 'a strictly Lacanian notion of constitutive alienation (or lack-in-being)', while 'Berlant is interested in the material and affective effects of more concrete forms of alienation' (135). By calling attention to these two distinct forms of alienation, Ruti differentiates between the two fundamental levels upon which people's lives often 'don't work'. As she points out, there is a vast chasm between a life that 'doesn't work' because, as Edelman observes, 'life, in some sense … is structurally inimical to happiness, stability, or regulated functioning' (Berlant and Edelman 2014: 11 in Ruti 2017: 137) and one that is structurally inhibited from 'working' by virtue of social class, race or gender. While acknowledging that negativity certainly does fundamentally constitute subjectivity through such a foundational lack or alienation from ourselves, Ruti argues that antisocial queer theory (such as Edelman's) too often 'turns entirely ordinary components of human experience into scenes of extraordinary suffering, thereby distracting attention from the kind of context-specific suffering that actually *is* unbearable' (141, original italics). Demarcating forms of suffering in this way acknowledges that while there are unavoidable forms of alienation and suffering, the trauma caused by systemic racism, sexism and global economic injustices is inherited from specific historical and socio-economic circumstances, which therefore can and should be addressed.

The fundamental mechanics of resilience discourse outlined by James are firmly rooted into *The Hunger Games*' imagining of the fictional future nation of Panem (an obvious reference to *panem et circenses*). James describes a 'cycle' of resilience which proceeds accordingly: first, adversity of some kind must be instigated, second, the adversity must be overcome, and, crucially, this heroic feat then broadcast to others. In this framework, resilience only matters if others can see it. At an individual level, a person who overcomes adversity accrues a higher status and increase in their social, economic, political or psychological resources. In *The Hunger Games*, the wealthy and technologically advanced Capitol operates at the centre of power, exerting a totalitarian regime over the surrounding twelve districts, whose residents live in varying levels of poverty. In addition to the already-harsh living conditions, the dominant power structures '*actively incite death and damage*' (James 2015: 9) by inflicting the Hunger Games upon the population, created as a punishment for past rebellion against the Capitol. However, each year one individual is afforded the opportunity to 'overcome' this adversity by winning the games, their victory broadcast to the nation, with mandatory viewing. Thus, systemic violence and suffering is generated and overcome in highly visible ways.

Resilience operates according to a feedback loop: any one individual's personal 'resilience labour' (i.e. the work they do to overcome their adversity) contributes in turn to overall societal resilience by generating value that sustains the dominant system (James 2015). As a result, the types of adversity produced by neoliberal economic and social policies and practices become naturalized as simply the way things are.[9] Likewise in *The Hunger Games*, by granting the victor access to improved living conditions, increased food rations and income, members of a disenfranchised population become nominally included within the dominant power structure. The victor's labour (participating in the games, killing rival children, creating a sensational media narrative) generates value for the government and its system of oppression while simultaneously cementing that system as natural and inevitable.

Of course, our inherited circumstances are not equally weighted. Histories of social control and oppression like slavery or patriarchy mean that some groups start out with fewer resources of resilience at their disposal. As James explains, individuals whose ways of living support dominant/hegemonic social structures are rewarded while others, whose lives do not in any way contribute towards the long-term sustainability of social institutions, are not considered worth investing in. Similarly, the topography of Panem society illustrates how even among the disenfranchised population, some groups stand a better chance of winning the games than others. Districts 1, 2 and 4, which are geographically closest to the centre of power, have more resources at their disposal. As a result, their children are healthier, stronger and train for the competition with a clear sense of purpose, considering it an opportunity to bring glory to their community. Katniss, of course, is from District 12, Panem's poorest region where residents who work in the coal mines are compensated with subsistence wages and subject to sickness, starvation and death (2008: 28), illustrating how the deck is stacked against the poorer districts so that their tributes are at a distinct disadvantage in terms of physical health and fitness. While a resilient population might recoup and repair itself, perhaps even gain a profit from their damage, *precarious populations exhaust all their resources in their constant struggles to stay barely alive*' (James 2015: 9) and are thereby actively diminished. At a core level, the distribution of resources and power across a society puts every citizen's life or death at stake.

This account of resilience provokes questions, therefore, about how to proceed when the very efforts we might make towards coping with socially inflicted suffering are, as Martin and Sunley suggest, all too 'easily captured by neoliberal ideology' (2015: 10). In a blog post on James's book, feminist scholar Natalia Cecire observes that although a perpetual cycle of trauma and healing may be harmful to perform, it remains 'the *best* deal on offer' (2015: n.p., original italics) for many people, as the alternative is to simply absorb trauma and gain nothing in return. James proposes one option: if resilience is the norm by which individual and societal 'health' are measured, melancholic practices might be capable of subverting it. As an update of Sigmund Freud's (1917) classic theory, melancholy is James's primary method of disrupting normative practices of resilience. Resilience, in turn, corresponds with mourning, or what Freud termed the ability to resolve and accept loss. Where trauma was previously to be resolved, James argues, it is now something we can recycle and exploit to gain social capital and inclusion. In this context, melancholia no longer means the failure to resolve loss, as it did for Freud; rather, James terms melancholy the failure to achieve resilience 'enough' or 'in the right direction' (2015: 19).[10] Of course, if resilience is the marker of inclusion into dominant hierarchies, then this categorically excludes those who are not resilient enough.

If some lives are already considered less viable to begin with, rather than striving to become socially viable through practising resilience, individuals can instead intentionally increase their unviability, or go 'into the death' (50), as James terms it. A deliberately counterintuitive approach to combatting the resilience imperative, James proposes that 'when power demands that you *live* … *death* seems like the obvious way to fight back' (11). Alternately, if 'power banks on your death' and a loss of life is already accounted for, then choosing the method, timing and duration of that death becomes a means of disruption (11). In this context, 'death' includes any practice that does not contribute to the overall health of dominant power structures. For example, 'one of the main ways to go into the death, to practice melancholic subversion, is to take care of yourself in non-resilient ways – for example, getting a regular, full night's sleep rather than constantly pushing the edge of burnout and exhaustion' (21). If we are compelled towards overcoming our trauma so that the structure that inflicted the trauma may reap the benefit, James suggests that perhaps a melancholic refusal to simply 'get over it' is the key to undermining resilience narratives.

So far, I have outlined the compatibility between James's understanding of resilience and how *The Hunger Games* formulates resilience. However, the series also complicates and diverges from the notion of resilience as a norm which melancholic practices are then capable of subverting (James 2015). Because while the novel *does* stage a scene in which Katniss goes 'into the death' (or threatens to), this is not a melancholic act but instead aligns more closely with Ruti's concept of defiant agency, or moments when we risk our social viability, as I will shortly revisit. As a result, while I agree that it is important to problematize resilience discourse (especially when deployed as an individualist solution that naturalizes oppression), I also argue that rather than giving in to a resilience/melancholy dichotomy, there are perhaps modes of resilience that are not only useful but also downright necessary to survival within both our own White supremacist capitalist patriarchy and in Collins's fictional totalitarian state. If Cecire is correct to assume that resilience is often the 'best deal on offer' (2015), then it makes sense to consider ways of performing resilience which acknowledge that systemic trauma is not (or should not be) natural and inevitable, but that it nevertheless currently constitutes the reality for many people. Furthermore, the imperative towards resilience naturalizes contextually specific forms of suffering (such as racism), producing them as individual, rather than structural or social problems. This speaks to why I find suffering resilience a more useful concept in this chapter: it foregrounds that systemic oppression is what naturalizes this contextual suffering, steering discussion away from resilience itself becoming the 'problem' to eliminate.

To elaborate on the concept of suffering resilience, I turn to Elliott's discussion of suffering agency. Arguing that the demand for subjects to embody and demonstrate agency has been exacerbated by rapidly increasing structural inequalities, Elliot uses the term 'suffering agency' to describe the intertwining of agency, choice and domination (2013: 88) through which neoliberal paradigms are reinforced. Agency here is a utopian ideal: we strive to capture it in our daily lives and to embody it in our interactions on personal and institutional levels, yet its availability grows ever more diffuse. The type of agency Elliott describes counterintuitively as suffering recalls Berlant's notion of sovereignty as an inadequate fantasy (2011: 97). Both call into question the fraught nature of agency itself (what does it look or *feel* like?) and complicate the simplistic binary that would suggest agency is either a fully installed and measurable characteristic (we are completely free agents) or is entirely absent (we are simply victims of oppression). Interrogating the ostensibly intrinsic value of agency as an 'index of the political good' (87), Elliott argues that the choices we make can be our own, and yet 'still feel both imposed and appalling' (84), meaning that they can be clearly read and even experienced as agency, while somehow becoming tantamount to self-inflicted subjugation. Elliott casts agency in its current incarnation as an elaborate neoliberal fiction, experienced as a suffocating trap rather than a clearly discernible – let alone fully graspable – form of power.

The neoliberalized agency Elliott identifies has great resonance with and offers a deeper understanding of resilience discourse as James defines it. Resilience is understood as having intrinsic value, yet it hinges on a false sense of the subject's sovereignty and can equally be experienced as a trap rather than empowerment or liberation. What James describes is how neoliberal culture captures and warps resilience as our capacity to resolve suffering is transformed into a capacity to extract value from it. Neoliberal socio-economic policies and practices inflict suffering on populations, who are then encouraged to be resilient and capitalize on their trauma, thus accruing further value that upholds those same neoliberal policies. In this model, both resilience and agency rely on suffering to create social value. I propose, therefore, that if all subjects are formed by and within resilience discourse to varying degrees, it makes sense to consider not how we can somehow repeal our social training but rather how we can use it in ways that allow us to preserve the benefits of our resilience rather than yield to it in ways that harm us.

Defiance

Where suffering resilience entails overcoming or capitalizing on trauma in ways that benefit the social order, defiant resilience, by contrast, describes the process of transforming suffering into something that does not create social value. To develop the concept of defiant resilience, I use Ruti's model of agency and then go on to analyse the climactic scene of *The Hunger Games* in which Katniss's threat of death allows her (and Peeta) to live, thus constituting an act of defiant resilience that the Capitol cannot profit from. Working within a Lacanian framework (and drawing on Slavoj Žižek's 2005 interpretation of Lacan), Ruti argues that

> even when we feel overwhelmed by the webs of power that surround us, we possess a degree of autonomy as long as we are willing to surrender our symbolic supports, as long as we are willing – even temporarily – to genuinely not give a damn about what is (socially) expected of us. (2017: 45)

This quotation explains that subjects are viable when they conform to dominant social expectation. Authentic autonomy, then, only arises when a subject is 'willing to honor its inner directive even at the risk of losing its social viability' (45). Being able to separate normative fantasies and ways of living from our own 'genuine' desires proves crucial to this formulation of agency but remains a task that Ruti admits is as challenging as it is necessary. If agency is enacted during moments when subjects risk their social viability (especially, though not only, on behalf of others), then accordingly any act of defiance that relies upon adhering to social expectation will eventually fail. Within this model, identifying and then following one's inner directive regardless of the expectations of the social order is key to defiant agency. Defiant resilience operates similarly, referring to moments in which individuals overcome or capitalize on trauma, but do so in ways that either risk their social viability or oppose normative power structures. As a concept, defiant resilience recognizes the existence of contextual suffering and oppression, while at the same time acknowledging that survival often requires us to be resilient against these forms of trauma.

When James refers to death, she means socially unviable or unproductive practices. However, because the concept of the Hunger

Games operates within the extreme genres identified by Berlant, the life and death stakes become literalized, thereby creating a society maintained and fuelled by death. To keep the system running smoothly, a specific type of death is required – a death that provides entertainment value. Emphasizing this, the games are designed in the style of a contemporary reality television series: from the lottery selection process to the interviews in which tributes are encouraged to win over the audience who will later 'vote' for them by sponsoring them in the arena. Through orchestrated media spectacle, audience enjoyment is maximized. The final tribute left standing effectively symbolizes 'life', not only their own or that of the games but also the life of society in its entirety. As far as the remaining twenty-three contestants are concerned, their deaths create more social value than their survival. Literalizing life and death in this way explicitly foregrounds the workings of biopolitics and how systems of power reproduce themselves through the deaths of some subjects that support the lives of others. Therefore, as James suggests, dying in the wrong way or at the wrong time has the capacity to upend this entire system.

Early on, the first novel delineates between 'right' and 'wrong' kinds of death within the Hunger Games system. Katniss's narration tells us that in an earlier arena with a barren landscape, 'half of [the tributes] died of cold' (2008: 40), which, she notes, does not provide the desired entertainment value of the brutal deaths the Capitol audience are accustomed to. Such 'quiet, bloodless deaths' (40) are not the affectively sensationalized type the Capitol is keen to promote because the same kind of value cannot be extracted for its regime of power. Similarly, 'cannibalism doesn't play well with the Capitol audience' (142) because although 'there are no rules in the arena' (142), a contestant who cannibalizes his fellow tributes renders their deaths inviable, not ethically, but aesthetically. When audience satisfaction is reduced, the overall 'health' of the society declines in turn.

Social viability within the Hunger Games system means producing the right kind of death (entertaining) or the right kind of life (as an exception). The first novel's climax, however, hinges on an act of defiant resilience which invokes entirely the wrong kind of death: by using poisoned berries to stage a double suicide, Katniss eradicates the prospect of a winner to symbolize the life of the system. During the competition, a rule change announces that two contestants may win the games (and their lives) if they are from the same district. This prompts Katniss to ally with Peeta, and together they make it to the end of the games, where the rule change is subsequently rescinded. The Hunger Games system compels Katniss and Peeta to live – to privilege their own life above the other's and for their victory to further sustain the Capitol's rule. To yield to this imperative would mean acting in accordance with the desire of the social order, demonstrating how individual resilience can become a sustaining force that preserves hegemonic power structures. By contrast, Katniss's character is keenly aware of the power that resides in creating the wrong kind of spectacle, of dying in the wrong way, or at the wrong time:

> Yes, they have to have a victor. Without a victor, the whole thing would blow up in the Gamemakers' faces. They'd have failed the Capitol. Might possibly even be executed, slowly and painfully while the cameras broadcast it to every screen in the country. If Peeta and I were both to die, or they thought we were … (2008: 338)

This scenario is also an example of suffering agency. The narrative compels Katniss to choose between two options (either kill Peeta and win the games or sacrifice herself), both of which are 'imposed and appalling' (Elliott 2013: 84). Instead, by devising a third option in which Katniss threatens to kill both Peeta and herself together by eating the poisoned berries, the novel demonstrates that one possible response to being compelled to resiliently live is to threaten death.

Here, the novel produces Katniss as a resilient subject who defies the social order. Or, as Žižek puts it, 'In a situation of the forced choice, the subject makes the "crazy," impossible choice of, in a way, *striking at himself*, at what is most precious to himself (Butler, Laclau and Žižek 2000: 122, original italics). Žižek is interested in how a 'radical gesture' (122) such as self-striking (including but not necessarily suicide) can constitute agency. Ruti explains that 'in such a scenario, the subject seeks to alter the basic coordinates of its predicament by destroying what it most values; it purchases its freedom at the cost of cutting itself off from what it holds most dear' (2017: 49). This is precisely what the poisoned berries signify: the willingness to destroy her own life is what grants Katniss her freedom, which is to live, but more importantly to live on her own terms and to act in accordance with her inner directive, rather than operating solely and wholly within the conventions of the games. For if Katniss and Peeta were indeed to destroy their own lives by committing suicide together, their deaths would in turn signify the death of the Hunger Games, with the absence of a victor exposing a broken system. Similarly, the narrative itself exposes the mechanics of defiant resilience by forcing its characters to make an appalling decision – namely, to perform agency (through the choice and act of killing the other) that feels like suffering rather than liberation and to perform resilience (by becoming the sole victor who symbolizes the life of the system) that naturalizes that suffering.

In this pivotal scene, Katniss's act of threatening suicide is certainly the wrong kind of resilience. However, she *is* performing resilience, and it is important to recognize this. Katniss's heroism stems from her resilience in this moment, manifesting as her defiance of the demand to suffer agency and her ability to transform her resilience into a spectacle the Capitol cannot extract value from. In capitalizing on the threat of death, Katniss and Peeta are both able to live. The system endures but is fundamentally altered as Katniss's resilience does not create the right kind of life. The system's production of a sole victor has been exposed as an arbitrary construction. Ruti's and Elliott's models of agency together are useful in making sense of the novels' formulation of resilience, as they are neither producing a melancholic subjectivity nor advancing melancholy as a mode of resistance in the way posited by James. For Katniss, going 'into the death' is not a melancholic act; it is a defiant one. It is critical here that Katniss is still produced as a resilient subject, one who uses and capitalizes on her suffering – and that *how* she does so is important, as she turns a traumatic scene of suffering agency to her own advantage and disrupts the power structures that orchestrated her suffering in the first place.

This scene is central to how the novel produces coming of age as not (only) about social inclusion, or the trajectory from girlhood to womanhood; rather, it is figured as simply managing to stay alive. Crucially, coming of age is not linked to Katniss's entry into and acceptance within society but her role in tearing down that society. Katniss's role as the instigator and figurehead of revolution recalls Ruti's observation that 'collective social mobilization relies on subjects who have the ability to stick to their desire in the face of the demand that they capitulate to the desire of the [social order]' (2017: 64). The novels suggest, much like Harris's idea of the future girl, that young women are perhaps particularly well-suited to this endeavour. If girls and women are trained in resilience discourse, as James proposes, then it makes sense that they might be uniquely equipped to use that training in ways that defy the social order. *The Hunger Games*' vision of girlhood acknowledges that resilience is often necessary to surviving systemic oppression at the same time as advocating defiance against that oppression. Just as Katniss's mentor Haymitch reminds her to 'remember who the enemy is' (2009: 159), equally we also must not lose sight of the enemy, that is, the neoliberal policies and practices that produce and perpetuate oppression – and not resilience itself.

In the first novel, coming of age is linked to Katniss's formation as a political subject and her increased willingness to risk her social viability. The catalyst for Katniss's heroic act of defiant resilience is the death of her friend and ally, Rue, who is brutally killed by another competitor. I read this scene, which highlights another form of unviable death, as significant in developing Katniss's inner directive through her ability to seize control of the processes of interpretation and meaning-making. It also raises questions about the narrative function of Rue's character in relation to the series' racial politics, as I'll later discuss. Ordinarily, Rue's murder would be precisely the kind of gruesome drama the Capitol would exploit for its own ends. However, Katniss's response in honouring Rue by wreathing her body in flowers and concealing her wound serves to highlight Rue's humanity, a show of solidarity that once again creates the wrong kind of spectacle. Katniss (rightly) suspects that the Capitol will not wish to broadcast this act of care:

> They'll have to show it. Or even if they choose to turn the cameras elsewhere at this moment, they'll have to bring them back when they collect the bodies and everyone will see her then and know that I did it. (2008: 234)

While the Capitol retains the ultimate power over whether Rue lives or dies, the novel presents a key moment in which Katniss seizes control over the interpretation of Rue's death. The generic conventions of the games dictate that each death is broadcast to generate maximum social value, a process that Katniss disrupts. Here, the emphasis is on seizing the means of production, and, for a fleeting moment, Katniss manages to shape the narrative asserted by the Capitol. She transforms the signification of Rue's death into loss and mourning, dignity and care, rather than simply an ephemeral and entertaining spectacle. Thus, the novel demonstrates that although the government maintains its control over the fate of its citizens and Rue's death cannot be prevented, Katniss's actions preclude the Capitol from extracting value from it. In other words, although we cannot extricate ourselves from systems of power and domination, our actions within those systems still matter immensely. We return to James's idea that timing and duration of death, while not exactly acts of resistance in the traditional sense, constitute a way of preserving some semblance of selfhood, an attempt at sovereignty even when denied autonomy. However, it is important to note that *The Hunger Games* does not afford all girls this semblance of sovereignty, the opportunity to die on their own terms and to create meaning. Instead, these opportunities cut across racial lines in both the novels and the films. It is therefore vital to examine the franchise's questionable racial politics.

Rachel E. Dubrofsky and Emily D. Ryalls give an incisive account of the post-racial politics at play in *The Hunger Games* films, critiquing the role Katniss plays as 'the person who gives Rue's death meaning'

(2014: 402). Their argument that 'race is configured as irrelevant, while at the same time whiteness is centered'[11] (400) applies equally to the novels. Dubrofsky and Ryalls highlight how Rue, as a Black character, serves the principal narrative function of 'innocent sacrifice' (401), a role which enables Katniss to shine as a 'great white saviour' (402).[12] In the berries example, Katniss threatens the wrong kind of death through defiant resilience. Rue's death scene proves more difficult to classify. Katniss takes care of Rue in a non-resilient way, which can be read along the lines of melancholy, the failure to capitalize in socially profitable ways rather than the defiant resilience Katniss performs later in the novel. Narratively, this moment is closer still to Ruti's defiant agency, as Katniss acts, for the first time, in a way that does not conform to the conventions of her social environment. However, although Katniss's act of care means that value cannot be extracted from Rue's death, the novel's structure relies on it to spark the growth of its protagonist. Rue's death marks a structural turning point in which the death of a Black child facilitates White self-knowledge and politicization. Or, put differently, Black death fuels White resilience. Rather than investing in minoritized populations (as James urges), the novel invests in the inevitability of White resilience. While female agency drives the series to a large degree, Rue's narrative role as the trauma that catalyses such narrative agency reveals that in a sense, her character function *is* death. *The Hunger Games* therefore not only centres the formation of White feminine subjectivity but also produces White coming of age as contingent upon the sacrifice of Black girlhood.

The novel itself extracts value from this sacrifice by using it to develop the protagonist's inner directive. Before Rue, Katniss is characterized by her ability to practise suffering resilience, to take 'negatives' like growing up in extreme poverty and turn them into 'positive' traits in the arena: 'That the Careers have been better fed growing up is actually to their disadvantage, because they don't know how to be hungry. Not the way Rue and I do' (Collins 2008: 206). By transforming childhood deprivation into resourcefulness, Katniss turns 'nothing into something' (James 2015: 1). For much of the first novel, Katniss's inner directive aligns with that of the social order; within the constraints of her world, survival is all that matters. Determined to present as worthy of investment, Katniss initially acts according to the rules of the Games. This is comparable to the ways in which most individuals act according to societal norms in order to earn, deserve and preserve a sense of social inclusion.

As a heavily surveilled subject, Katniss is keenly aware of how the Capitol audience (or ruling social order) perceives her. For example, when Katniss is injured and temporarily deaf in one ear, the narration emphasizes her active performance of restraint, not in her own mind but in her facial expression: 'I can't let my fear show. Absolutely, positively, I am live on every screen in Panem' (2008: 220). In line with Arlie Hochschild's (1979) work on emotion management, Katniss knows that concealing negative emotion and managing affect will play better on camera, indicating that how she feels is irrelevant compared to whether she conforms to the Capitol's model of a valuable tribute, someone worth investing in. As Kanai puts it, 'For Hochschild, feeling rules require the right feelings on the right occasion; and if one does not have the right feelings, one must work to have them' (2019: 31). Being intelligible as a valuable tribute means carefully controlling anything that may be perceived negatively, such as frustration or disappointment, and presenting a capable front. Initially, then, there is no conflict between the desires of the Capitol and Katniss's own desire to stay alive.

After Rue, however, Katniss's veneer of social acceptability begins to crack. Where previously her main priority had been 'the acquisition of food' (2008: 307), she now develops her own inner directive as she begins to behave in ways that demonstrate Ruti's observation that 'there are parts of our being that the [social] order tries to discipline but that it can never completely colonize' (2017: 48). Abandoning her performance of affective restraint, Katniss openly grieves for Rue, noting that 'for several hours, I remain motionless', having 'lost the will to do the simplest tasks' (Collins 2008: 237). Here, Katniss performs the 'wrong' affect, indicating that her focus on creating social value in exchange for her life has evaporated. In contrast, Katniss's earlier characterization as a calculating cost/benefit analyst is summed up in her exchange with Peeta the night before they enter the arena. Katniss struggles to understand Peeta when he tells her, 'I want to die as myself. Does that make any sense? ... I don't want them to change me in there. Turn me into some kind of monster that I'm not' (Collins 2008: 140). Initially, Katniss doesn't understand Peeta's perspective at all; she is only interested in her immediate survival, telling Peeta to focus on 'staying alive' (140). It is only after Rue's death that Katniss finally understands Peeta's desire to 'maintain his identity. His purity of self' (140). This shift in characterization develops as the result of Katniss's social bonds, namely with Rue and Peeta, but also her experience of the trauma inflicted in the arena. Crucially, it is also the point at which she becomes aware of the power of symbolism, and of ideology. Wreathing Rue's body in flowers does not alter either Rue's or Katniss's own material circumstances in any tangible way. Katniss remains trapped in a system not of her own making in which she will have to fight to kill in order to win. Yet Katniss's politicization shows that she can act within the framework of the games to broadcast the idea that Rue is a person, and her death is not entertainment. Rue's death therefore marks a structural narrative turn, the point at which Katniss's emerging inner directive takes precedence and her suffering resilience turns to defiance. She continues to overcome her trauma, to turn weaknesses into strengths, but in ways that those in power cannot extract value from. It is the development of Katniss's inner directive (i.e. her capacity to act according to her own desires) that enables her to redirect resilience in this way.

Intensification

In this final section, I examine the relationship between narrative structure, resilience and intensified trauma in *The Hunger Games* novels and George Tillman Jr's film adaptation of *The Hate U Give*. Drawing on Jeffrey Nealon's (2002) work, James observes that intensification is 'the underlying logic of resilience discourse' (2015: 46). According to Nealon, 'in a world that contains no "new" territory – no new experiences, no new markets – any system that seeks to expand must by definition *intensify* its existing resources, modulate them in some way' (2002: 82, original italics). In James's analysis of musical patterns and song structure, she finds there are 'different tactical approaches to the same underlying strategy of building and exacerbating sonic and affective tension' (2015: 29). Similarly, I argue that *The Hunger Games* and *The Hate U Give* take different approaches to consolidate narrative tension through the escalation and exacerbation of trauma. Unlike *The Hunger Games*, which produces White resilience through imaginary traumas in a futuristic setting, *The Hate U Give* centres Black female subjectivity and grounds its protagonist's political awakening within the realist context of racism and police brutality in contemporary America. From the outset, the stakes are life and death for Black teenage protagonist Starr Carter, who develops her inner directive and political agency after witnessing a police officer murder her childhood best friend. Following Khalil's murder, Starr, like Katniss, is no longer willing to sacrifice parts of herself in exchange for social acceptability.

Both protagonists are introduced in a state of 'crisis ordinariness' (Berlant 2011: 10): Katniss lives in extreme poverty under near-constant surveillance, and Starr lives in the contemporary United States, where the structural history of racism and colonialism shapes 'everyday life, policies, spaces, economic systems, and social norms' (Lavalley and Robinson Johnson 2020: 1). The narrative point of departure (Katniss volunteering for the Hunger Games to spare her younger sister and Starr witnessing Khalil's death) is therefore not the incitement of trauma, which is both systemic and entirely routine. Katniss's and Starr's character trajectories, then, are not from a relatively 'undamaged' state to a 'damaged' one; rather, their a priori damage is intensified. Each narrative relies on an intensified model of continually inflicting and overcoming damage. Katniss's horrific experiences in the first novel set up the newly intensified status quo of everyday crisis in which the second novel begins. *Catching Fire* repeats the same basic narrative formula as the first novel, with Katniss entering a second Hunger Games arena to face new and more appalling horrors. The basic structure of the trilogy follows a trajectory of everyday crisis, an intensified trauma, which in turn intensifies the everyday crisis, a re-intensified trauma, which in turn re-intensifies the everyday crisis, and so on.

The Hate U Give is similarly structured by trauma and heightened emotion. The opening sequence introduces the racist norms organizing Starr's life in the predominantly Black neighbourhood of Garden Heights. At age nine, Starr, along with her brothers, receives 'the talk' from their father, Maverick, about how to conduct themselves when stopped by the police: 'When it happens, don't act mad. You gotta look calm.' This form of emotion management is what Hochschild refers to as 'inhibiting feelings so as to render them "appropriate" to a situation' (551). Starr is instructed to inhibit any anger she might feel, to appear appropriately non-threatening to law enforcement. Expanding on Hochschild's work, Williams, Bryant and Carvell describe this kind of emotional masking as a 'racialized feeling rule' (2018: 4), or one of many 'racial strategies that people of color have adopted for survival in a culture that actively reinforces White supremacy' (3). In another early scene, Starr explains that dual identities help her navigate the Black local spaces of her neighbourhood versus the predominantly White educational space of the private school she attends. The feeling rule Maverick teaches Starr thus permeates every sphere of her life, shaping and splitting her sense of self along racial lines.

The social norms at school demand that Starr mask and dilute her Blackness; she must be careful not to use slang, lest she appear 'ghetto', and she must be non-confrontational, lest she appear aggressive. Tanisha C. Ford observes that while cinema has given attention to external markers of code switching – language, for example, in *Sorry to Bother You* (Riley 2018) – '*The Hate U Give*'s treatment of identity politics goes beyond the outward social performance to depict both the weight of bearing witness and the emotional toll of burying trauma' (2018: n.p.). This kind of affective masking is a typical strategy used by Black subjects to navigate White spaces, as Roxanna Harlow (2003) finds in a study of Black professors' emotion management while teaching at predominately

White institutions. Harlow explains that Black faculty use strategies like suppressing their experiences of structural racism, minimizing race in the classroom and concealing their anger. Starr notes that her school friends' use of slang has no bearing on their social viability, whereas for Starr to be accepted, she must turn the signifiers of her Blackness (slang) into non-threatening Whiteness (civility). Complying with racialized feeling rules thereby shapes Starr into someone who cannot speak or act freely in any environment, illustrating the emotional burden of complying with White supremacist norms.

The Hate U Give generates intensely heightened affect through visual spectacles of racist trauma, a protest scene and the climactic scene between King (a local drug dealer Khalil worked for, and who threatened Starr for speaking out) and Starr's family. The climax follows King locking Starr and her brother into their father's shop and setting fire to it, which, although they escape relatively quickly, itself creates extreme dramatic tension. The confrontation escalates when Starr's seven-year-old brother, Sekani, takes their father's gun and aims it at King. In turn, two White police officers arrive and aim their weapons at Sekani, and Starr raises her hands, using her body to shield Sekani, who drops the gun. It is this, along with Starr's dialogue ('How many of us have to die before y'all get it?'), that causes the police to lower their weapons. Earlier scenes suggest that speaking out is vitally important regardless of whether it achieves the intended outcomes. Yet in the climactic scene (which is not adapted from the novel), Starr's political agency *does* have the power to affect material change and save her brother's life, something Starr couldn't do for either her friend Natasha (killed in a drive-by gang shooting when they were both ten years old) or for Khalil. Therefore, in addition to raising the emotional stakes almost to their breaking point, the scene gives Starr a significant 'win' against the police that would have been otherwise absent. Prior to this, however, the film suggests that speaking out in advance of the grand jury trial and appearing as a witness are crucial to Starr's formation as a political subject, and of course to the mechanisms of justice, even when, as in this case, justice is not served.

Emotion is similarly amplified during a chaotic protest scene (likely inspired by the Black Lives Matter protests in Ferguson in 2014) after a grand jury decides not to indict the officer who shot Khalil. Here, Starr's transformation from a reticent witness to a powerful orator crystallizes as she takes a megaphone and climbs onto a car to address the crowd. Ford observes that before Starr delivers her speech, she layers a 'Rest in Peace Khalil' T-shirt over her school uniform, thus visually integrating her dual identities and signifying 'her refusal to live as a fractured being: a "hood" girl in one instance and a "whitewashed" preppy black girl in another' (2018: n.p.). Self-cohesion is reiterated in the closing sequence when Starr informs us that she only has one identity now. Apparently no longer subject to the racialized feeling rules that ordered her life prior to Khalil's murder, Starr is pictured in the final scenes (immediately following the harrowing climax) enjoying the sun with her family in Garden Heights, then laughing with her boyfriend at school. Starr's natural hair (as opposed to the braids she wears during most of the film) signifies her newfound ability to 'be herself' at school, thus neatly tying up the messy politics and intense overflow of affect the film has worked so hard to generate.

When considering the narrative structure of resilience, it is important to examine the function that inflicting such extraordinary trauma serves. While Rue's murder catalyses White resilience and a fantasy of revolutionary overthrow, Khalil's murder catalyses Starr's ability to defy White power structures through a comparatively realist style of protest. For while Katniss helps tear down an oppressive regime, the structures Starr speaks out against remain in place by the film's close. However, Khalil's murder plays two other important narrative roles. First, it offers a fictionalized account of the real-life police violence perpetrated against Black people in the United States. The film draws this link overtly when Starr posts photographs of Tamir Rice, Sandra Bland, Eric Garner and Emmett Till on social media, and again when Starr asks why her friend Hailey unfollowed her afterwards: 'Was it Emmett Till's picture that did it?' The second role Khalil's murder plays is to 'mirror' Natasha's murder (Levin 2020: 157). Writing about the novel (Thomas 2017), Adam Levin observes that Natasha's murder 'is erased from communal memory' (2020: 157), demonstrating how law enforcement and the media often fail to address violence committed within Black communities, and that women and girls' stories are often overlooked. One of the major turning points for Starr in deciding to speak up for Khalil is when she admits to knowing who murdered Natasha, but that she 'wasn't gonna snitch', both because she feared for her life and because she felt compelled to comply with the 'street rules' which demanded her silence.

The film suggests that as a Black subject caught up in White structures of power, Starr does have recourse, and her voice has the power to affect change. But does she have the capacity to transform her conditions of living, as well as transforming herself? The film's tidy resolution in which order is restored by the police arresting King suggests a structural pattern of damage that is incited only to be superficially healed (James 2015). The film's story and complex political motivations appear almost stymied by the strictures of its realist genre, which appears to preclude tearing society down. In a structure which demands consonance following a climax, the options are slim. For the narrative to progress, Starr must move on from and incorporate the events that changed her, which is exactly what happens; familiar structures produce familiar resolutions.

The Hunger Games similarly resolves its narrative intensification with a familiar sense of gendered closure produced through marriage and children. In the series conclusion and epilogue, Katniss returns home after the war and slowly learns to cope with its aftermath. The series' love triangle is resolved by reuniting Katniss and Peeta because he symbolizes 'rebirth instead of destruction. The promise that life can go on, no matter how bad our losses. That it can be good again' (Collins 2010: 371). However, the epilogue, which reveals a glimpse of Katniss and Peeta's life twenty years later, complicates this understanding of 'rebirth' and 'destruction', or life and death. Susan S. M. Tan notes a frustrated reader response (2014: 30) to the trilogy's epilogue, and that such an ostensibly happy ending rings false, given the prior narrative events. Tan quotes Katherine R. Broad, who argues that 'Katniss' rebellion serves to keep her an appropriately gendered, reproductive, and ultimately docile subject' (2013: 125 in Tan 2014: 30), a reading that echoes my own response upon reading the trilogy for the first time.

However, in terms of resilience, *The Hunger Games*' epilogue is notable in its refusal to overwrite the damage inflicted over the course of the trilogy. Tan presents a compelling argument that 'Katniss' nameless, faceless offspring, who should suggest the continuation of life, point instead to its continual potential for disruption' (30). The evocation of life typically signified by the figure of the child is undermined by Katniss's admission that 'it took five, ten, fifteen years for me to agree. But Peeta wanted them so badly' (Collins 2010: 372). This reinforces Collins's early establishment of Katniss's aversion to having children (2008: 10), as even winning the Hunger Games would not ensure her children's exclusion from them (2008: 307). That such a domestic outcome is not necessarily one that Katniss herself desires thus disturbs any reading of reproductive fulfilment. In another example, the epilogue's present tense narration makes it clear that Katniss's survival is ongoing, that it, like her nightmares, 'won't ever really go away' (373). The final paragraph explains that Katniss will tell her children 'how I survive it' (373). Using historical present tense here would situate 'it' – the games and the war – as firmly in the past, something endured and overcome. Instead, signifiers of 'life' and 'death' accumulate and uneasily settle together in the epilogue, and nowhere more so than its final line: 'There are much worse games to play' (373), which recalls the past horror of the games while suggesting that the present is only a marginal improvement.

I have argued that *The Hunger Games* and *The Hate U Give* are both structured by ever-increasing trauma. Resolution is uneasy in *The Hunger Games*, which focuses on the persistence of trauma that cannot be simply overcome, and that does not serve to present a unified self whose goal is to transform suffering into social capital. *The Hate U Give*, however, offers Starr's integrated subjectivity and promotes superficial healing attained through uncomplicated narrative closure. Yet regardless of whether their protagonist's personal suffering is overcome or endures, both works exact trauma and create narrative spaces in which feminine subjectivity is produced through a cycle of suffering and resilience. Girlhood is therefore imagined as an ongoing struggle to stay alive, and the coming-of-age narrative produces a female subject whose heroism is derived from profound trauma.

5

Relationality and transformation in *Girlhood*

Resilience, as I have outlined, has a distinct resonance with girlhood coming-of-age genres. Chapter 4 established the resilience paradigm as a newly conventionalized femininity, demonstrating how Katniss's character must first endure trauma and suffering before defiantly overcoming it by strategically risking her social viability. In this chapter, I build on my prior reading by using the French film *Bande de Filles/ Girlhood* to define two contextually specific modes of resilience. First, transformative resilience, which operates in service of dominant power hierarchies, and second, relational resilience, which operates intersubjectively in service of affirming girlhood itself.

While the aftermath of postfeminism may not be entirely restricted to the United States and the UK, its affective influence is heavily tied to this context. However, as Handyside and Taylor-Jones (2016) note, in a globalized cultural economy, it is essential to look beyond dominant British and North American perspectives to give a more comprehensive account of girlhood in popular culture. For although the iterations of postfeminism I analyse in the book are primarily Anglo-centric, as with any discourse operating in a globalized world there are overlaps and slippages across multiple national settings. *Girlhood* therefore provides a rich example of the intersections and discrepancies between French and Anglo-American cultures with respect to how girlhood cinema mobilizes resilience discourse in its formulation of subjectivity. This chapter aims to widen the scope of my discussion on girlhood genres and demonstrates the expansive reach of resilience discourse across national contexts.

Notably, while *Girlhood* is firmly rooted in a French context in terms of both cinematic tradition and the spatial-geographic focus of the film, its audio-visual construction of girlhood also works in a distinctly transnational register. One example is Rihanna's song 'Diamonds', used to score the pivotal dancing scene. As Lisa Jansen and Michael Westphal observe, Rihanna's cultural production has a global appeal, and its worldwide circulation transcends 'national and social boundaries' (2017: 46). Will Higbee likewise notes that this kind of music 'is avidly consumed by a global youth audience' that is 'as much white and middle-class as it is black and *banlieusard*' (2018: 170). What I find especially interesting here is the way that transnational global youth culture becomes the primary mechanism of the girls' (temporary) escape from their everyday lives. The film therefore exploits the aspirational appeal of a pop star like Rihanna, which lies, at least partially, in the universalizing fantasy of freedom from national boundaries.

Before I move on to define relational and transformative modes of resilience, I want to briefly compare *The Hunger Games* and *Girlhood*. Discussing their modes of address and methods of producing meaning will clarify their different approaches to formulating girlhood resilience. Transformation plays an especially important role in each text. As discussed in Chapter 2, transformation is central to the postfeminist paradigm and the coming-of-age narrative which often presents change or epiphany as the key to emancipation or completion of identity. In *The Hunger Games*, Rue's death scene is the fundamental transformative moment, changing Katniss's perception of the world and inciting her to act within harshly limited circumstances. The events of this scene prove vital to Katniss's coming-of-age arc, marking the activation of a political consciousness that enables her to defy and play a pivotal role in abolishing her tyrannical social order. This scene is further illuminated by Huehls's interest in and differentiation between

> those authors who replace representational forms of meaning-making, which use referential language to depict, reflect, or say

something about the world, with more ontological forms of meaning-making, which derive value from the configuration and interrelation of beings, human or otherwise. (2016: xii)

In *The Hunger Games*, the transformative moment that marks Katniss's ideological shift transpires through representational forms of meaning-making, as Katniss proves able to seize some semblance of control over the referential interpretation of Rue's death, using symbolism to make it signify differently, despite (and because of) the tightly controlled system she must operate within. The novels' mode of address is vital here, as the first-person narration provides us with insight into Katniss's interiority; the reader is offered direct access to her transition from calculating cost/benefit analyst to the figurehead of a revolution. In this sense, the series' production of meaning, subjectivity and coming of age all prioritize a representational politics. What this means is that *The Hunger Games* operates on the assumption that Katniss's beliefs must change so that she can change her world, suggesting that social reformation is predicated on the transformation of individual subjectivity.

Structured around its protagonist's central moments of self-reinvention, *Girlhood* at first appears to adhere to a similar trajectory. However, where *The Hunger Games* uses first-person narration to give insight to the interiority of girlhood and to chart the politicization and subsequent identity formation of its protagonist, *Girlhood*'s transformations are motivated by survival and access to different ways of living and forms of social inclusion, rather than the traditional identity-formation typical in coming-of-age genres. *Girlhood* is far less interested in providing audioviewers[1] entry to Marieme's inner world. In fact, as I will go on to explain, rather than giving a sense of unmediated access to girls' subjectivity, the film often distances us from Marieme's character during significant moments when we might typically expect to be afforded insight into her emotions or interiority. Hence Huehls's definition of an ontological form of meaning-production appears to make a more useful reference point in this context. Huehls suggests that 'ontology is meaningful because of the way beings exist in relation to each other and to larger assemblages of beings' (xii). Following this, *Girlhood*'s imaginary of the girl coming of age manifests as a process characterized by the connections and interactions among girls and their spatial relations to sociality.

Girlhood is very much concerned with the conditions of possibility that arise from interactions, change, encounters with and occupations of space. The narrative charts sixteen-year-old Marieme's transformation into the self-assured Vic ('for Victory')[2] over three significant periods of her life. Meaning is produced primarily through a vibrant colour palette and effervescent music sequences, as well as narrative and structural moments of transformation. Through its four transitional sequences, each signalling epiphanies, turning points or opportunities for reinvention, the film produces Marieme's coming of age visually through striking use of costuming and aurally through French composer Para One's evocative electronic score. As Marieme chooses different paths, she assumes and performs different identities. Transition (movement from one position to another) is thereby structurally linked to transformation (a change in form or appearance). Max Thornton observes that *Girlhood* 'lack[s] full structural coherence' because 'growing up, after all is not a tightly-plotted three-act hero's journey with clear turning points, tidy linear progression through the successive stages of personal development, and a satisfying ending' (2013: n.p.). The film proves especially attuned to the intensities and indeterminacies that are fundamental to coming of age.

In a study of Sciamma's first feature film *Naissance des pieuvres/Water Lilies* (2007) and Mia Hansen-Løve's *Un amour de jeunesse/Goodbye First Love* (2011), Handyside suggests that non-diegetic music is their primary method of providing character insight. Featuring teenaged girl protagonists, these films use music as a 'vector of meaning and affect' to 'give form and expression to girls' emotions' (2016: 121) during their first experiences of love and heartbreak. In both films the music is outside of the girls' worlds, usually non-diegetic, and is not the literal expression of their voice. Rather, it is a disembodied, non-identical expression of their feelings, and thus a paradox can be maintained, whereby the films simultaneously offer us insight into the heightened, disoriented sensations of the girls' encounters with intimacy, but allow the girls to retain their opacity and privacy. (Handyside 2016: 121)

Here, Handyside does not propose that music offers access to the interiority or subjective worlds of the protagonists; rather, their 'encounters with intimacy' are the central concern. This phrasing prioritizes the encounter or the associations, relations and forms of contact girls create and experience in the world. At the same time, the music provides freedom from scrutiny and relief from the tendency towards attributing and fixing meaning. Music therefore affords insight while also concealing information, suggesting that perhaps we do not require intimate knowledge of a character's interior world for our attention to hold.

Building on Handyside's work, Isabelle McNeill argues that in *Girlhood*, 'Para One's score thus harnesses the potential of extra-diegetic music to be both narratively significant … and yet indeterminate …, allowing the girls and their lives to affect us while retaining the "opacity" that Handyside identifies in *Naissance des pieuvres*' (2017: 5). *Girlhood*'s project is not, therefore, in deciphering or revealing the meaning of girlhood or attempting to define and represent descriptive categories such as 'Black girlhood' or 'French girlhood'. This is not to suggest that its fiction bears little or no relation to our own world, but rather that the film's aesthetic qualities signal that its interest does not lie in an attempt to represent or communicate the 'reality' of French Black youth culture and, more specifically, the world of Black girls growing up in the Parisian banlieue.[3] Instead, the film charts Marieme's transformations and maps out the types of spaces and forms of sociality that she gains access to as a result. In doing so, *Girlhood* therefore presents (one) way of being a girl.

Relational resilience

To analyse relational resilience, I focus on two key scenes, both of which operate in what Julia Dobson describes as an 'avowedly non-realist, performative mode' (2017: 40). In Chapter 4, I discussed suffering and defiant modes of resilience, each of which is predicated on a subject's social viability. For example, each involves overcoming socially inflicted trauma; where the purpose of the former is to gain social capital, the latter risks that capital. In this chapter, relational resilience manifests in moments or circumstances in which overcoming (or at the very least withstanding) trauma transpires as a result of social connection. To further clarify, I will first briefly analyse the anthemic opening scene of a brightly lit and tightly shot American football game, before paying closer attention to the film's core musical sequence in which Marieme and her friends dance to Rihanna's 'Diamonds'. As Dobson suggests, the banlieue is the film's primary setting, yet 'these two stylized scenes remain at the very centre of the affective and sensual mappings of the film, creating an overwhelming impact on the spectator that overwrites other spatial exclusions' (2017: 40). It is no coincidence that the two scenes with the greatest affective impact are also those affirming the collective power of girlhood relationality. In each scene, the film works formally to reproduce the affective impact of girls' collective potency (Colling 2017; Ringmar 2017). Thus, in *Girlhood*'s opening scene, vivid colour, slow motion and the powerful rhythm of Light Asylum's fiercely cathartic track 'Dark Allies' (2010) unite to create an intensely heightened and kinetic sequence invoking the physicality and collective team spirit of girlhood.

Prior to introducing its protagonist, the film emphasizes the complex dynamics and connections between the girls on the field. The football game can be understood as a form of organized social opposition, rehearsing conflict designed to be resolved within set boundaries and structures. However, the relative security of the training ground does not endure for long. Immediately following the football game, Sciamma makes effective use of space and sound to articulate a sense of the structural hierarchies that encapsulate the film. As the stadium lights are extinguished, the bold image of the two teams celebrating as they chant and cheer is cut to darkness. The camera follows the girls through their neighbourhood, the excited post-game conversation collectively dominating the soundscape, until they abruptly fall silent. Although the girls continue to dominate the screen visually, gradually two or three male figures come into view in the background of the frame. Despite their relatively insignificant presence on-screen, Sciamma makes it clear that all it takes to silence a large group of physically strong, athletic girls is the presence of a much smaller number of the neighbourhood boys. Visually foreshadowing the trajectory of the film, the groups break apart until Marieme finds herself walking alone. This opening sequence provides an effective summary of the postfeminist dilemma in which feminine/feminist energies are dispersed by the persistence of patriarchy. As Ringmar notes, 'Each individual body attunes itself to the bodies of others and together these bodies attune themselves to the situation in which they find themselves' (2017: 11). The freely assertive fantasy occupied by the girls in the football training ground, a traditionally masculine space, is quickly eclipsed by an oppressive reality dominated by masculinity, allowing no room for female self-expression.

While the opening scene emphasizes the anonymous collectivity of the football team, the Diamonds sequence[4] focuses on the relationship between Marieme and her newfound friends (Lady, Adiatou and Fily). Their friendship is central to the film, especially the second act, which concentrates on the interplay between Marieme's individual subjectivity and the intersubjectivity she experiences through becoming a member of the group. It is during this second act that Marieme's transformation into Vic is set in motion. The girls plan a party in a Paris hotel room, where they try on their glamorous shoplifted dresses (security tags intact), smoke, drink and dance to Rihanna's electro-pop ballad 'Diamonds'. Much of the film's action takes place in the public spaces of the banlieue or central Paris shopping district, but as the film's opening scene conveys, these communal spaces do not belong to the girls. Instead, the intimacies of their friendship are played out in a hotel room; the only privacy they can hope to attain is in a space they have rented for the night. When renting a hotel room, there is a reliability to the prescribed rules for interacting with a space (e.g. in the expectation of specific times for checking in and out) which contrasts with the inherent instability of gaining access to a space for a restricted period. As a stage for intimacy and friendship, the hotel room invokes the sense that their freedom is on loan, creating a visceral awareness that there is an expiration date attached to their shared strength and happiness. This sense of uncertainty is part of how the film generates tension, creating apprehension about the direction taken by Marieme's story, as her world is in constant flux, and nothing seems to offer any security or permanence.

Marc Augé's term 'non-place', which describe transient spaces like hotels, airports or supermarkets, is significant to how girlhood is produced here as a liminal space, one that is slipping from Marieme's grasp. Such spaces, Augé explains, 'cannot be defined as relational, or historical, or concerned with identity' (1995: 77–8). A non-place, then, is primarily characterized by its anonymity; it is decontextualized from the specificities of any particular social conditions. As such, according to Augé, social connection or identity formation is unlikely to thrive in a non-place. Nonetheless, in *Girlhood*, the hotel room proves crucial to both Marieme's intensifying connection to her friends and their formation of both group and individual identities. Perhaps the ahistorical nature of the non-space is even what helps to cultivate the girls' growing connection with one another. Moreover, what Augé describes as 'places for living' ... where individual itineraries can intersect and mingle' (66–7) are, if not entirely off-limits to the girls, most certainly hostile to their presence.

By setting the Diamonds sequence in a hotel room, *Girlhood* illustrates how the girls must resort to finding their freedom in a nondescript non-place. On the one hand, this may seem an essentially desolate situation, in which the four girls are so constricted by their social environment that they must rent an anonymous space in which to dance, drink and flourish, and only for one night. On the other hand, the chosen setting can be read as an appropriation of space, celebrating how the girls' occupation of the hotel room transforms non-place into place, where organic feminine sociality can thrive. As Augé notes, 'A person entering the space of non-place is relieved of his usual determinants' (103). This relief from their everyday may in fact be exactly what Marieme and her friends need: freedom from the weight of their social histories and daily environment. After all, as Dobson points out, 'the domestic, familial space is seen, not as a space of retreat, but as [a] problematic site of an oppressive policing of girls' appearance and behaviour' (2017: 39). The sequence therefore speaks to the urgency of their need for a space in which they can truly relax, express their affection for one another and the pleasure they take in one another's company. Indeed, the time spent in the hotel room is the only part of the film in which all four take reprieve from the restraints placed on them by their masculine-oriented social environment.

Much like Starr's coming of age in *The Hate U Give*, finding her voice is crucial to Marieme's trajectory. Prior to the musical sequence, the film includes a quiet moment in the hotel hallway as the girls walk towards their room, the use of a long shot rendering them small in the frame. Although we can see that they are laughing and chatting, their voices can barely be heard, diluted by the generic hotel soundtrack (thus setting this scene in clear parallel to the opening scene in the banlieue). Yet, as soon as the door is opened, their voices ring out loudly, in excitement and anticipation of the night ahead. A quick cut follows, showing the four of them, immediately playful and relaxed, as Marieme dives onto the bed to join her friends. Their raucous delight is in direct opposition to their much quieter demeanour in the hallway. This transition from quiet to loud not only recalls but also reverses the opening sequence's transition as the large group of girls are silenced by the presence of the boys. It also emphasizes their need for a room of their own, in which they can partake in the everyday pleasures to be found in eating, drinking and dancing together, as well as the ability to laugh and talk without censure.

The audiovisual soar

The editing and composition of the Diamonds sequence is typical of the group-individual dynamic seen throughout the film. When characters are alone in the frame, they command centre screen, taking up space and demanding our attention, such as with the radiant close-up of Lady as she lip-syncs the opening lyrics of the song. Yet equally, the dynamic fast-paced camera movement and editing remind us that the girls are never far from one another. As the first verse begins, the camera pans back to accommodate Adiatou's presence. The editing here transitions to a spare, balanced two shot, as Lady and Adiatou join hands, showing that when characters occupy a frame together, they truly share the space. The sequence continues in tight close-ups, bodies shifting in and out of frame. Aligning and realigning with one another, they become almost indistinguishable from one another, invoking the pleasure of what Colling calls 'the spectacle of girls moving in synchrony' (2017: 87). Colling cites William McNeill's (1995) work on 'muscular bonding' (6), a term he coins to describe the enjoyment we take in collective movement. *Girlhood*, with its intensely kinaesthetic sequences, promotes exactly this kind of pleasure. Importantly, although this sequence creates unity between Marieme and her friends, it does not allow either the girls' bodies or their identities to merge; close-ups of their faces convey that although they are interconnected, they are not interchangeable.

The sequence momentarily pauses the narrative flow, its distinctive audiovisual style contributing to a sense of discontinuity. As McNeill finds, 'the performance of "Diamonds" in the film destabilizes diegetic space by borrowing from a music video aesthetic' (2017: 7), which is characterized by the 'blue-filtered lighting, glamorous head shot' and 'apparent awareness of and interaction with the camera and lip-synched performance of a pop song' (1). The blue filter stands out in particular: although the colour echoes the visual motif used throughout, this is the only scene that diverges from the warmer and more naturalistic lighting used in the rest of the film. Equally, the decision to play out the entirety of 'Diamonds' is significant here. Allowing us to experience the song as the characters do creates further immersion into their world, aligning audioviewer and character in the same temporal space. The musical sequence creates a time out of time, in which the viewer is suspended outside the ordinary world of the film, just as Marieme and her friends are suspended in an experience outside the familiar rhythms of their everyday lives.

Rihanna's 'Diamonds', a song that critics found 'dull' and 'bland' (James 2015: 146), is reinterpreted by James as an example of what she terms a melancholic practice, capable of undermining our expectations of (suffering) resilience.[5] Just as the asynchronous queer narratives of films like *Appropriate Behaviour* may be underappreciated or unintelligible to critics because they deliver something unpredictable, James argues that 'Diamonds' sounds 'directionless' (2015: 146) because neither the song nor Rihanna is practising resilience in the way we have come to expect. Although Rihanna *does* capitalize on her 'damage' (James 2015: 154) – in this case, domestic abuse within the context of her personal and professional relationship with American R&B artist Chris Brown[6] – she does not do so 'in the "right" way, i.e., in a way that amplifies listeners' experience of privilege' (James 2013b). Privileged listeners might expect a resilient overcoming narrative, but, as James shows, Rihanna instead produces a melancholic refusal of resilience by amplifying the 'wrong affects' (2015: 144). Nicole R. Fleetwood finds that 'instead of abiding by the protocols of the black female survivor of violence who repudiates her abuser, Rihanna sticks close to the scene of her assault and continues to rehearse and restage the interplay of love, violence, and erotic attachments in deliberately shocking ways' (2012: 419). Instead of amplifying an experience of overcoming abuse, 'Diamonds' practises melancholia, prioritizing an attachment to damage rather than a triumphant display of simply 'getting over it'.

Musically, 'Diamonds' makes promises it never intended to keep. It does this by building towards, and subsequently undermining, the musical climax, or soar (James 2015). James describes a musical pattern of consonance-dissonance-consonance common to popular music, and which is analogous to the formula of the hero's quest that *The Hunger Games* and *The Hate U Give* adapt. At its most basic, this kind of harmonic structure requires a movement between musical rest (consonance) and musical tension (dissonance) before returning to consonance. Pop songs typically use the tonal relationship between consonance and dissonance to build and release affective tension. In a sense, the return to consonance 'resolves' any conflict or tension that is intentionally created by the dissonant sounds. 'Diamonds' works within this pattern, priming listeners to expect an affective release, but instead continually producing melancholic sounds.

In contrast to the genre conventions of a typical pop song, which dictate that form and structure be oriented towards the goal of musical climax, 'Diamonds' 'doesn't go anywhere' (James 2015: 146). Associating the musical climax or soar with the listener embodiment of resilience, James argues that Rihanna's deliberate refusal of the soar is what produces a melancholic subjectivity. Typically, the verse-chorus-verse formula would be followed by a 'break' in the pattern where the musical crest transpires (2015: 147). In EDM-pop, a 'pause-drop' immediately follows the soar.[7] This pause (in which most of instrumental and/or vocal sound is reduced) is designed at once to delay and exacerbate the rapid musical descent that creates the most effective catharsis for the listener (147). 'Diamonds', however, includes a pause-drop after the second verse, yet subsequently omits the soar (James 2015: 147–8). Without an escalation of aural intensity to precede the pause, the song simply maintains its musical threshold rather than crashing through and overcoming the intensity usually created by a soar. Capitalizing on genre assumptions, 'Diamonds' uses strategies that rely on musical and compositional climaxes while ultimately neglecting their delivery. In a context in which 'success, optimization, investment, and capitalization' are ethically and aesthetically idealized, 'Diamonds' is noteworthy because it adopts these compositional aesthetics but subsequently 'fails to fully exploit and optimize' them, constituting a *'failed musical investment'* (James 2013a). Melancholic musical techniques, therefore, sound like loss and deficiency, or a failure to maximize and reap the rewards of the resources at one's disposal.

I suggested earlier that the consonance-dissonance-consonance works similarly to the hero's quest, which is structured around the disruption of the protagonist's everyday world, creating tension to be eventually resolved by the narrative's close. The coherence of their world is rendered dissonant by events beyond their control until the protagonist's own agency can resolve the tension and conclude by returning to a state of central coherence. Conclusions of this nature offer a kind of resilience in which protagonists do not 'bounce back' to their original state; instead, they integrate the dissonance they experience, become fundamentally altered by it, but also in the end manage to cohere again around a new state of play. This kind of consonance is distinct from the type at the beginning of the narrative but still produces coherence for the characters and subsequently the reader. The generic expectation of a fundamental transformation that produces a coherent subject evidently works across multiple modes of cultural production. This is one of our primary collective cultural narratives, which shapes our own expectations of identity-formation to be structured around a trajectory of growth.

Building on James's analysis of 'Diamonds', I examine *Girlhood*'s use of the song and the kinds of resilience its musical sequence produces. Sciamma uses a narrative 'break', and what I describe as an audiovisual soar, thereby generating quite a different reading of resilience within the film. In Rihanna's performance, the break section is haunted by an absent soar, and the song gestures towards a catharsis it does not provide. At first, *Girlhood* and Rihanna are in visual-aural alignment: during the pause-drop section of 'Diamonds', as the camera slows, so do Marieme and Lady as they dance. Immediately after the song's break section, however, *Girlhood* creates its own soar by staging an aural intervention as the girl's own voices break out, merging with Rihanna's in the diegetic soundtrack. Although different to the soar-pause-drop formula, this pattern delivers an affective surge of intensity, nonetheless. All four characters are framed together, as they jump and sing exuberantly to the song's final chorus and coda, a four shot once again emphasizing their intergroup intimacy. The power of the girls' voices coming to the fore of the soundtrack, in tandem with the image of their dancing and the physicality of their movement as they jump in time to the music, thus equates to the visual manifestation of the musical soar Rihanna omits.

Prior to the musical break in 'Diamonds', *Girlhood* includes a visual break in the sequence, cutting away from Lady, Adiatou and Fily to show Marieme as she watches them dance together. Here, the camera dollies in to a close-up of Marieme; this technique of drawing gradually closer to her is one of only a few in the film that invites the audioviewer into Marieme's interior emotional world. Marieme's facial expressions as she watches her friends dance evoke a complex mix of emotions, perhaps akin to what Laura Carstensen et al. refer to as 'poignancy', that is, the combination of both positive and negative feelings that arise with the awareness of one's 'limited time in the context of meaningful experience' (2008: 158). The colourful aesthetics and visual soar produce a girlhood that feels joyful and carefree, an animating force. Yet the film constructs Marieme as aware that her joyful experience is finite; thus, girlhood sociality feels momentary, produced to some degree as an exceptional experience that cannot endure for long beyond the bounds of their hotel room.

There are several moments in the film when Marieme's horizons open up, such as the pivotal first transition when the camera draws away from her, increasing our field of vision much as Marieme's own world is about to expand. Conversely, in the Diamonds sequence, the combination of camera movement towards Marieme and the extended focus on her facial expression work together to further the sense of restriction that pervades the film, even in moments as carefree as this one. McNeill notes that during the musical sequence 'the girls momentarily become "stars," like Rihanna', though at the same time, 'the traumatic melancholia of the video and Rihanna's fragile persona contribute a sense of unsettling transience' (2017: 12). This along with the visual break, then, suggests Marieme's own sense of a genre with a limited shelf life. At a time in her life when Marieme would be expected to be focused on acquiring skills, gaining knowledge, growing up and outward into the world, her horizons instead contract. Not only will the song end, but this chapter of her life is also soon to close. Breaking away from the exhilaration developed in the first part of the sequence, especially during this rare moment highlighting Marieme's interiority and the 'poignancy' of her emotional landscape, works to generate an intensified affective pleasure in the final moments of the sequence, as it dawns on us that Marieme's happiness here will likely be all too fleeting.

By creating its own soar, *Girlhood* does not diminish Rihanna's undermining of one. Rather, the two appear to harmonize. The characters perhaps find a more traditional form of resilience in 'Diamonds', a song that refuses to let listeners overcome and recycle their damage. This suggests that melancholic practices such as 'Diamonds' are in fact crucial to forming the kinds of resilience that work against oppressive hierarchies rather than for them. What makes the Diamonds sequence so powerful is that it produces resilience in service of girlhood itself. By this, I mean that the resilience it produces affirms feminine sociality, rather than the dominant hypermasculinity that pervades the film from the outset and is the primary power dynamic structuring Marieme's everyday world. The moments in which Marieme's agency is most restricted are when the men in her world exercise their power over her, for example, her brother's abuse. Equally, for much of the film Marieme's actions work towards her gaining patriarchal acceptance and entry into the very same hierarchies that oppress her. This scene is notable for its construction of relational resilience derived from girlhood community; however, it also hints at the complexities of how girls interact with one another.

On the one hand, Marieme and her friends draw their strength from one another in this striking sequence. On the other, Marieme's inclusion within the group is cemented by her intimidation of a younger girl, whose stolen euros help pay for their night of fun. This is one of multiple instances where Marieme capitalizes on the oppression of other girls, with the film's third act providing the primary example of a fight against a girl from a rival group, which works narratively to complete and consolidate Marieme's transformation into Vic. Winning the fight gains Marieme brief acceptance from her brother, whose dispassionate offer to play video games with him is in stark contrast to his physical and verbal abuse of Marieme in the rest of the film. Unlike the structured opposition of the football game, here the conflict is resolved through violence and the humiliation of Marieme's opponent. We begin to see the ways that relational resilience as the capacity to overcome the strictures of the everyday – even although it does provide the support structure Marieme needs – comes at the expense of the hostile exclusion of other girls. Relationality, then, is not so clear-cut. While constructing social bonds between girls as central to their subject formation, *Girlhood* also acknowledges that, as Ruti puts it, 'relationality is not necessarily any more pure, any more devoid of power struggles, than any other component of human life' (2017: 81).[8] Initially appearing to affirm girlhood and feminine sociality as they resist or undermine the status quo in which girls are undervalued, relational resilience becomes somewhat compromised by these scenes in which Marieme's narrative agency is driven by her role in other girls' suffering.

Transformative resilience

Having examined some of the aesthetic strategies the film uses to create relational resilience, I now want to think about how its structure produces transformative resilience, or the capacity for change that enables one to overcome adversity in 'socially profitable ways' (James 2015: 15). Transformation is central to the film's structure, which unfolds over five segments, stylistically demarcated by four extended cuts to black. Four key moments of transition are scored by an urgent minimalist electronic composition that develops intensively throughout the film. The affective energy of the score advances Marieme's transformations, as each segment concludes with a transitional sequence that signals turning points or opportunities for reinvention. The soundtrack is therefore vital to charting Marieme's trajectory as she joins a girl gang ('Néon'), forcefully declines the opportunity to follow in her mother's footsteps as a low-paid hotel cleaner ('Néon reprise'), initiates a sexual relationship with her brother's friend Ismaël ('Girlhood'), then leaves her neighbourhood to work for a local drug dealer ('Le Départ'). In addition to the atmospheric soundtrack, the film produces Marieme's coming-of-age process visually through striking use of costuming, foregrounding the concept of identity formation as a performative construction.

In Chapter 1, I discussed how *Gone Girl* presents the process of transforming oneself to align with postfeminist social norms as damaging to the formation of feminine subjectivity. Chapter 2 analyses *Girls'* use of formal and narrative strategies to establish and disavow expectations that growth and coming of age will be achieved through self-transformation. *Girlhood*'s approach to transformation diverges significantly in two important ways. First, the film suggests that transformation is key to gaining much-needed access to social spaces and accruing social value, and second, it interrogates the notion that external transformation is intrinsically linked to the formation of subjectivity or identity in the way we might expect of coming-of-age genres. Instead, the transitions work to produce Marieme as a resilient subject who overcomes adversity. I therefore situate the transitions within a framework of continual adversity and overcoming through analysis of the first and final sequences.

In its first act, the film establishes that Marieme's home life is abusive, and her educational opportunities are limited. Her brother's abuse makes the domestic space untenable, and Marieme's poor grades prevent her entry into the instructive space of the lycée, foreclosing an academic path that might lead her beyond the banlieue. Having established in the first act the conditions Marieme must surmount in her coming-of-age quest, the first transition creates a sense of affective resilience by using the score and camerawork to suggest that transformation might be the key to overcoming her limited opportunities. In this

Figure 12 Profile close-up of Marieme (Karidja Touré) during *Girlhood*'s first transition sequence (Sciamma 2014). *Girlhood*, directed by Céline Sciamma © Hold Up Films/Lilies Films/Arte France Cinéma 2014. All Rights Reserved.

sequence, Marieme is washing dishes; she hesitates before slipping an ornate knife into her pocket. The camera then tracks up from her hands placed firmly on the edge of the sink to a close-up of her face in profile (Figure 12). Though Marieme remains the primary subject of the shot, her features are only partially revealed to us. As discussed, this is one of several important moments in the film that shields Marieme's character from the camera's scrutiny. Where a typical close-up of a character's face might offer insight into their emotions or at the very least access to a facial expression, *Girlhood* invites us to accompany its protagonist on her journey but does not offer her interiority for our inspection. The camera then draws slowly away, allowing Marieme (with her back to us) some breathing room as the Néon theme intensifies, announcing that something new, something exciting is on the horizon. As the soundtrack soars, Marieme's potential emerges, encouraging us to imagine futures of possibility for her, irrespective of external constraint.

Early scenes suggest that girlhood friendship has similar potential to open up new spaces and ways of being in the world. At the same time, these scenes in which Marieme spends time with the other girls express a sense of quiet foreboding, drawing on the popular trope of the impressionable young girl led astray by the bad influence of a rebellious new friendship group.[9] This tension between potential and risk aligns with the two contrasting discourses of late modernity Harris identifies, which produce girls as either 'can-do' capable achievers or alternatively as 'at-risk' and vulnerable (2004: 9). For example, Marieme's first trip to Paris with the girls (which immediately precedes the transition) composes a complex dynamic of risk and potential, both of which arise from a series of confrontations that demonstrate their 'taking pleasure in a noisy display of protest and dominance' (McNeill 2017: 8). First, after Marieme declines the invitation to visit Paris and subsequently changes her mind, Lady confronts her, hard-faced, demanding whether Marieme is afraid of her. For an anxious moment, the camera holds on Marieme's face before Lady bursts into laughter, defusing the tension. Laughter breaks out similarly when the girls intimidate a White shop assistant who suspects Marieme of shoplifting, and following their confrontation with a rival group of antagonistic girls on the opposite side of the Métro platform, scenes which McNeill reads as the girls 'acknowledging the event as performance' (2017: 8). In these cases, the girls' posturing grants little sense of actual violence or aggression. However, when read in tandem with the knife Marieme pockets, or the setting of the banlieue as an indelible cultural image of crime and deprivation, there is certainly room to interpret these scenes as portents of imminent risk or violence. Nevertheless, the film's emotive transitions and colourful aesthetics evoke the expansive potential the figure of the girl so often yields (Harris 2004; McRobbie 2008). The girl, then, generates feelings of buoyant optimism, while also carrying a heavy sense of trepidation. Therein lies the central conflict in *Girlhood*'s vision of girls as irrepressibly luminous, capable and imbued with potential, and at the same time severely limited by their social environment.

If clothing is typically read as marker of identity providing insight into the construction of selfhood, the costuming in *Girlhood* diverges somewhat from this understanding. Costuming, as well as music and narrative, plays a significant role in the transitions, especially the first and final, which are the most distinctive. While clothing does still read as identity-driven in some respects (connoting Marieme's youth, for instance, in the first act), Marieme/Vic's clothing cannot be read solely or even primarily as 'signs' of her internal world or identity. Rather than visual markers of identity transformation, then, I suggest that the costume changes signal Marieme's ability to access different ways of being. The American football uniform, for instance, is the first costume Marieme wears. Bulky shoulder pads and a cage-like helmet facilitate an embodied way of being in the world, one that enables the girls to take up more space and participate in the rough and tumble of the game without coming to harm. In turn, the training ground gives the girls space to revel in their physical abilities. Once they have shed their protective armour, however, they transform from whooping, cheering athletes to cautious young girls who must be vigilant at all times in their own neighbourhoods.

In the first transition, Marieme sheds her nondescript long-sleeved tops and long braids and emerges with straightened hair, fashionable clothing and a newfound confidence (Figure 13). When the domestic and educational spaces are restricted or excised altogether, Marieme's first costume change marks her initiation into a space for feminine sociality to thrive. Here, dressing and acting like 'one of the girls' is what indeed makes Marieme one of the girls. By the final transition, Vic makes her way up a flight of stairs, pausing to adjust her short, tight red dress, hinting at her discomfort in this new costume. Far from the exciting sartorial transformation of the first transition, here Vic's attire

Figure 13 Marieme's fashionable new clothing and hairstyle in *Girlhood*'s first transition sequence (Sciamma 2014). *Girlhood*, directed by Céline Sciamma © Hold Up Films/Lilies Films/Arte France Cinéma 2014. All Rights Reserved.

is a uniform of sorts, providing entry to a high-class party to sell drugs to White guests.

However, this particular transformation is momentary, as once the transaction is complete Vic immediately exchanges the hyper-feminine dress for trousers and a sweatshirt, removing a platinum-blonde wig to reveal short, braided hair (Figure 14). The film hints at complex gender politics as Vic eschews her feminine clothing and instead binds her chest, wearing loose clothing and close-cropped braids that allow her to blend in and move freely within the masculine spaces of her new neighbourhood, effectively becoming, in this segment of the film, 'one of the guys'. If Marieme's home life and schooling leave her with 'nothing' (James 2015: 1) to work with, *Girlhood* suggests, it is only through transformative resilience that she can grasp at 'something' (1). Traditional spaces of identity formation are hostile or foreclosed; therefore, to gain access to new spaces, Vic must look the part.

During the transition sequences, the film's score plays a crucial role in generating affect, and also, therefore, in my interpretation of the costume changes. Unlike the elevating Néon theme of the first transition, which imbues Marieme's exterior transformation with a sense of triumph, in the final transition the music takes a minatory turn, creating an urgent sense of threat through discordant tones

Figure 14 Vic's masculine attire in the final act of *Girlhood* (Sciamma 2014). *Girlhood*, directed by Céline Sciamma © Hold Up Films/Lilies Films/Arte France Cinéma 2014. All Rights Reserved.

and rhythmic sounds reminiscent of a heartbeat. This ominous affect created through the soundtrack is further compounded by the camera, which follows Vic's feet, tracking her steps in a slight slow motion that contributes to the threatening atmosphere. Here, the music generates fear for Vic, associating her transformation with a sense of foreboding rather than the joyful sense of potential in prior transitions. The returned emphasis on risk suggests that transformative resilience might be necessary for Vic's survival but not necessarily something to be celebrated in itself.

The central role of transformation indicates that girlhood genres are perhaps uniquely influenced by postfeminist empowerment rhetoric avowing its emancipatory potential. However, *Girlhood* aesthetically connects transformation to both uplifting and fearful registers in its transition sequences, thereby affectively conveying that transformation after postfeminism does not necessarily always feel liberating. Although, as I've suggested, *Girlhood* does not discount Marieme's internal world, the transition sequences reveal that the film's primary interest is in the kinds of spaces and socialities her costumes provide access to, making where Marieme goes and who she connects with more important than our sense of 'who' she is.

Aesthetics of sociality

Having established a distinction between transformative and relational resilience, I now want to discuss the fourth transition sequence, which blurs the boundaries between the two modes as they become narratively and formally imbricated. Its very status as a transition connects it to the notion of change enacted by the film's structure. The music creates a sense of forward momentum in line with Marieme's narrative position at this point, having triumphed in her fight with a rival girl and asserted her sexuality with Ismaël. Yet, the transition also emphasizes girlhood sociality in much the same way the Diamonds scene did. Taking place in La Défense, the Paris business district, it situates Marieme within a wider social sphere, thus extending the scope beyond her primary friendship group. Beginning with Vic in close-up as our central reference point, the camera then tracks slowly left past her friends and along a line of girls chatting excitedly and expressing their affection for one another through casual physical contact.

In combination with the tracking shot, the soundtrack creates and articulates the relations between Marieme as an individual subject and her wider social group. McNeill notes that the 'Girlhood' theme used here bears some structural and formal resemblance to the Néon theme of the first two transitions, but that unlike the 'ambivalence of "Néon," "Girlhood" expresses a more positive sense of rising momentum that echoes Vic's growing sense of agency within the narrative' (2017: 5). Observing that the shot 'asks us to admire the girls' youthful vibrancy, beauty and connectedness whilst defying our desire to know them or guess their trajectory' (5), McNeill suggests, like Handyside, that music is used to express the girls' emotions, while allowing them to retain opacity and privacy. We are invited to witness their relational intimacy, but the film does not extend our insight to the girls' individual subjectivities or the paths their lives may take. As a relational image of girlhood, it underscores the joy emerging from and within the girls' relationships to one another. Structured as part of a key transition sequence, it is clear that connection and sociality are integral to Marieme's subject formation, her capacity for transformation and for transformative resilience especially.

Whereas the sequence opened with Marieme, beginning with the individual before broadening the scope to map out her social relations, the final shots situate her character as one girl among many, recalling once again the concept of muscular bonding (Colling 2017; McNeill 1995), or the temporary loss of our individual boundaries, which, Colling suggests, 'creates the feeling of becoming something bigger, giving the individual the opportunity to stretch out beyond their isolated capacities' (87). Panning slowly forward over a crowd of girls, Marieme and her friends are included but not privileged by the camera. Instead, they are part of a multitude of girls occupying the entirety of the frame, thus cementing the film's understanding of Marieme as a relational subject whose coming of age is produced by and through the connections she makes with others. The girls walk away from the camera, which follows at a slow pace, allowing them to slip beyond the camera's scope so that others may enter the frame. This composition enables the audioviewer to follow and observe from a distance, while once again hinting at the girls' unknowability.

In a reversal of the opening scene, the girls' indistinct chatter comes to the fore in the final shot of the sequence. Now walking towards the camera, their collective voices slowly supersede the dominance of the non-diegetic 'Girlhood' theme. Girlhood sociality once again finds its most vivid expression in the anonymity of the non-place. Against the grain of Augé's assertion that social connection is unlikely to flourish in a non-place, these spaces in fact prove crucial to feminine relationality, as the domestic sphere which ought to yield 'places for living' (1995: 66–7) instead inhibits the girls' self-expression. At once demonstrating the characters' resourcefulness in seeking out spaces in which they might thrive, if only momentarily, this scene also reveals that social identity is a key determining factor in one's experience of a non-place. Augé's argument that airports, hotels and shopping centres are decontextualized from social conditions is essentially accurate. However, his proposal that they conclusively therefore 'cannot be defined as relational, or historical, or concerned with identity' (1995: 77–8) perhaps overlooks the importance of paying attention to the specificities of the identity and associated historical weight each individual subject brings to a non-place, and furthermore, the relationality that can transpire between the individuals inhabiting them. Dobson too identifies the non-place as important to *Girlhood*'s spatial topography, interpreting such spaces as lacking in their 'capacity to function as social places as they encourage self-designation as individuals defined by transitory function for example, consumer, commuter' (2017: 41). Perhaps, then, if one holds strong social ties to familial, educational or other social institutions, the atomizing force of the non-place feels especially anti-relational as it encourages such individualized identities. If, however, one's social history or identity are in fact 'roadblocks ... to their flourishing' (Ruti 2017: 137), the non-place might function, as *Girlhood* suggests, as one of the only settings in which relational bonds can be initiated and sustained.

Instead of focusing on the particular speech or interiority of an individual, the La Défense transition audiovisually produces a collective relationality. Like the affective resilience created by the Diamonds sequence, it therefore places value in taking up the space of the frame and the soundscape, while at the same time giving privacy to who these girls might be and what they might be saying to one another. To value girls, the film suggests, we do not require access to the inside of their heads. This last point has important implications for resilience discourse, which typically encourages female subjects to reveal and overcome their suffering so that they might gain social capital. A minor point of convergence arises here between *Girlhood* and *The Hunger Games*, recalling the moment Katniss begins to preserve her privacy and the integrity of her selfhood by withholding her affective responses from the cameras in the arena. However, while this highlights the importance of privacy in terms of Katniss's characterization, readers are in fact granted continuous insight to her inner world by virtue of the simultaneous present-tense narration. In contrast, there is little clue as to whether Marieme's character values privacy precisely because the film's aesthetics are designed to shield her interiority from the scrutiny of our gaze. *Girlhood* is far less interested in the 'content' of the girls' identity and in figuring out or pinning down who they are, or what this might mean (the 'truth' of their subjectivity and or/girlhood), than it is preoccupied with imagining girls as simply being. The film values their collective (and individual) voice but suggests that the content of their speech is far less important than the very fact that girls ought to be afforded opportunities to speak. Whether aesthetically or narratively, girlhood genres are evidently invested in both the enhanced scrutiny girls face from social others and affording them opportunities to retain opacity and privacy (Handyside 2016).

Finally, while transformative resilience remains complicit in the postfeminist paradigm of continual self-improvement and flexibility, I argue that *Girlhood*'s thorough entanglement of transformation and relationality makes it far more difficult to read a transformative mode of resilience as an absolute capitulation to a restrictive status quo. This is not to say that transformative resilience is therefore a liberatory practice, and nor does it need to be. The film is clear that transformation comes at a price, but it is also how Vic gets where she is going, offering her far more opportunities and experiences than the normative paths she rejects (or that reject her). Each mode of resilience can be alternately caught in a restrictive liberatory/complicit paradigm with plenty of convincing evidence for either. Transformative resilience *is* complicit with postfeminist norms, yet at the same time, it liberates Vic from an unwanted marriage and a life of low-paid work. Within the confines of Vic's world, transformation may not be as wholly emancipatory as postfeminist rhetoric often suggests, yet there are evidently ways in which postfeminist conventions offer more potential for freedom than the alternatives available to her. Rather than arguing for/against each model, I have instead explained how the film produces resilience aesthetically, and what each mode offers Marieme's character. Relationality of both kinds (with other girls, and against them) opens up Marieme's world and allows her access to different ways of living.

In this respect, there is an odd angle of intersection between *Gone Girl* and *Girlhood*. Both works emphasize that self-transformation is the socially desirable route to rewrite one's story and change generic outcomes. Each protagonist tries on the identities their respective societies have fashioned for them, and both narratives speak to the unsustainability of available norms and subjectivities, as well as the impossibility of fashioning a wholly new identity, or forging a new path out of nowhere and with nothing. In *Gone Girl*, postfeminist modes of identity formation are more likely to exhaust potential than fulfil it. Meanwhile, the ambiguity of *Girlhood*'s approach to costuming, music and narrative suggests that the film is less interested in the impact of transformation on individual subjectivity and more in what the various identities allow Vic to do and where they allow her to go. I have given shape to two cultural manifestations of resilience discourse that appear at first glance to be in opposition. Yet, as we have seen, transformative and relational modes of resilience – predicated upon flexible self-reinvention and social ties, respectively – are in fact thoroughly entwined, necessitating methods of analysis that resist the temptation to make arguments within a liberatory/complicit binary.

6

Feel-bad femininity in *Catch Me Daddy*

While *Girlhood* delivers on its promise of a resilient coming-of-age narrative, this chapter explores the bad feelings generated by a film that breaks this contract of spectatorial expectation. Adapting Nikolaj Lübecker's concept of the 'feel-bad film' (2015: 3), this chapter primarily analyses *Catch Me Daddy*, a British thriller following sixteen-year-old protagonist Laila's quest to evade capture by the two groups of men hired by her father, Tariq, to retrieve Laila and bring her home.[1] The film's closing stages a horrific confrontation between Laila and her father, culminating in his attempts to coerce her to commit suicide. Following a protracted sequence in which Tariq fluctuates between rage towards his daughter and regret for his actions, Tariq instructs Laila to stand on a chair and place a noose around her neck. Here, the film ends abruptly, offering no narrative or emotional catharsis and literally leaving us hanging over the question of Laila's capacity to determine her own fate. In doing so, it finds resonance with Lübecker's genre of feel-bad films, which work in an 'unpleasant register' (2015: 2), using narrative and cinematographic devices to produce a desire for catharsis or satisfaction, and then continually preventing closure. Several scenes early in the film affectively produce a sense of resilient femininity, thus establishing expectations that Laila's self-determination will prevail in the face of adversity. The subsequent failure of the closing sequence to perform resilience is what denies narrative closure and instigates an affective feel-bad experience.

Although Lübecker identifies several feel-bad modes, including abjection and cringe comedy, he concentrates on four in particular: '"assaultive films", "desperation films", "suspension films" and the "feel-bad farce"' (2015: 4). What each of these categories share is the creation and ultimate frustration of a desire for catharsis, although their modes of address and affective registers vary considerably. Across each of the four modes, Lübecker identifies films in which

> the intensification of the feel-bad climate is so radical that the spectators begin to worry where things are going. They begin to wonder about the 'intentions' of the film, about the nature of the spectatorial contract. (3)

It is the 'destabilization of the spectatorial contract' (3), as Lübecker puts it, that is central to the production of bad feelings, though each mode achieves that aim using different methods.

Lübecker's interest in feel-bad genres lies in their 'political and ethical potential' (4). Working in the assaultive mode, films like Lars von Trier's *Dogville* (2003) 'go through the body of the spectator to her intellect' (16), by deliberately provoking discomfort or unpleasant sensorial affects, while at the same time inviting an intellectual engagement with the political and ethical questions they raise. Suspension films, by contrast, convey unpleasant feelings indirectly, causing a sense of unease through their uncertainty or indeterminacy. Films such as Gus Van Sant's *Elephant* (2003) engage with our desire to explain and understand a difficult or traumatic social conflict or problem, and then endlessly defer any clarity of closure (Lübecker 2015). What truly defines all feel-bad modes is when 'the film produces a spectatorial desire, but then blocks its satisfaction; *it creates, and then deadlocks, our desire for catharsis*' (2015: 2, original italics). Generic expectation, one of the central concerns of this book, proves essential to the identification of the feel-bad film. If, as Lübecker points out in his discussion of the art film, disturbing subject matter and an 'open ending' (Bordwell 1999 in Lübecker 2015: 3) are in fact defining features of the genre, then expectation can dictate that catharsis or closure may not necessarily be forthcoming.

Lübecker observes that many mainstream genres portray and generate negative emotion, 'but most will make sure that such emotions are diffused at the end of the film' (2015: 2). See, for instance, the film *Precious* (Daniels 2009), in which horrific acts of rape, sexual abuse, familial neglect and systemic violence are perpetrated against the eponymous protagonist, a teenage Black girl who is continually failed by the education and social welfare institutions that ostensibly exist to support her. Near the end of the film, Precious learns she has tested positive for HIV, which, as Mark Blankenship (2009) points out in his *Huffington Post* review, would almost certainly be a fatal prognosis in 1987 when the film takes place. Despite this, the film closes with an upbeat musical sequence set to LaBelle's 'It Took a Long Time' (1974), first underpinning the resolution provided by the coming-of-age trajectory and then ameliorating any negative or unpleasant emotions generated by the film's horrific events. What Lübecker's model suggests is that as spectators, many of us are prepared to invest time and emotional energy into films that make us feel bad; however, by their close, we then wish to feel better. Yet in some cases, this 'narrative containment' (3) as Lübecker terms it, is not always successful. In the television series *The Handmaid's Tale* (2017–present),[2] set in a near-future dystopian society founded upon systemic ritualized rape, the severity of the violence perpetrated against women pushed some spectators beyond their emotional limits (Bernstein 2019; Reid 2018; Sturges 2018). Upbeat musical numbers were stretched to their own breaking point, proving incapable of containing and ameliorating the emotions generated by the on-screen violence.

The Handmaid's Tale exacts extreme levels of sexual, psychological, physical and emotional brutality upon its female characters (Bernstein 2019; Gilbert 2018). Jennifer Maher's critique illustrates both the severity of the violence and its affective power:

> The emotional stakes of *The Handmaid's Tale* are amped up to such an extreme degree that the attempted suicide of an innocent woman who has already had her eye gouged out for disobedience elicits relief from its (feminist) audience because *at least the baby didn't die*. (2018: 210, original italics)

In its first season alone, *The Handmaid's Tale* features systemic mass rape, sexual coercion, imprisonment, public executions, torture and genital mutilation. Several episodes close with pop songs many critics found inappropriate, given the series' subject matter. Two episodes in particular stand out, both featuring slow-motion 'power walks', which Emily VanDerWerff describes as scenes where 'Handmaids would stride toward the camera in formation, in ways that seemed designed to underline their force as a potential army against their oppressors' (2018: n.p.). In the fourth episode of season one, the protagonist, June, is suffering the effects of being locked away for weeks in isolation and finally manipulates her captor into allowing her to leave the house, a victory that Constance Grady points out is 'a very basic, tiny freedom' (VanDerWerff and Grady 2017: n.p.). For Grady, the relatively minor triumph does resonate, on the one hand, as it demonstrates the labour that goes into achieving it, but on the other, the 'final shot of the Handmaids power-walking down the street inflates the victory' (2017: n.p.). Similarly, VanDerWerff finds that although she appreciates the use of pop songs as an aesthetic choice, they are ultimately 'jarring' and 'out-of-sync' with the brutality depicted (2017: n.p.).

The season one finale similarly attempts to create a sense of victory using a slow-motion power walk and upbeat music. In this case, the series formulates a moment of defiant agency when a group of women, led by June and a character named Ofglen, refuse to stone another handmaid to death – the innocent woman noted by Maher, who has survived her suicide attempt only to be sentenced to death for endangering her child. Harnessing the power of collectivity, June and the rest of the group risk their lives to save one of their own, and their insubordination is framed as a triumph. As the handmaids make their way through snowy grey streets, the power walk conveys their unity (Figure 15). Yet this too is diminished by the way the women gradually break from the group, only to return to the houses where they are each held captive by a state-sanctioned rapist. This scene is scored by Nina Simone's 'Feeling Good' (1965), a song which expresses the kind of euphoria that 'comes with liberation from oppression' (Cheal 2020).

Feel-Bad Femininity in Catch Me Daddy 173

Figure 15 June (Elisabeth Moss) leads a group of handmaids in a power walk following a defiant act of suffering agency (*The Handmaid's Tale*, Miller 2017: 1.10). © MGM Television 2017–20, MGM/UA Television 2020–.

David Cheal observes that, 'released during the ferment of the civil rights protests, Simone's "Feeling Good" was a manifestation of that movement's burning desire for freedom' (2020). Given this context, it is no surprise that some critics, such as Kristin Iversen, take issue with *The Handmaid's Tale* using a song emblematic of the civil rights movement[3] to soundtrack fictional White women's emancipation (2017), a critique which recalls the way *The Hunger Games* uses Rue's death to fuel its fantasy of White resilience. It also ties with Angelica Bastién's argument that the show is 'more concerned with the interiority of white women at the expense of people of color who recognize that Gilead isn't a possible horrifying future, but the reality of what America has always been' (2017: n.p.). Musical sequences in this case are not only ineffective but also exacerbate the excess of bad feelings the show aims to produce.

Catch Me Daddy constructs expectations of feminine resilience and agency roughly in line with the generic conventions of the quest narrative. Teresa de Lauretis argues that quest narratives (and in fact all narrative structures) feature male heroes as active subjects whose desire drives the action. Female characters, by contrast, tend to be 'immobile' or 'personified obstacles' (1984: 118). In the Oedipus myth, the Sphinx's only narrative function is 'to test Oedipus and qualify him as a hero' (1984: 112). Essentially, male heroes come of age, or achieve their identity as masculine subjects, by overcoming female obstacles. This coming of age, in which the female is the matrix for male identity, is conceived as the point at which narrative closure is achieved. De Lauretis's argument resonates deeply with the gendering of resilience discourse, in which the way to become an acceptable female subject is to overcome one's femininity, and even better, to capitalize on this overcoming (James 2015). This suggests that even within female-focused resilience narratives, the 'object' to defeat remains feminine, regardless of the characters' gender.

Catch Me Daddy stages a quest narrative in which its female protagonist occupies the active role of the hero, and the obstacles standing in the way of her coming of age are the desires and decrees of male characters (particularly her father). Using this structure reifies, de Lauretis argues, a traditional gender binary, even with a female character in the subject position (1984). Yet Laila is not produced as an integrated member of her society and does not in the end achieve any self-completion or successful coming of age. Where *The Hunger Games* and *Girlhood* produce harsh but hopeful coming-of-age narratives – for better or worse, their protagonists have potential to find a place in their worlds – there is nowhere for Laila to go within her quest narrative. The obstacle from the traditional quest narrative – her father – remains undefeated and so does the obstacle one finds within resilience discourse – Laila's perceived fragility and passivity. In essence, the film works its way through the quest narrative, only to arrive at a conclusion in which the genre is incapable of producing a feminine subject.

Resilience in *Catch Me Daddy* manifests through the aesthetics of agency. Broadly speaking, I use the term 'agency' to refer to the ways we exercise our capacity to act, not necessarily in order to have a concrete effect on the world or transform our material realities but encompassing any endeavours towards doing so. I also return to James's notion of resilience, which refers to a hegemonic or aspirational imperative for women and girls to overcome the deficits associated with traditional conceptions of femininity. As James explains, to become socially viable subjects, there are two requirements female subjects must fulfil: 'Femininity is first performed as damage, second as resilience' (2015: 82). I examine scenes in which the film fulfils the terms of James's model by performing both requirements successfully, before turning to scenes in which feminine damage is performed but *not* overcome, thus affectively instigating feel-bad femininity.

The film aestheticizes agency through motion, affect and choice. First, I will show how the film creates and initially delivers on expectations of agentic femininity by characterizing Laila in relation to forms of sound and motion that signify freedom. Then, I examine how the film both performs and overcomes 'feminine damage' by envisaging Laila within the confines of traditional femininity from which she must break free. Once I have outlined agentic expectations, I analyse resilient affect in *Girlhood* to illustrate how the intensification of damage in *Catch Me Daddy* that is *not* overcome results in feel-bad femininity. Finally, I consider the aestheticization of choice, returning to Elliott's concept of suffering agency to show how even making appalling choices can feel 'good' when compared to abstaining from the choice-making paradigm altogether.

Catch Me Daddy and *Girlhood* both feature emblematic dancing sequences in which the central thematics of agency and resilience become uniquely entwined with girls' bodies in motion, and with the music they dance to. The intersection between music and girlhood agency and resilience is central to films like *Fish Tank* (2009), *The Fits* (2015) and *Assassination Nation* (2018). Set in a working-class estate in Essex, *Fish Tank* features a young protagonist who dreams of becoming a dancer. However, as Sarah Hill notes, while social class is something girls in films like *StreetDance* (Giwa and Pasquini 2010) can overcome, Mia is likely to 'remain dancing in car parks that are a far cry from the glamorous cityscapes that provide the backdrop for teen girl dance films' (2020: 77). Yet although the prospect of a feel-bad ending for Mia's story looms large throughout the film, it swerves at the last minute, offering her an escape Laila is never afforded.

Kinetic agency

By characterizing Laila in relation to forms of sound and motion that signify freedom, *Catch Me Daddy* creates the expectations of agentic femininity it will later undermine. The song Laila dances to is Patti Smith's 'Land: Horses / Land of a Thousand Dances / La Mer (De)' from her 1975 album *Horses*. Our sense of Laila as a resilient subject comes into focus here, as despite the cluttered and claustrophobic close-ups used to constrict her immediate environment, Laila is clearly someone who knows how to make the most of what little space she has at her disposal. By transforming the interior of a cramped, ramshackle caravan into a playful space for creative self-abandon and pure joy, her character manages to resiliently 'turn nothing into something' (James 2015: 1). The result is a form of girlhood grounded in making the best of one's circumstances and creating enjoyment despite the restrictions of life on the run.

While aesthetically constructing Laila's freedom and agency, the dancing sequence is, at the same time, structured and scored to signal that this agency is under threat. Whereas *Girlhood* uses sound, colour and the extended duration of its chosen song to create a narrative refuge or cinematic space that belongs to the four girls alone, *Catch Me Daddy*'s dancing sequence, by contrast, is structured so that although Laila occupies most of the audiovisual space, her agency and freedom are not the sole focus. The Diamonds sequence reserves space for Marieme and her friends alone, affording us a privileged view as they enjoy their freedom. It also addresses the spectator from firmly within Marieme's perspective, rooting the sequence in her interior world, enhanced by Sciamma's use of colour and duration. *Catch Me Daddy*, by contrast, uses trans-diegetic music, therefore not allowing us to inhabit a sole perspective as we are constantly shifting between two soundspaces. We first hear 'Land' non-diegetically during a shot of the two groups of men as they continue their pursuit of Laila. As we join Laila and Aaron in the caravan, the music becomes diegetic. With each cut between the pursuers and the pursued, the music transitions between non-diegetic and diegetic sound. For Robynn Stilwell, such transitions constitute 'a place of destabilization and ambiguity' (2007: 186), which we see here in the shifts between non-diegetic and diegetic music, as well as objective and subjective spaces. Visually, the sequence cuts between Laila's dancing, Aaron watching until he eventually joins her and the men as they drive through the moors. Opening, closing and interrupting Laila's dancing with shots of the men pursuing her effectively situates Laila as trapped between them, communicating that the song does not belong to Laila alone, and that the freedom her dancing signifies is acutely under threat. Laila inhabits the agentic space of the song, but the transition between non-diegetic and diegetic sound must also ascribe agency to the men: they too have the power to act, and their agency has the capacity to disrupt, subdue and potentially eliminate Laila's.

These constraints are further conveyed by the way that, unlike *Girlhood*'s preservation of the hotel room as a sacred space, Laila is not afforded a room of her own; she instead shares a cramped caravan in the middle of nowhere with her boyfriend Aaron. Laila's dancing is structured as a part of her everyday world rather than the escape from the ordinary that Sciamma stages when Marieme and her friends retreat to the anonymous hotel room to create their own freedom and find their own voices for the night. Laila, by contrast, is confined to the caravan, having been instructed by Aaron not to accept an invitation to go out dancing with her friend to a club. Neither Laila nor Marieme is pictured dancing in a nightclub environment, which would more firmly align their characterization with the social and public space. Crucially, both dancing scenes take place in spaces transgressing the boundary between public and private: the hotel room being both one and the other, while the claustrophobic privacy of the caravan appears too fragile to sustain the border. In different ways, these scenes suggest a hostility of the external world towards both characters, acknowledging that the private worlds they create for themselves are marked by their wholly improvised momentariness and transience. *Catch Me Daddy*'s dancing sequence is emblematic of Laila's momentary escape from patriarchal confinement, extricating herself from her 'real' world by running away and living in hiding with her boyfriend; yet the real world never quite recedes from view.

Laila's agency is first and foremost produced by her capacity for initiating movement despite (and because of) external limitations. When Laila dances, the film constructs her kinetically, obscuring her features in rapidly cut, hazy, blurred-out frames. There is one segment of the sequence reserved solely for Laila, in which she appears at her most uninhibited as she twirls, twists and drops, the camera in close, following her movement. Through shallow depth of field, extreme close-ups and rapid cutting, motion (and therefore, it is intimated to us, agency) becomes linked to distortion and dissolution. There is a kind of freedom in losing oneself in affective sensation, as Laila does when she dances. It also renders her a character who, although constrained by circumstance, is – at least potentially – in command of her own bodily autonomy and narrative agency. Although the narrative tension and sense of foreboding created by the cutaways to the bounty hunters is effective, the overall sense is that despite the shadowy figures of patriarchy closing in on Laila, she has the capacity to resiliently overcome.[4]

This portrayal of kinetic agency through dance is compounded and complicated by two scenes that rehearse the link between damage and resilience. If we assume that 'damaged' femininity refers to instances in which qualities of passivity or fragility are emphasized, this is encapsulated by a scene in which Laila's brother Zaheer finds her alone in the caravan and tries to persuade her to come home. Once again, the film invokes agency in relation to motion; however, in this instance the power initially rests with Zaheer rather than Laila. After lecturing her about family responsibility, Zaheer's attempt to physically overpower Laila backfires fatally, as their struggle culminates in his fall and accidental death, which triggers Laila's first escape (the first of four, as I will discuss). The difference is striking between the Laila who dances and twirls freely, the camera mesmerized by her movement, and the Laila immediately afterwards, framed statically as she sits motionless, staring impassively as her brother reprimands her. The framing and editing indicate that Zaheer's capacity to act is greater than Laila's, his agency being linked to his capacity to move while Laila must remain still, and to speak as she must remain silent.

In this scene, Laila is framed in an eye-level close-up, which would typically promote spectatorial intimacy with her character, but because her eyes are downcast, it instead reads as passivity. This is exacerbated by the static framing of Laila in comparison with the kinetic shot of Zaheer, who paces frantically back and forth, the camera following his movement to keep him in centre screen. Reverse shots between Zaheer and Laila in this short scene further compound the relationship between male kinetic agency and female static passivity. Reverse shots are typically designed to show smooth spatial continuity between characters in conversation, usually with eyeline matching which makes transitions appear seamless as well as manufacturing a kind of emotional continuity. The reverses between Laila in close-up and Zaheer in medium framing, however, show the acute imbalance in their relationship, further contrasted by Laila's immobility and Zaheer's continual movement. The blocking in this scene reinforces Zaheer's curtailing impact on Laila's agency. The frame remains focused on Laila as its subject, yet Zaheer's movement as he paces directly in front of the camera impedes our view as he literally takes over her space in the narrative, which we see is beginning to contract. Evidently, the space allotted to a protagonist is already significantly reduced when her character is envisaged within the confines of a traditionally feminine paradigm. Static framing, reduction of narrative space and silence all function to portray Laila as passive and inhibited from taking action, thus articulating the feminine damage she must overcome.

Laila's passivity in this scene does not ultimately diminish our perception of her as a potentially resilient subject; rather, the scene that follows enhances the notion of her as a socially viable subject worthy of our affective investment. Traditionally feminine qualities must first, as James argues, be performed before they can be overcome. In this case, Laila breaks the stillness by lunging to grab her phone and flees out of the window onto the moors, leaving behind Zaheer who is accidentally killed trying to restrain her. This marks the first of four times Laila narrowly escapes from the men pursuing her. Immediately after, Laila escapes the grasp of Shoby as she runs into the darkness of the moors, and then she unwittingly evades Barry as he searches for her in a packed nightclub. Finally, when a suspicious taxi driver seems to know too much about their situation, Laila and Aaron rush out of the car and into the dark hills. As part of the thriller genre, these scenes increase the tension of the chase. More importantly, they also intensify our sense of Laila's determination and agency, characterizing her as someone capable of taking flight and persevering in the face of adversity. When read along with the kinetic agency of the dancing scene, these escapes create an expectation that against all odds, Laila's determination and perseverance will prevail later in the film when Laila does return home to her father.

These escapes also offer Laila the opportunity to reclaim her narrative space. In doing so, the film draws a link between traditional feminine fragility and contemporary feminine resilience. Within the resilience paradigm, femininity remains a burden, albeit no longer one that prevents women from taking action; instead, as James argues, it 'provides you the very materials with which you *can* do something' (2015: 84). Early on, the dancing scene reinforces our initial expectations of the kind of subject Laila is – namely, free and uninhibited by restraint. Then, the scene with Zaheer articulates traditionally feminine attributes of immobility and passivity that directly challenge and contrast the film's initial formulation of agency in motion. Attributes like passivity, which have traditionally been ascribed to women and prevented them from owning and mobilizing agency, are now the very basis from which women can act – and – through their actions – 'prove' their resilience and viability as social subjects. Hence, Laila's ongoing movement from one scenario of escape to another becomes the way in which she can prove her resilient viability. The norms of traditional femininity remain powerfully intact; however, their parameters and manifestations shift so that traditional femininity no longer *feels* good – unless accompanied by an act of overcoming.

Resilient affect

When traditional femininity is performed without the requisite overcoming, it can only generate feel-bad femininity. As part of its closing sequence, which takes place primarily in Tariq's restaurant and culminates in his attempt to coerce Laila to commit suicide, *Catch Me Daddy* unleashes an intensification of feminine damage. Laila's femininity becomes feel-bad during a scene of prolonged crying, a signifier of feminine excess. This is especially striking when read alongside *Girlhood* which features a protagonist who cries but ultimately displays what I call 'resilient affect', or strong emotion eventually overcome in such a way that communicates self-control. To explain what I mean by resilient affect, I want to draw connections between what Stephanie Shields terms 'manly emotion' (2002: 85) and Shonni Enelow's definition of a 'restrained but resilient' (2016: n.p.) acting style. Each explores the legibility of emotional registers and identifies a cultural ideal demanding a strong affective response expressed through containment or restraint.

For Shields, manly emotion is the dominant ideal within contemporary US society and the standard by which both men's and women's expressions of affect are measured (Shields 2002; Shields and Warner 2007). Neither synonymous with male emotion nor 'an expression of normative or natural emotion' (2002: 85), manly emotion is instead 'the expression of deeply felt emotion under such control that it can be telegraphed by the minimal gesture, tone of voice, language, or facial movement' (85). Manly emotion, then, is a cultural imperative dictating that affect be strong and authentically felt but minimally expressed. Similarly, Enelow observes an intensely contained contemporary American acting style she labels 'restrained but resilient' (2016: n.p.). Demonstrating a 'resistance to and evasion of spectacular emotionality' (n.p.), this style of restrained resilience recalls Berlant's definition of flat affect as an 'underperformed emotional style' (2015: 199).[5] Enelow finds that contrary to a prior generation of American teenagers on film who fought to 'express their true selves', the contemporary performances she examines offer no such 'emotional release or revelation' (n.p.), fighting instead to control rather than reveal affect.[6] The emphasis placed on affective control associates this ability with one's agency and capacity for self-determination.

Before I compare the feel-bad femininity of *Catch Me Daddy* to the resilient affect in *Girlhood*, I first want to look at Arthur Koestler's distinction between weeping and crying:

> *Weeping* has two basic reflex-characteristics which are found in all its varieties: the overflow of the tear-glands and a specific form of breathing. ... *Crying*, on the other hand, is the emitting of sounds signalling distress, protest, or some other emotions. It may be combined with, or alternate with, weeping. (Koestler [1964] 1989: 271–2, original italics)

Julian Hanich's (2008) use of Koestler's heuristic definition gives further insight into how we distinguish between socially acceptable and unacceptable displays of emotion. Although Hanich is interested in the difference between crying and weeping at the movies, his analysis helps explain how girls' emotions are constructed as something to display and visibly overcome, and why emotions that are *not* overcome can generate an intensely uncomfortable mode of spectatorship. Hanich argues that weeping is a primarily silent activity allowing the cinemagoer to avoid the 'isolating effect of shame' (2008: 29) which overt (noisy) crying would likely provoke.[7] Within the space of the cinema, visual manifestations of distress are more socially acceptable than aural signs, as the shame of crying aloud makes us vulnerable to the 'potentially embarrassing gaze of others' (29). Hanich also differentiates between the real-life tears of cinemagoers and fictional tears on-screen, noting that while in our everyday lives we tend to 'avoid, by and large, the tear display *of* others' (32, original italics), 'tears on the screen can have a highly pleasurable effect on us by making us weep in empathic mimicry' (32). What this suggests is that we might enjoy fictional weeping but draw the line at overt crying, which we no longer experience as pleasurable.

Feel-Bad Femininity in Catch Me Daddy 183

Figure 16 Profile shot of Marieme crying in the final scene of *Girlhood* (Sciamma 2014). *Girlhood*, directed by Céline Sciamma © Hold Up Films/Lilies Films/Arte France Cinéma 2014. All Rights Reserved.

In *Girlhood*'s final scene, Marieme weeps and thus remains within the realm of socially acceptable resilient affect, as opposed to Laila's overt and therefore socially undesirable crying. The impact of Marieme's audible sobs and the visual signs of her distress are reduced by framing her from afar, and with her back to the camera. When we do see and hear Marieme crying, her face is in profile, and she remains framed from a distance, thus also creating a dissociated spectator position (Figure 16). As the camera draws in closer, it also pans away from Marieme, slowly edging her out of shot. There is potential to read this as leaving Marieme behind; the camera is perhaps no longer interested in her story, as if Marieme has exhausted her options and is no longer capable of the transformations required of her. However, as I suggested in the previous chapter, there is room for a reading in which the camera's shifting gaze in fact offers Marieme privacy as well as shielding us from her affective overflow.

When Marieme finally reappears by stepping forward into close-up, she is no longer crying. Although the question of what lies ahead for Marieme is left open, there is an assurance of perseverance in her look of stoic determination (Figure 17). Most of all, Marieme is shown capable of regulating her affect, which reads as her being in control of her fate, much like Katniss's carefully calculated withholding of emotion in the

Figure 17 Marieme looks determined, after stepping back into the frame (Sciamma 2014). *Girlhood,* directed by Céline Sciamma © Hold Up Films/ Lilies Films/Arte France Cinéma 2014. All Rights Reserved.

first *Hunger Games* novel. In their study on the 'social value of tears', Leah Warner and Stephanie Shields suggest that a

> moist eye in a sad context … signals that a strong emotion is being expressed in response to an uncontrollable loss but also that the emotion is sufficiently under control so as not to produce an overflow of emotion and full-blown crying. (2007: 95)

While their study suggests that a 'moist eye' is most effective at conveying emotion that we perceive as authentic and justifiable, the ability to control one's affect is equally important. Marieme's crying is more intense than mere weeping, but her eventual ability to regulate emotion cements that she is competent and in control, positioning her safely within the norms of acceptability for crying.

While *Girlhood* ameliorates Marieme's crying using editing and composition, *Catch Me Daddy* does not shy away from or attempt to mitigate Laila's distress. On the contrary, Laila sobs (rather than resorting to stoic weeping), and her crying is not aestheticized; instead, she is framed in a close-up that emphasizes her tear display (Figure 18).[8] In spite of the given norms of resilient femininity which demand that girls overcome or control their affect, here it is Laila who is overcome by her emotions. The resulting combination of visual and

Figure 18 Close-up of Laila crying in *Catch Me Daddy*'s closing sequence (Wolfe 2014). *Catch Me Daddy*, directed by Daniel Wolfe © EMU Films/Film4 2014. All Rights Reserved.

auditory distress equates to an almost intolerable sensation of intimacy. Within resilience discourse, Laila's unmitigated overflow of tears signifies that she possesses an excess of what James labels 'feminine fragility' (2015: 82). Moreover, a performance of resilient affect remains absent by the narrative's close and is consequently unavailable to us as spectators.

Girlhood offers the pleasures of emotional empathy and embodiment of resilient affect, all the while keeping intact the fantasy of a coherent and controlled subjectivity. In *Catch Me Daddy*, Laila's uncontrollable crying threatens to disrupt any such illusion. Crying in this instance is an undignified, relational 'cry for help' in which one solicits external assistance; it signifies a reliance on and interdependence with others, as well as communicating a devastating lack of control over oneself. An idealized contemporary femininity is supposed to be fragile but not *too* fragile. This explains why Laila's femininity feels bad: she does not overcome her fragility in the way we expect of a female heroine. The film creates an expectation that any fragility or passivity will be either narratively overcome or formally mitigated (or both). However, while the protracted scenes featuring Laila's crying are indeed incredibly uncomfortable, it is the abrupt ending that truly makes this film a feel-bad experience as it denies us the opportunity to watch Laila overcome her excessively feminine damage. Laila's crying not only violates an unwritten social contract, but it also violates the spectatorial contract established by the film's endlessly deferred promise of resilience. The social damage generated by the crying scenes could likely be tolerated were it in the end ameliorated or transformed into the affective resilience the film leads us to anticipate, yet which it, as we shall discover, ultimately withholds.

Agency, interrupted

The final aesthetic of agency the film mobilizes and undermines is that of choice. Here, I compare the film's conclusion, which cuts to black in medias res before Laila can make a choice or determine her fate, to the turning point of the film, in which Laila chooses to return home to her father (in exchange for the release of Aaron's kidnapped mother). This latter decision aligns with Elliott's concept of suffering agency, or 'the way in which choices made for oneself and according to one's own interests can still feel both imposed and appalling' (2013: 84). Suffering agency is a recurrent motif in the post-apocalyptic television series *The 100* (Rothenberg 2014–20), which is almost pathologically preoccupied by the problematic of choice and personal interest under imposed restraint. As Clarke, one of the teenage protagonists, remarks, 'Whatever choice I make, somebody always dies' (4.12 'The Chosen'), indicating the kind of futility identified by Elliott in which systemic domination is uniquely connected to our individual capacity for choice, action and agency.[9]

Elliott, as discussed, identifies a type of personhood that is constituted through neoliberal logic positing 'interiority as the possession of interests; interests as the motivation for choice; choice as the engine of action; chosen action as measure of agency; and agency as a sign of personhood' (2013: 88). I interpret this as a linear, additive set of propositions which establish a self-reinforcing ('common sense') rationality wherein agency becomes the sole defining factor of personhood. To become socially intelligible within this framework, one must demonstrate personhood through actions that function as a measure of agency. Action is instigated by choices, which we make according to our personal interests or stake in our own welfare. To maintain social viability (within the neoliberal paradigm), one must make choices and act within one's own interests. Within this framework, *which* choice is irrelevant; what *is* important is that Laila *must* choose.

If suffering agency refers to circumstances in which we must decide between two unbearable choices, this is precisely the kind of no-win situation the film stages at its point of no return. Hiding with Aaron in the darkness of the moors, Laila is presented with a choice: she can keep running and risk Aaron's mother being killed by the men that hunt her, or she can return home and face her father. Here, suffering agency illustrates how power works upon subjects, not through denying the opportunity to act as such but rather through turning our choice-making capacity into a no-win catch-22 nadir. While this scene offers a potent example of suffering agency, it is not designed to make us feel bad in Lübecker's sense of the term. It's true that we might experience negative or unpleasant emotions at the thought of Laila returning home to her domineering father. In scenes like this, however, suffering agency begins to feel, if not *good* exactly, then perhaps satisfying, because it delivers on our expectations of a resilient heroine who overcomes adversity by making choices and taking action under duress. As I will argue, it is any interruption of agency that feels bad, because it denies us the manifestation of resilience that the film has led us to anticipate.

Catch Me Daddy's final scene orchestrates another situation in which the 'choice' of action is left up to Laila. Tariq instructs Laila to climb up onto a chair, physically manoeuvring her when she refuses. This recalls Tariq's earlier displays of dominance – for instance, scenes in which he repeatedly assaults Laila by violently kicking her or forces her to drink alcohol. Here, however, although we are aware by now that Tariq can exert his will through physical violence, he instead shouts at Laila to place a wire noose around her neck. This is what tells us that the film is not simply about a father's control over his daughter; if that were the case, it could present Tariq looping the wire around Laila's neck

Figure 19 Tariq (Wasim Zakir) ceases active coercion of Laila and cries (Wolfe 2014). *Catch Me Daddy*, directed by Daniel Wolfe © EMU Films/Film4 2014. All Rights Reserved.

himself. Rather, the film is interested in Laila's complicit agency. When Laila complies and slips her head through the wire, we are aware that she does so under duress, yet it is also understood that she is making a choice. Unlike the earlier staging of suffering agency, Laila makes a choice that is decidedly not in line with her own interests. We are presented with a scenario in which Tariq could kill Laila as he has threatened to, but instead he wants her to actively embrace or enact her own complicity in his violence against her. Tariq wants Laila to make the *right* choice, which is of course a choice of *his* making. The quandary of Laila's agency is further emphasized as, after setting the situation in motion, Tariq walks away. In contrast to his previously dominant position in the frame, Tariq is now small, slumped over and crying in the background of the shot (Figure 19). Tariq's power within the frame (and therefore over Laila) is considerably diminished, especially when compared with earlier shots where he dominates Laila's physical space, obscuring her from view (Figure 20) or appearing almost demonic in his rage (Figure 21).

In its closing sequence, the film stretches out a series of reverse shots between Laila and Tariq. Through its extended duration, the film suspends and defers the moment of reckoning, opening up potential to imagine alternative courses of action: Laila could remove the wire, make further appeals to her father, run – or even step forward from the chair.

Figure 20 Tariq forces Laila to drink gin, his body obscuring hers within the frame to communicate his power over her (Wolfe 2014). *Catch Me Daddy*, directed by Daniel Wolfe © EMU Films/Film4 2014. All Rights Reserved.

Figure 21 Tariq, shouting at Laila (Wolfe 2014). *Catch Me Daddy*, directed by Daniel Wolfe © EMU Films/Film4 2014. All Rights Reserved.

Figure 22 Close-up of Laila's feet as she stands on a chair with a noose around her neck (Wolfe 2014). *Catch Me Daddy*, directed by Daniel Wolfe © EMU Films/Film4 2014. All Rights Reserved.

Figure 23 Laila standing, motionless, calling out to her father (Wolfe 2014). *Catch Me Daddy*, directed by Daniel Wolfe © EMU Films/Film4 2014. All Rights Reserved.

While an act of coerced suicide would make a horrific conclusion to an already bleak film, it would not be a feel-bad film, as it would provide a form of satisfaction arising from subjective self-determination. Just like the scene on the moors, if Laila were to jump, her choice would be imposed and appalling (as Elliott might say), yet it would still read as a determination of her own fate within limited circumstances. Instead, the film offers a close-up of Laila's feet, motionless in the frame (Figure 22), and a long shot of her standing, arms by her sides (Figure 23), indicating clearly that although Tariq is no longer actively coercing her, Laila remains passively in place, sobbing and calling out for her father. The diminishing focus on Tariq recalls Sumi Madhok, Anne Phillips and Kalpana Wilson's Foucauldian observation that 'agency and coercion cannot be understood in a binary relationship of presence/absence, where the one is present only by virtue of the other's absence' (2013: 2–3). Tariq is no longer actively coercing Laila's compliance, yet that does not consequently mean her capacity to act freely and of her own accord necessarily increases. The perceived contradiction between Laila passively complying with and actively resisting her father's will points to this complication of the relationship between agency and coercion, yet also creates frustration, as the film's feel-bad qualities partially arise from the ways it creates a perception that Laila is capable of overcoming, yet in the end 'chooses' not to.

It is often much easier to find value in narratives that portray protagonists (successfully) navigating worlds that aren't designed for their flourishing (as Berlant might put it), just as we see in *The Hunger Games* and *Girlhood*. It becomes more difficult to parse the value in a film like *Catch Me Daddy*, in which the odds seem far less insurmountable than those faced by Katniss or Marieme, and yet Laila's character appears to regress to an almost pre-feminist sensibility, one that the film's structure will not allow her to overcome. Despite this, I argue that it is an idealized version of resilient agency that the film's closing illuminates. If traditional forms of resilience and agency have been co-opted, and the suicidal act is not a truly viable alternative, then there is clearly an impasse of some kind at play. My intention in reading the film through the framework of resilience and scrutinizing the different forms of agency it works with is not to assign moral value to resilience and declare that performing resilience makes us 'bad' (neoliberal) subjects. James points out that '*because resilience discourse is hegemonic, your "choices" will be judged against an ideal of resilience whether you like it or not*' (2015: 20). In an everyday context, most female subjects cannot afford to opt out of performing resilience. However, while we may not be able to bear the loss of our social viability, a fictional character certainly can. I want to raise the question here of whether watching a character perform an excess of feminine damage, without being eventually rewarded with the requisite overcoming, creates a spectatorial fear of losing our own social viability. More importantly, how might such an impact on the spectator be productive within the film's generic framework? If, as I have argued, resilience is a newly conventionalized feminine norm, I want to reflect on the potential value in feel-bad femininity, as it opens an opportunity to consider the forms that a refusal to participate in societal expectation might take.

To this end, I'll draw a loose parallel between Lübecker's understanding of negativity in cinema, James's notion of resilience and Edelman's (2004) celebratory reclamation of the alignment between queerness and the Freudian-Lacanian death drive. Advocating an embodiment of that which impedes our social viability, Edelman calls for a queer politics that embraces rather than attempts to refute negative associations with death and social disruption. His central argument is that death-driven queerness poses a threat to the heteronormative reproductive sexuality symbolized by the figure of the child, for whom we must secure a brighter future. The promise of a better future, Edelman proposes, operates as a fantasy of stability, wholeness and self-coherence, where death drive is figured as that which disrupts our efforts towards maintaining such a fantasy (2004: 10). Turning towards negativity, Edelman proposes, is a method of refusing the false optimism of reproductive futurism and 'the insistence of hope itself as affirmation' (2004: 4).[10] In *Sex, or the Unbearable* (2013), Edelman and Berlant define negativity as 'the relentless force that unsettles the fantasy of sovereignty' (vii–viii), and which has the capacity to undermine our sense of self-continuity, 'fixity of identity' (vii–viii) or coherence as social subjects. In this formulation, not only are we severed from any complete understanding of ourselves, but any fantasy of ourselves as autonomous agents is also shattered.

Within this paradigm, it is possible to conceive of *Catch Me Daddy*'s scenes of immobility and self-dissolving crying as productive of precisely this kind of negativity, which troubles the fixity of Laila's identity as a resilient subject and reminds us that the sovereignty resilience discourse purports to offer is a fantasy. When read in relation to resilience discourse, Edelman's theory of death-driven negativity might advocate that rather than attempt to overcome the trauma associated with femininity, we ought instead to embrace its negative associations.[11] Similarly, the concept of the feel-bad film engages directly with our relationship to negativity. Just as James observes that we can cope with the negativity of traditional femininity if it is surmounted, Lübecker too suggests that we can bear negativity momentarily, as long as it is eventually narratively and/or formally contained. The feel-bad film refuses this containment of negativity, instead exacerbating and intensifying unpleasant affect, disavowing closure and satisfaction in a way that corresponds to Edelman's refusal of social viability. Likewise, the film increases the negativity of femininity, refusing us the release of overcoming.

In this framework, queerness (which for Edelman is virtually synonymous with negativity) ostensibly becomes 'ethical' through 'its figural status as resistance to the viability of the social' (Edelman 2004: 3).[12] Resisting the viability of the social is the chief aim here – seemingly at any cost. This would also appear to dovetail with much of the work of this book, which has engaged with the problematic of postfeminist social viability across various narratives and genres. I find Ruti's interpretation helpful here, as she explains that Edelman's theories are considered ethical (rather than simply nihilistic) because within discourses of queer theory, the 'antinormative almost automatically carries an ethical force' (2017: 28). Ruti is concerned that

> the kind of radical self-dissolution that Edelman celebrates can only be undertaken from a position of relative security, that deprivileged subjects – many women, racialized subjects, and those who lead economically precarious lives (that is, subjects whose claim to symbolic identity is shaky to begin with) – simply cannot afford to abandon themselves to the jouissance of death drive in the way that more secure subjects might be tempted (or even compelled to do). (2017: 125)

Ruti argues that each subject's claim to symbolic identity – that is, her ability to align fully with social norms – is inevitably a determining factor in her capacity to oppose or violate those social norms. This resonates with James's (2015) acknowledgement that deprivileged subjects are precisely the ones who have the most damage to recycle and who need to hold on to what little social capital they manage to acquire.

The difference between resilience (as a hegemonic marker of social viability) and agency (as the way in which resilience manifests) is important. If *Catch Me Daddy* had opted for a closing scene in which Laila removes the wire, it would have created a potential for conventional forms of agency and resilience to emerge. Whereas were Laila to jump, even though a suicidal act has the potential to read as a form of agency, it is difficult to imagine interpreting it as a straightforward act of resilience. On the one hand, the potential for overcoming in this scenario remains wholly unclear. On the other, if – as I have argued – contemporary feminine resilience manifests in making choices and acting upon them, then even the suicidal act could be read as a form of overcoming.

In Chapter 1, I argued that the dead girl figure articulates the paradox in which self-annihilation becomes the most effective method for securing a subject's social viability. The dead girl often manifests as an escape from conventional femininity; in this instance, however, the possibility of Laila choosing death would only further affiliate her with contemporary feminine norms. Both *Catch Me Daddy* and *Gone Girl* position suicide as an act that might secure their protagonists a measure of social viability, albeit under different postfeminist paradigms and with different narrative functions. *Catch Me Daddy* presents the suicidal act as entangled within a discourse of self-determination and agency, where self-striking is a requirement of social acceptance in the narrative world of the film and legible as a resilient choice within a contemporary postfeminist framework. Here, then, are two narratives in which suicide is imagined as a potentially socially viable act – preserving rather than shattering our alignment with the social order.

For Laila to be read as a viable feminine subject it does not actually matter which choice she makes – only that she does make one. Social expectation ceases to be about making the 'right' choice and instead simply demands that we make any choice at all. The way to become an acceptable female subject is to overcome perceived gender deficits, illustrating that for female subjects to successfully come of age in a postfeminist setting, the narrative obstacle they must defeat is femininity itself. By contrast, Laila's opportunity to complete the coming-of-age process is suspended by the film's abrupt cut to black, following its final image of an extreme shallow focus close-up from

Feel-Bad Femininity in Catch Me Daddy

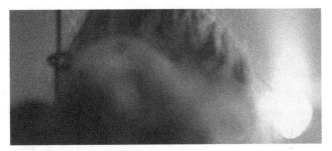

Figure 24 *Catch Me Daddy*'s final image, an extreme close-up of the back of Laila's head (Wolfe 2014). *Catch Me Daddy*, directed by Daniel Wolfe © EMU Films/Film4 2014. All Rights Reserved.

behind Laila's head (Figure 24). The closeness of the camera exceeds the intimacy of a typical close-up: not only is there little information regarding Laila's interiority or motivation, but the distorted image does not even invite our consideration. The film shifts to a form of depersonalized intimacy which, along with the cut to black, suggests a waning interest in Laila's character and what she might or might not do. Instead, the film structurally opts out of the choice-making resilience paradigm, disengaging from the problematic of female characters and their agency or lack thereof. In doing so, the film removes the predicament of Laila's choice from the aesthetic field of interpretation. We can interpret and find meaning in this formal decision, but not in the choice itself, which is excised from the film's narrative, denying her character and the spectator access to the very terms of the debate.

Whereas the resilience model encourages us to *use* our negative feelings, our excessively affective femininity, and create surplus value, Laila's feel-bad femininity generates negativity but denies us a positive or cathartic experience of overcoming. The film's very structure suggests that there is nowhere for Laila to go within the narrative – as there are simply no choices left to make. If, as I have argued, the genre itself proves incapable of producing socially viable feminine subjects, then classic narrative structures like the hero's quest are in fact fundamentally hostile to the production of female subjects, who are encouraged to overcome not just traditional forms of adversity but also conventionalized femininity.

When considering the prospect of a genre's viability and where it can take us, Emerald Fennell's film *Promising Young Woman* (2020) offers another perspective on feel-bad femininity. As VanDerWerff (2021) notes, genre plays a key role in the film's most critically divisive twist, which sees the protagonist Cassie brutally murdered by her best friend's rapist. The film opens as a revenge thriller – a genre which rubs uncomfortably against the bright future we are constantly reminded that Cassie was supposed to have. Instead of living the good life of a middle-class doctor, we learn that after her best friend Nina's rape and subsequent suicide, Cassie dropped out of medical school and became utterly consumed with seeking vengeance. The opening scene explains Cassie's main preoccupation: with her makeup expertly smeared, she pretends to be drunk, then lures unsuspecting men into taking her back to their place, where they attempt to assault her. After snapping back to stone-cold sobriety, Cassie pours scorn on her targets, who, at one point she notes, never want to have sex with her once they realize she is sober enough to consent.

As Grady observes, Cassie appears to be trapped in entirely the wrong genre. Cassie's 'life does not quite suit her', and the tragedy she experienced has resulted in 'a state of suspended animation' (2021: n.p.). Cassie lives at home with her parents and works in a cafe, both of which are presented as signifiers of a life stalled firstly by trauma but also by Cassie's refusal to get over it. Her childhood bedroom in pastel pinks and her flowery, girlish clothing are all signs that Cassie has been unable to complete her coming of age in the expected ways. Cassie's femininity feels bad because she ought to have outgrown it by now, and not only has she *not* done so, but neither does she especially care to. Much like Rihanna's song 'Diamonds' discussed in the previous chapter, the film is interested in the tragedy of someone who cannot or will not let go of the worst thing that happened to them. Although plenty of reviews celebrate the film's darkly comic aesthetic and the pleasure it takes in its revenge tale (Morris and Wortham 2021; VanDerWerff 2021), many critics express a desire and expectation of overcoming, empowerment or healing (McAndrews 2021; Stevens 2021; Willmore 2021) – none of which *Promising Young Woman* truly provides.

The third act appears to hold potential for Cassie's bright future to rematerialize. A fantastical montage of Cassie's new relationship with Ryan, an old friend from school, briefly conjures the sense that the rom-com might offer a way out – a new genre, a new life. As Cassie falls in love, the film hints at the possibility of leaving the revenge schemes behind – reorganizing her life around the future, rather than continually picking at old wounds. But the rom-com was never truly viable; this is not her genre, as Cassie suspected all along. The candied sweetness of the romantic promise grinds to a halt when Cassie discovers that Ryan witnessed Nina's rape and did nothing to help her. Shattering the fantasy of romance as an escape hatch that might steer Cassie back towards the good life she was, it is implied, supposed to inhabit all along, enables the film to step into its final act unencumbered by the promise of a new beginning.

Having exacted several counts of revenge on people who were sympathetic towards Nina's rapist (named Al Monroe) at the time, Cassie's final act of revenge is to be carried out against Al himself. Disguising herself as a stripper in a stereotypically sexualized nurse's costume and rainbow-coloured wig, Cassie infiltrates Al's bachelor party and handcuffs him to the bed where she intends to carve Nina's name into his skin (recalling Lisbeth in *The Girl with the Dragon Tattoo*, who successfully tattoos 'RAPIST PIG' on her rapist's chest). Al breaks free and easily overpowers Cassie, smothering her with a pillow in an agonizing two-minute scene which plays out the entirety of her gruesome death in near-silence. With her brutally protracted death, Cassie is hardly a romanticized dead girl embodying lifeless serenity on the cover of a young adult novel. However, unlike *Catch Me Daddy* which withholds any final moment of agentic triumph, *Promising Young Woman* does attempt to extract catharsis from Cassie's murder by hinging its final twist on a moment of agency from beyond the grave.

In the final scene, Al's wedding is disturbed by sirens in the distance, and he is subsequently arrested. Cassie's (and the film's) parting shot is a series of scheduled text messages to Ryan, which read:

C: Enjoy the wedding

C: Love,

C: Cassie & Nina

C: ;)

These text messages, critics note, attempt to elicit pleasure and resolve any bad feelings generated from Cassie's death by granting her agency and by punishing Al's crimes. In the *New York Times* podcast *Still Processing*, hosted by Jenna Wortham and Wesley Morris, Wortham describes the affective impact of the police sirens as a cathartic moment:

> It's supposed to fill the viewers with this relief. It does. It works. You're like, oh, my god. Thank god, right? There's one side of me that's like experiencing that relief of, quote, help. And then there's the other part of me that's much larger and much more sentient, aware that's like, the police? What are the police going to do? The police ain't shit. And I was like, well, that's also how you know this movie is made by white people, because I don't know anybody who hears the arrival of police sirens and experiences the feeling of relief. (2021: n.p.)

Strikingly, despite noting that in reality she would not feel relieved, for Wortham the film's cathartic moment *works* – even if only for a moment. As Lübecker suggests, the film's affective impact is felt first, before the 'larger and much more sentient' level of critical thought kicks into gear, demonstrating exactly the kinds of cultural training Berlant describes. For much like the sitcom correlates the happy family with the happy ending, in a culture saturated with detective dramas and police procedurals, sirens and safety are 'one and the same' (Needham 2009: 148). Wortham's comment about the

Whiteness of the police as a signifier recalls my discussion of *The Hate U Give*, which relies similarly on the state to serve up both justice and catharsis, with divisive effect.

Just as *Promising Young Woman*'s pleasure in the state-as-solution is undercut by analytical thinking, any pleasure elicited by Cassie's agency is similarly negated as Dana Stevens notes:

> It's as if the movie wants to provide the audience with the satisfaction of a successful revenge plot while robbing its main character of everything the quest for vengeance was meant to give her in the first place: agency, freedom, the chance to get on with her life and make it about more than the worst thing that ever happened to her. (2021: n.p.)

While I am partially drawn by Stevens's argument, I want to make the case that the film simply is not interested in the socially viable subject who heals from her trauma and moves on – it is interested, evidently, in the subject who cannot or will not move on and rejoin society, the subject who would rather die than get over it.

Fennell describes Cassie as 'heroic, even if that heroism is distressing in lots of ways' (Aurthur and Donnelly 2021: n.p.). Cassie *does* sacrifice her life for a greater good – in defiance of everyone in the film who wants her to 'let it go' and move on and in defiance of generic expectations of empowerment. Yet although Cassie's character refuses to turn her trauma into a spectacle of overcoming, the final twist steps in to do it for her. Once again, music is deployed to triumph over negativity, with Juice Newton's sweeping ballad 'Angel of the Morning' playing while Al is arrested. This and the text messages – which signify Cassie's agency from beyond the grave – are what manage to turn 'nothing' (no future, no genre, no life) into 'something' (vengeance, justice, restored order). Yet as Mary Beth McAndrews rightly notes, 'two women had to die for a man just to get arrested' (2021: n.p.), making the triumph ring hollow.

Although the shape it takes is different, Cassie, like *Girls*' Hannah, is stuck in an impasse she cannot reconcile. If impasse is something that 'cannot be worked through or overcome' (Schoene 2017: 96), this is certainly the case for Cassie by the end of the film, which has worked through competing genres that lead Cassie nowhere, and tied itself in knots doing so. Ultimately, none of the genres *Promising Young Woman* inhabits can accommodate the needs of its protagonist, who, like Laila, finds there is simply nowhere left for her to go. Colleen Kennedy (2021) and Anna Menta (2021) interpret the film as a tragedy, noting that its five-act structure is reminiscent of Shakespearean classics like *Hamlet*. According to Tanya Pollard, tragedy is a genre in which 'revengers are typically frustrated victims who want retribution for a crime that goes unpunished, a crime either committed or protected by the highest power in the land' (2010: 59). In *Promising Young Woman*, as with the Renaissance tragedy, 'the moral is seldom straightforward' and 'the revenger is always eventually punished for taking the law into his or her own hands' (59). It is precisely because tragedy is *not* one of the many genres *Promising Young Woman* mobilizes that Cassie's death is so shocking. For as Duncan A. Lucas points out, 'If we are handed a text and told that it is a tragedy, we might reasonably expect a "sad" story' (2018: 9). In this case, there is a degree to which the audience contract has been breached. By thinking of the film as a tragedy, however, it becomes evident that death is the generically expected and, indeed, the only place left for Cassie to go.

Interestingly, the original script envisions the final scene as Al (and his friend Joe) burning Cassie's body. When the financial backers had reservations, Fennell flirted with 'the big, fuck you, cathartic ending' in which Cassie triumphs by donning a 'sexy outfit' to 'kill a ton of guys' (Fennell in Aurther and Donnelly 2021: n.p.). This ending went unwritten, 'because the moment Cassie is in that room, I realized that there is no way of honestly showing that. Because it's not true. And it was important to me to play out as realistically as I could, what this would look like' (Fennell in Aurther and Donnelly 2021: n.p.). What we have here is a generic struggle on our hands. The original ending would have withheld catharsis entirely – the ultimate feel-bad ending from a genre which promises, if not a heroine who always lives to tell the tale, then at least justice or retribution of some description (VanDerWerff

2021). The rejected 'fuck you' ending would have delivered on the film's generic promises of cathartic revenge. Instead, the feel-bad and the fuck-you have been smashed together; we are to feel bad that Cassie dies (in the film's two-minute gesture to generic realism) and then feel better once she manages to take the bad guys down with her.

Inverted resonances emerge between *Promising Young Woman* and *Gone Girl*, with both protagonists making outlandish revenge plans that could (and do, in Cassie's case) culminate in their death. However, despite Amy's unhappy postfeminist viability, she recognizes: 'It's not fair that I have to die. Not really die. I don't want to. I'm not the one who did anything wrong' (Flynn 2012: 314–15). Amy, stuck in postfeminist impasse, demands social viability and pays the price with her happiness. She draws the line, however, at sacrificing herself and would rather return, alive, to the unhappy postfeminist promise than die a perfect death. Whereas Cassie, stuck in an entirely different but no less damaging impasse, strikes back at the social order that wronged her and pays the price with her life. The suggestion that Cassie *could* have taken other paths – as signalled by the rom-com tropes in the third act – makes it feel that much worse when she does not. Reading *Catch Me Daddy* and *Promising Young Woman* through the feel-bad mode illuminates a collective attachment to an idealized version of resilient agency. Fantasies surrounding the attainment and implementation of agency and resilience are evidently complex. What these two films have demonstrated is how essential it is to investigate what makes feminine subjects socially viable within their culturally and historically specific contexts and, most crucially, to question the price we are willing to pay for social inclusion.

Conclusion

This book has aimed to examine how 1990s–early 2000s postfeminist empowerment discourses have shaped contemporary post-2008 genres and emergent female subjectivities. As I have argued, fantasies of postfeminist empowerment have begun to feel bad and are growing increasingly strained, a feeling which is further aggravated by a post-recession culture of precarity and insecurity that poses a significant threat to the postfeminist promise of personal autonomy and liberation (Negra and Tasker 2014). The book has illuminated a major cultural turn in which postfeminist empowerment in popular genres has begun to drastically shift from an affective register of enjoyment, carefree pleasure and fun to one in which postfeminism is articulated as a site of rage, horror and resentment. This finding suggests that although postfeminist ideals remain culturally prevalent, there is a profound shift in constructions and perceptions of the capacity for postfeminist empowerment discourse to deliver a path to fulfilment. At the very least this opens up additional or alternative affective registers through which to understand postfeminist empowerment discourse. It also constitutes an important step in rendering postfeminist empowerment ideals not only as unattainable but also, more importantly, as undesirable.

I have argued that there are two distinct but overlapping strands of postfeminist culture, namely the empowerment genres prevalent in the 1990s to mid-2000s and their continuing legacies in post-2008 resilience genres. As with any kind of periodization, determining a precise beginning and ending to any particular era must inevitably be fraught. Nonetheless, a conceptual periodization of postfeminism has enabled me to create a descriptive abstraction of the postfeminist era typified by choice, autonomy and individualized empowerment and provide a framework for understanding its primary subject positions, generic elements and ideals. Furthermore, it offers a conceptual framework for understanding resilience discourse as being intimately entwined with, yet distinct from empowerment genres. It is worth clarifying here that my intent has not been to use the term 'postfeminist resilience' for the purposes of rigidly classifying yet more cultural works as postfeminist. Rather, in line with Berlant's (2008) conception of genre as a set of mutating conventions that evolve in response and relation to shifting social and historical conditions, my delineation between empowerment and resilience genres is made with a view to understanding the intersections and divergences between them. Chapters 2 and 5 demonstrate the centrality of transformation to both paradigms, yet in *Girls* this process leads to circular repetitions that hold little sense of fulfilment or completion of subjectivity, whereas *Girlhood* retains some (cautious) optimism for transformation as a survival tactic that facilitates connection and mobility. This illustrates the affective ties between the different genres aimed at women and girls, at the same time as showing the ways in which their priorities diverge significantly.

Chapters 1 and 2 give insight into the shape of a new discursive field in which fictional millennial women are seen working through their experiences of growing up with the fantasies of postfeminist empowerment discourse as the primary mode of address structuring their lives. Efforts to maintain social viability within a postfeminist framework lead either to the exhaustion of subjectivity seen in *Gone Girl* or else the fractured disappointments in *Girls*. Rather than dismiss continued investment in postfeminist culture, I instead examined the bonds we form to things that harm us, and how difficult, even impossible, it can be to sever our attachments to the genres that sustain and contain us.

I have also found it crucial to give space to narratives like *Appropriate Behaviour* in which the postfeminist dilemma is felt along the peripheries (if at all), demonstrating that whether one views postfeminism more as a genre, a sensibility or an ideology, its dominance is not all-pervasive, and in no way captures every sphere of life or infiltrates every corner of female subjectivity. While *Appropriate Behaviour* is often read as analogous to *Girls*, the impasse it produces stems less from an inability to cut loose from harmful genres and more from a desire for a generic path to follow. I have therefore aimed to show that while analysis of postfeminism remains vitally important, it is far from the only frame of reference, and nor are postfeminist ideas and ways of living the total sum of feminine culture. However, Chapter 3 finds its connection with the previous two by articulating how contemporary genres are producing subjectivities in disalignment with their social environments.

Having established the argument that traditional postfeminist pleasures have begun to decay in the cultural imagination, I explored the emergence of resilience as a defining characteristic of contemporary girlhood genres. I argued that the growing ubiquity of resilient femininities spanning multiple genres and expressed through numerous affective registers has necessitated a heightened focus in the book. By extending James's analysis of pop music, I have developed an account of the audio/visual, narrative and structural aesthetics of resilience across film and popular literature. The book develops an affective lexicon to better understand contemporary modes of suffering, defiant, transformative and relational resilience, as well as a framework through which future research might expand on further modes that are specific to the genres they emerge within.

Affect is central to the ways fictional genres make sense of the innumerable postfeminist contradictions women and girls are subject to. The key tension of empowerment discourses is the imperative for female subjects to present themselves as wholly autonomous, while at the same time concealing a performance of traditional femininity. As Gill (2007) explains, self-discipline and surveillance are among the tactics women undertake to ensure compliance with cultural feminine norms, while simultaneously perceiving and presenting these tactics as a freely made choice. *Gone Girl*'s significance lies in its structural and generic articulation of the paradoxes inherent to trying to maintain social viability within a postfeminist landscape. Similarly, while reading *Catch Me Daddy*, I noted the tensions generated by resilience genres which demand that traditional femininity must be performed and visibly overcome for female subjects to achieve social viability. In relation to different postfeminist paradigms, both *Gone Girl* and *Catch Me Daddy* go to extreme lengths (narratively and aesthetically speaking) to articulate and expose the 'bad feelings' postfeminist discourses cultivate and suppress.

The concept of cruel optimism teaches us that if we are to reject postfeminist fantasies of fulfilment altogether, we must have viable alternatives waiting in the wings. It is therefore unsurprising that many of the works analysed here struggle to find satisfactory resolutions to their protagonists' stories. In 1985, Rachel Blau DuPlessis argued that once women collectively confront gendered social norms, quest narratives might cease to imagine all women's narratives ending in marriage or death (1985: 4). Over thirty years later, it is remarkable to find such a scarcity of alternatives in our collective imaginary. In Chapter 4, I discussed the gender politics of the *Hunger Games*' epilogue, in which Katniss settles down as a wife and mother (and to children she did not especially want, no less). Like Broad (2013), I remain frustrated at times by the durability of achieving traditional narrative closure for femininity through marriage and motherhood. Although characterizing Katniss as ambivalent towards her fate significantly complicates the notion of closure in this instance, it nevertheless appears to be presented as the 'best deal on offer' (Cecire 2015: n.p.).

The Hunger Games is one of three texts analysed in this book that concludes with motherhood (*Girls*) and marriage (*Gone Girl*). While *Girls*' narrative and structure continuously stall even the slightest sense of progression, the series finale somewhat complicates the notion of endless arrested development. The final episode (6.10) offers a glimpse of what the future might hold for Hannah's character, suggesting that, to some degree, she may finally be equipped to complete her coming of age. Exploring motherhood, the episode wraps up the major storyline of season six, that of

Hannah's unplanned pregnancy and her decision to keep the baby, to the bafflement of the show's characters and critics alike (Gilbert 2017). Much as Edelman argues, the child and the heteronormative nuclear family 'is the governing fantasy of achieving Symbolic closure through the marriage of identity to futurity in order to realize the social subject' (2004: 13). This is precisely the fantasy of future closure *Girls* invokes to signal Hannah's entry into woman/adulthood, her formation as a socially viable subject realized via her maturation, which in turn is achieved by having a child. The way out of impasse, the series suggests, has been under our noses all along. Hannah's task is simply to properly realign herself and reinvest in normative good life promises. Of course, whether those promises are presented as fulfilling or not *is* important. However, even across vastly different genres, this synchronicity indicates the enduring power of traditionally feminine ways of living. For even when produced as profoundly frustrating (*Gone Girl*) or quietly unsettling (*The Hunger Games*), marriage remains the primary device through which their narrative arcs are finalized. Therefore, while it might be notable that a mainstream novel like *Gone Girl* produces marriage and motherhood as a nightmare rather than a dream come true, there remains an urgent need for stories which abandon this traditional framework altogether.

Of the works analysed here, it appears that independent and arthouse films are perhaps currently best equipped to reject normative resolutions. In *Appropriate Behaviour*, Shirin's central problem remains unsolved, and in *Girlhood*, Marieme is out of options. Yet each film's open ending suggests that although the path ahead is unclear, a path *does* exist, and these characters will find their way. In both films, marriage and motherhood are present only along the margins. In *Appropriate Behaviour*, Shirin's brother and his fiancée represent a conventional, heteronormative life trajectory, which is neither maligned nor aspired to by the film. *Girlhood* notably outright rejects marriage and motherhood when Ismaël offers to marry Vic and she tells him that this isn't the kind of life she wants. In this case, it appears that perhaps alternatives are *not* required, as Vic doesn't need to know exactly what she does want, only that it isn't to settle down as a wife and mother. As a relatively mainstream production, *Fleabag* proves an exception here, by rejecting the generically expected romantic closure. Similarly, Fleabag's messy, fractured subjectivity does not require radical transformation for the narrative to progress. Instead, the series offers a queerlinear trajectory for Fleabag, who chooses to walk away from her most intimate relationship with the camera/audience. These works decisively reject normative resolutions based in identity transformation or romance, while acknowledging that, much like their protagonists, the way ahead may not always be entirely legible.

In Chapter 6, I read *Catch Me Daddy*'s final image of Laila, standing paralysed on a chair with a noose around her neck, in relation to the hard cut to black which leaves the audience hanging on the verge of the choice-making paradigm. Here I want to revisit this final image to further consider the suggestion that it may offer potential resistance to the 'viability of the social' (Edelman 2004: 3), a key concern of this book. As indicated by Ruti, any resistance of this kind tends to be championed as automatically having ethical value. Yet it feels disingenuous to wrest something ostensibly positive from a scene of such utter despondency. As I have argued, the image of paralysis in *Catch Me Daddy*'s final scene destroys any fantasy of resilient girlhood we may have held. The feel-bad femininity generated by the film certainly unsettles fixity of identity, and its narrative structure undermines any sense of subjective sovereignty. Yet when read in terms of resisting social viability, the film orchestrates a scenario in which it becomes impossible for its protagonist to do so. Irrespective of which choice she makes, in making any choice at all Laila retains her claim to symbolic identity as a resilient subject. Furthermore, we must consider the feel-bad aesthetics that precede Laila's standing on the chair. Crying, silence and paralysis in the face of patriarchal violence do not simply feel bad because they deny us an aesthetic experience of resilience. Or, to put it another way, resilience does not simply feel good because it facilitates our alignment with social expectation (though this is certainly part of the equation).

Rather, it feels good because resilience is bound up in our ability to survive and at least attempt to thrive within social environments that are often not designed for us to do so. Ruti writes that

> the strand of queer theory that advocates various versions of the ethics of opting out often promotes the ideal of antinormativity so indiscriminately that one act of defiance seems just as good as any other, irrespective of the 'content', let alone the outcome, of the act in question. (2017: 37–8)

This suggests that perhaps the value of negativity, antinormativity, incoherent subjectivities and threats to fantasies of sovereignty is not in fact as self-evident as queer theory so often suggests (Bersani 1995; Edelman 2004; Halberstam 2011).[1] While *Catch Me Daddy* can serve as a productive theoretical exercise in exploring the limits of agency and the devastation of stripping its protagonist of her viability, it would be controversial to suggest that the negativity generated by Laila's fictional pose constitutes an ethical ideal. As Chapter 4 shows, resilience discourse cannot be reduced as simply being tantamount to the neoliberal/postfeminist status quo. Furthermore, as Huehls (2016) suggests, it is possible to accept the ongoing hegemony of dominant hierarchical structures without surrendering entirely to them. Therefore, even as I might find Edelman's exaltation of negativity conceptually intriguing, its critical sustainability must remain in question.

A reading focused on the value of negativity captures the girl's coming-of-age genre within a paradigm in which female suffering is intensified, not to be overcome but to be celebrated as an antinormative act of self-dissolution. Such a reading valorizes this fragmentation of girls' subjectivity when, as Ruti suggests, it is 'women, racialized subjects, and those who lead economically precarious lives (that is, subjects whose claim to symbolic identity is shaky to begin with)' (2017: 125) from whom such dissolution is most often demanded. Instead, the image of Laila presents the ultimate impasse, highlighting the impossibility of free choice and demonstrating that in situations where 'webs of power … surround us' (45), sometimes the costs of resisting the viability of the social are simply too much to bear. Furthermore, perhaps it is not always strictly necessary. As the book has aimed to demonstrate, it is instead worthwhile making the effort to 'inhabit the world the way these texts and their characters do' (Huehls 2016: xi). Rather than resisting and critiquing our social circumstances, we are likely better off trying to adapt to and explore any impasse we find ourselves in (Huehls 2016; Schoene 2017).

With the above in mind, future research might consider the question of what it means to be a feminine subject following the gradual collapse of the fantasy of the happily empowered, freely choosing, self-scrutinizing subject of postfeminism. If, as I suggested in the introduction to this book, postfeminism has already irrevocably altered the conditions in which feminine subjectivity is formed, then it is imperative to give further consideration to what relationality, agency and resilience look and feel like in our contemporary context. The aftermath of postfeminist empowerment produces a diverse range of contradictory subject positions, each of which offers productive complications and ambiguities for further study.

James's (2015) work, used in Part 2 to explore the different modes of resilience produced by girlhood genres, provides a framework for understanding the pleasures resilient femininity can generate, as well as the bad feelings produced when our expectations of resilience are thwarted. In Chapter 4, the concept of defiant resilience offers insight into the ways subjects might risk their social viability in opposition to the expectations of their social order. Because the resilience imperative naturalizes contextual forms of suffering, suffering resilience gives a useful reminder that systemic oppression is the 'problem' to eliminate, and not resilience itself. Expanding on this framework, Chapter 5 proposes that while transformative resilience enables us to overcome adversity in ways which benefit dominant hierarchies, and relational resilience affirms our social ties, each of these modes offers elements of both complicity with and liberation from postfeminist and capitalist paradigms – often simultaneously. This model acknowledges the complexities of existing histories of trauma and oppression, while at the same time proposing that survival often necessitates resilience against these forms of suffering. I have therefore offered a contextually specific and flexible set of theoretical concepts and frameworks through which make sense of the continuing endurance of resilience genres.

One especially productive area to explore further would be the distinctive role sound plays in formulating resilient subjectivity and producing resilient affect. I have concentrated on how music is used in narratives genres and is especially linked to moments of closure or catharsis. This provokes further questions about media which does not rely on the structures of narrative typically used in film and television. What kinds of resilience are generated by digital modes of production? The research I have conducted on resilience would make a productive ally to work such as Dobson's, which analyses the YouTube 'pain memes' created by girls using 'handwritten flash-cards and an emotive music soundtrack to narrate personal experiences of bullying, abuse, grief, and often also self-harm, eating disorders and anxiety' (2015: n.p.). Pointing out the tensions between the videos as a form of self-expression, and their use of silence, Dobson notes that the silence constitutes 'a feminine display of weakness, muteness, and passivity', but that in this case the girls' feminine damage is broadcast, not to be overcome but 'as a kind of symbolic rebellion against the educational, psychological and medical institutions that have served to promote disclosure, confession, and the speaking of one's problems as the means of healing and self-actualisation' (n.p.). The relationship between silence and femininity is especially contested within feminist scholarship (Parpart 2010). For as Jane L. Parpart observes, 'voice, or the act of speaking out' is often characterized as 'one of the key conditions demonstrating women's empowerment' (2010: 13), while silence tends to be perceived as 'passivity and powerlessness' (Gal 1991: 175 in Parpart 2010: 13).

In the concluding chapter of *The Ethics of Opting Out*, Ruti and Jordan Mulder explore the potential of silence as a mode of resistance.[2] Working from a Lacanian perspective, they outline the various forms silence can take, and the different interpretations of silence that are on offer. Mulder asks:

> Does silence involve an automatic acquiesce to the misrecognitions of the Other? Or can it perhaps be read as a form of resistance, as a refusal to open one's interiority to the interpretive, probing attitude of the Other (or other)? (2017: 215)

In response, Ruti asserts that silence always has the capacity to damage or even destroy our social viability (216). Yet Ruti is also interested in whether the refusal to expose one's interiority can possibly also be read as a 'sign that the subject has learned not to heed the desire of the Other, which in most social situations, especially ones involving authority of any kind, elicits the subject's speech (active participation)' (216). Silence can therefore signify a refusal to actively participate in, let alone respond to, normative social enactments of authority. However, it seems that silence must occur at particular moments, in specific contexts, in order to function as and/or be perceived as a form of resistance.[3] This is where shifting norms of femininity complicate matters. If traditional femininity demands passivity (manifested as silence), then a refusal to speak is more likely to signal acquiescence to convention. By contrast, the demands of the contemporary resilience model are twofold: first, silence is required, which must then be broken, but only with the 'right' kind of sound/speech. Further investigation in this area might touch upon the fraught and shifting nature of the complicated relationships that emerge in feminine/postfeminist culture between silence, femininity, resilience and agency.

This book demonstrates a variety of ways in which postfeminist empowerment discourse has profoundly shaped contemporary fictional genres aimed at women and girls and their expressions of feminine agency and subjectivity. The genres I consider in this book vary considerably – including a crime thriller, a single-camera American comedy, an independent film, a series of young adult novels and two art house films – and each text brings a unique generic history to bear on its narrative. What this shows is that in their ever-shifting guises, postfeminist discourses in both their empowerment and resilient formations retain significant currency in our contemporary culture across popular and independent genres alike, as well as across a range of media and modes of address. Through its affective approach to postfeminism, the book uncovers the relationship between normative genres, on the one hand, and social and cultural formulations of femininity, on the other, by exploring the ways we collectively conceptualize desirable modes of being and agency in our current moment.

Notes

Introduction

1 To periodize the inception of our current configuration of neoliberalism, I follow David Harvey, who suggests that 1978–80 constitutes 'a revolutionary turning-point' (2005: 1) in neoliberalism's social and economic history, as political leaders in China, the United States and the UK instituted economic strategies to privatize public services, deregulate industry and repudiate social provision.
2 The notion of 'having it all' is endemic to postfeminist culture and usually refers to the widespread belief that, having reaped the benefits of liberation promised by feminism, women who may not previously have entered the workforce are now able to secure professional careers at the same time as marriage and motherhood.
3 Based on Candace Bushnell's eponymous 1997 anthology.
4 Based on Helen Fielding's eponymous 1996 novel.
5 There are synergies between cruel optimism and the Marxist notion of false consciousness, which emphasizes the illusory nature of ideology and the way ideology functions to mystify and obscure the realities of exploitative and inequitable social relations in capitalist societies. For Berlant, however, it is not necessarily that our consciousness is false – we are often all too aware that our investments in normative culture and social institutions are in tragic misalignment with our own interests. What the concepts of cruel optimism and, in particular, impasse both account for is a relation in which subjects may well possess at least a partial awareness of the futility of their investments, yet these attachments remain stubbornly intact precisely because they provide a sense of optimism and self-continuity.
6 My understanding of genre derives from Berlant's arguments about the relationship between aesthetics and affective expectation, rather than in relation to genre theory as is typically understood in film and literary studies, though there is some overlap. Genre scholar Steve Neale's proposal that 'genres are instances of repetition and difference' (1980: 48) corresponds with Berlant's interest in the ways that genres are shaped

and reshaped in accordance with specific social and historical contexts. Similarly, both focus on the relationship between genre and pleasure. Neale suggests that audience pleasure stems from recognition of familiar generic elements as well as from seeing those elements used in new ways. Equally, Berlant understands genre as an aesthetic structure promising those who engage with it that they 'will experience the pleasure of encountering what they expected', although the details themselves may vary (2008: 4).
7 All further italicizations included in citations from James's work are her own.
8 Falguni Sheth (2009) explores the former US Secretary of State Condoleezza Rice's role with regard to the controversial US military prison in Guantanamo Bay, arguing that privileging a woman of colour within the US government obscures and contributes to the White supremacy at the heart of political institutions. Similarly, Jasbir Puar's (2007) concept of homonationalism details how 'good' gays and lesbians who will adapt and contribute to society's existing status quo are nominally included and accepted within it.
9 Critical reception of *Gone Girl*, for example, includes debate over whether or not the novel and film ought to be classified as either feminist or misogynist (Burkeman 2013; Cappello 2014; Dobbins 2014; VanDerWerff 2014) and therefore overlooks the novel's contribution and commitment to exploring, in ugly detail, the affective impact of postfeminist culture.
10 Based on Angie Thomas's eponymous 2017 novel.
11 In this book, I follow the practice of capitalizing all racial groups, including Black and White. I acknowledge that capitalizing White risks legitimating the beliefs of White supremacists who also follow this same practice (Ewing 2020). However, as sociologist Eve Ewing points out, Whiteness is a 'specific social category that confers identifiable and measurable social benefits', and therefore ignoring such specificity runs a much greater risk of continuing to construct Whiteness as a neutral and invisible category (2020: n.p.).

1 Feel-bad postfeminism in *Gone Girl*

1 The economic crisis quickly gave rise to a still-growing body of work exploring its impact. Katy Shaw's *Crunch Lit* (2015) examines the contemporary 'recession writings' of authors such as Jonathan Franzen

and Don DeLillo. *Gender and Austerity in Popular Culture: Femininity, Masculinity and Recession in Film and Television* (ed. Davies and O'Callaghan 2016) gives a wider analytic view of the relationship between gender and precarity.
2 I return to this quotation and provide more detail later in the chapter.
3 See Tina Chanter, who argues that any social construction makes space for subjects to subvert, rebel against or reject such constructions, yet there remains 'a sense in which those injunctions govern individual reactions, albeit negatively or indirectly. If a woman prefers wearing black leather to pink flowery dresses, this choice is far from incidentally related to the ideal of femininity that culture upholds for her' (1997: 47).
4 Here, Ruti is drawing on Žižek's assertion that normative power and hegemonic expectation are not incompatible with oppositional acts of 'radical autonomy' (2005: 140). For Žižek, the 'negativity of freedom' (140) can manifest in the Lacanian 'act' (Lacan [1973] 1981: 50), which cannot be defined as simply any action or behaviour that may be irreconcilable with hegemonic expectation; rather, it must also be an act in accordance with one's own desire or 'inner directive' (Ruti 2017: 45).
5 Ruti acknowledges Butler's view that Lacan's act of defiance is impossible, as even the idea that we might reject normative power is simply 'one ideological fantasy among others' (2017: 48). Moreover, Ruti explains, even if we were capable of saying 'No!', this would equate to the kinds of anti-relational solipsistic heroism Butler frequently disavows (2017: 55). Yet, drawing on the classic example of Antigone's defiance of the law, Ruti counters Butler by arguing that because Antigone risks her viability as a social subject on behalf of her brother, individuals are indeed capable of effectively defying normative power.
6 Flynn's Cool Girl finds countless cultural counterparts in films like *There's Something about Mary* (Farrelly and Farrelly 1998), *500 Days of Summer* (Webb 2009) and *Drinking Buddies* (Swanberg 2013). Strikingly similar to the Cool Girl, the female characters in these films are typified by their ability to successfully tread the line between behaving like 'one of the guys' while still conforming to stereotypical feminine beauty norms.
7 Ahmed turns to bell hooks, who points out that when *The Feminine Mystique* was published in 1965, over a third of American women were

already in the workforce (hooks 2000: 2 in Ahmed 2010: 50–1). Therefore, it was a specific section of society, that is, 'only women with leisure time and money who could actually shape their identities on the model of the feminine mystique' (2000: 2). hooks's analysis points out the ways in which the fantasy of the happy housewife was determined by the intersection between race and social class, an insight which equally applies to Cool Girl femininity.

8 This recalls Joan Riviere's article 'Womanliness as Masquerade' (1929) in which she argues that, particularly among professional women in male-dominated workplaces, a mask of femininity must be performed in order to escape masculine judgement.

9 See further discussion of self-annihilation and social viability in the conclusion to Chapter 6.

10 Key examples within this genre also include Paul Albert Steck's painting *Ophelia Drowning* (1895) and *The Young Martyr* by Paul Delaroche (1855).

11 There are countless examples of this popular contemporary publishing trend: *Envy* (Olsen 2011), *The Unbecoming of Mara Dyer* (Hodkin 2011), *Throat* (Nelson 2011), *The Dead-Tossed Waves* (Ryan 2010) and *Imaginary Girls* (Ren Suma 2011). See also what might be considered an exemplar dead girl novel *The Lovely Bones* (Sebold 2002), narrated by a teenage girl in heaven following her brutal rape and murder.

12 The retro noir films Farrimond identifies all draw upon the classics of the 1940s noir genre, an exemplar of which is Daphne Du Maurier's novel *Rebecca* (1938) and its subsequent film adaptation of the same name (Hitchcock 1940), where the title character is afforded agency and influence, despite having died prior to the events of the narrative. See Tania Modleski for further examination of Hitchcock's fascination with the trope of the dead woman who 'exerts an influence from beyond the grave' (1988: 1) and Deborah Jermyn's (2004) discussion of the female corpse in film noir and classical Hollywood.

13 The psycho bitch has roots in the femme fatale figure of classic 1940s and 1950s film noir, such as Brigid O'Shaughnessy in *The Maltese Falcon* (Huston 1941), along with the neo-noir films of the 1980s and 1990s such as *Basic Instinct* (Verhoeven 1992). The classic film noir era was the focus of psychoanalytic, feminist and film studies theorists, who

primarily critiqued the femme fatale figure as a 'symptom of male fears about feminism' (Doane 1991: 2–3). For analysis of the neo-noir era's incarnation of highly eroticized and sexually dangerous femininities in films like *Fatal Attraction* (Lyne 1987), see Elaine Berland and Marilyn Wechter (1992). Contemporary investigations of the femme fatale include Farrimond (2017), who examines the retro noir film (as discussed above), as well as adolescent, bisexual and monstrous manifestations of the femme fatale. For a specifically postfeminist analysis of the femme fatale, see Samantha Lindop (2015).

14 The happy postfeminist subject is of course still in cultural circulation, as Gill (2016) points out, since new feminisms do not displace 'older' postfeminist ideas. Equally, examples of feel-bad postfeminism do not supersede or overwrite cultural texts in which postfeminism continues to be positioned as the categorical path towards feminine fulfilment and/or emancipation.

2 Postfeminist impasse and cruel optimism in *Girls*

1 In *Love Actually* (Curtis 2003), ten-year-old Sam races through Heathrow Airport security to confess his love for classmate Joanna, while *Two Weeks Notice* (Lawrence 2002) and *When Harry Met Sally* (Reiner 1989) both feature runs through New York streets. I compare *Girls'* rom-com run sequence to *When Harry Met Sally* later in this chapter.
2 This quotation references the first season tagline accompanying the promotion of the series, 'Living the Dream. One Mistake at a Time' (*Girls*. 2012. Season 1 [DVD]: HBO).
3 For an account of the central role hunger, food and eating plays in *Girls* see Jane Hu's (2012) article in *Los Angeles Review of Books*, 'Reality Hunger: On Lena Dunham's "Girls"'.
4 The term 'neoliberalism' is used in Berlant's work mainly as a heuristic for understanding the transformation of political and economic norms of social reciprocity and meritocracy since the 1970s (2011: 9).
5 In a *TIME* interview, Dunham confirms the influence of *Sex and the City* on *Girls*, stating that her own characters 'are women who couldn't exist without *Sex and the City*' (Poniewozik 2012).

6 That *Girls* presents obsessive-compulsive disorder (OCD) as distressing for both the character and the audience is especially notable in a television landscape in which OCD is typically used as a source of humour. For examples, see *Glee* (Murphy, Falchuk and Brennan 2009–15) and *The Big Bang Theory* (Lorre and Prady 2007–19). For a study of OCD tropes in comedy, see Paul Cefalu (2009).

3 Searching for belonging in *Appropriate Behaviour*

1. *Girls'* success has seen the rise of an extraordinary number of female-led US television series like *Insecure* (Rae and Wilmore 2016–present), *Crazy Ex-Girlfriend* (Bloom and McKenna 2015–19), *Unbreakable Kimmy Schmidt* (Fey and Carlock 2015–19) and *The Mindy Project* (Kaling 2012–17), as well as British shows like *Fleabag* (Waller-Bridge 2016–19), *Killing Eve* (Waller-Bridge 2018–present), *Chewing Gum* (Coel 2015–17) and *I May Destroy You* (Coel 2020). There are also comedies exploring female experience like *Search Party* (Bliss, Rogers and Showalter 2016–present), *Catastrophe* (Delaney and Horgan 2015–19) and *I Hate Suzie* (Piper and Prebble 2020–present).
2. This dilemma is perhaps indirectly linked to the dominance of postfeminist media culture, which is detrimental not only due to its false ideological promises but also in the way that it stifles or subsumes anything that does not correspond to its conventions – mirroring the way that the discourse on *Girls* seems to subsume *Appropriate Behaviour* into its own orbit.
3. *Fleabag*'s script refers to this character as simply 'Priest'. However, press coverage of the series dubbed him 'Hot Priest'. On this note, another point of convergence emerges between *Gone Girl* and *Fleabag*, both of which are interested in the conscious performance of subjectivity. Yet where *Gone Girl* uses the 'Cool Girl' construct to capture a specific configuration of postfeminist femininity, *Fleabag*'s unnamed characters like 'Priest', 'Bank Manager' or the derogatory 'Bus Rodent' are, as Emily Saidel (2020) argues, a narrative strategy expressing the (also unnamed) protagonist's avoidance of intimacy.

4 Suffering, resilience and defiance in *The Hunger Games*

1. See Harris, who describes escalating social concern regarding the self-esteem (or lack thereof) in 'white, middle-class young women who are supposed to succeed, or who are perceived to have everything and yet cannot overcome psychological obstacles to their own guaranteed success' (2004: 32). The 'problem' is located within young women themselves, whose 'personal, psychological barriers to feeling confident and optimistic, being able to achieve, and developing internal resilience, strength and self-belief' (32) are perceived as holding them back from achieving success.
2. Ben Whitham (2013), by contrast, argues that resilience came to be an integral feature of security discourse rather than supplanting it. Regardless of whether it displaced the prior discourse on security entirely, what is important is that resilience becomes a primary focus across multiple social, political and cultural spheres at this particular historical juncture.
3. The Centre for Military Health Policy Research published a report titled 'Promoting Psychological Resilience in the U.S. Military' (Meredith et al. 2011) which states that the CSF programme 'features a strategy to increase the overall resilience in the force by enhancing soldiers in the physical, social, spiritual, and family dimensions' (33), thus demonstrating the pervasive reach of resilience discourse into all spheres of life.
4. Much like Berlant, James considers neoliberalism to be hegemonic, a pervasive set of 'common sense' ways of thinking about the world and its power structures without being an entirely totalizing force.
5. Although the use of language like 'damage' is redolent of trauma theory, James's concept resonates more with Berlant's 'crisis ordinariness' (2011: 10), designed to capture the unremarkable absorption of such damage into the everyday. As James puts it, the damage inflicted by neoliberalism manifests not as the shock of a singular traumatic event but rather is always already incorporated in the routine of the entirely unexceptional everyday.
6. This type of thinking is affiliated with what Barbara Ehrenreich identifies as a 'mass delusion' (2009: 13) within contemporary America in which positive thinking is advanced as the primary method for achieving personal and professional success.

7 Young adult dystopian fiction with female protagonists includes works like the *Delirium* trilogy (Oliver 2011–13), the *Divergent* trilogy (Roth 2011–13), *Uglies* (Westerfeld 2005) and Julie Bertagna's trilogy (*Exodus* 2002; *Zenith* 2003; *Aurora* 2011). See also *Female Rebellion in Young Adult Dystopian Fiction* (edited by Sara K. Day, Miranda A. Barteet and Amy L. Montz 2014), which discusses the wider impacts of this dystopian girlhood genre.

8 *The Hunger Games*' primary intertextual reference point is the 'death match' genre, which includes films like *Death Race 2000* (Bartel 1975) and *The Running Man* (Glaser 1987). While the death match in these films is primarily a form of entertainment and population control, in *Battle Royale* (Fukasaku 2000) – the film to which *The Hunger Games* is most often compared – the death match originates from harsh economic conditions and anticipation of youth rebellion. What distinguishes *The Hunger Games* from these examples is its emphasis on televised spectacle and surveillance culture.

9 Emphasizing that individual resilience generates social value enables James to successfully differentiate between her theory of resilience and other personal forms of recovery or therapy. As such, James does not touch upon the tension between critiquing the practice of resilience itself and what such a critique might mean for those individuals who (must) practise resilience.

10 For James, one way of practising melancholy is to invest in those who are excluded from or less able to practise resilience as they have fewer resources at their disposal. James details how a group of Occupy activists bought $14.7 million of Americans' personal debt and absolved the debtors from the burden of repaying exorbitant medical bills. If government or social systems are not investing in their citizens' well-being, either financially or through the provision of healthcare, then, rather than encouraging individuals in financial debt to be resilient and overcome their difficulties, other better-off individuals can invest their own resources into eliminating the original adversity once and for all.

11 The novels describe Katniss as having 'olive skin', 'straight black hair' and 'gray eyes' (Collins 2008: 8). However, the casting of Jennifer Lawrence (a White, blonde, blue-eyed actress) in the film adaptations cements the popular conception of her as a White character. Iris Shepard and Ian

Wojik-Andrews note that Lawrence's casting is typical of 'Hollywood-centric movies that employ white actors and actresses to play non-Caucasian roles' (2014: 197).

12 For further analysis of the 'narcissistic fantasy' (2003: 33) of the White saviour in Hollywood cinema see Hernán Vera and Andrew M. Gordon's *Screen Saviors: Hollywood Fictions of Whiteness* (2003).

5 Relationality and transformation in *Girlhood*

1 In this chapter I use the term 'audioviewer' (Chion 1994: 56) in place of spectator, following Colling, who finds that 'the term spectator seems inadequate' (2017: 15) when addressing the relationship between sound and image, as this chapter in particular does. See also Vivian Sobchak's (2012) discussion of the tendency within film analysis to prioritize visual aspects of cinema over sound design or music (2012: 25).

2 Ginette Vincendeau suggests Vic's name is 'a reference to the Sophie Marceau character in the classic French teen film *The Party* (*La Boum/ The Party*, Pinoteau 1980)' and quotes Sciamma as saying that since the original Vic 'was the French little fiancée of the 1980s', the objective was to find her contemporary counterpart (2015: 27).

3 *Girlhood* is also part of the banlieue film genre (Vincendeau 2015). Will Higbee explains that although 'technically the French word *banlieue* signifies "suburbs," it is an extremely loaded term in its contemporary socio-cultural context' as it typically refers to working-class housing projects 'dominated by violence, unemployment, criminality, social exclusion and populated by alienated male youth' (2007: 38). As Vincendeau notes, the Parisian banlieue, home to communities of first- and second-generation immigrants, are 'central to narratives of multicultural France' (2015). Although a number of banlieue films were released in 1995, such as *État des lieux* (*Inner City*, Richet 1995) and *Douce France* (Chibane 1995), *La Haine* (Kassovitz 1995) remains the chief point of reference, achieving a markedly high critical and commercial profile, praised for its examination of social stratification and its distinctive visual style. For an in-depth examination of *La Haine*, see Vincendeau (2005). For wider discussion of the 'banlieue film' genre, see Higbee (2007).

4 I use single quotation marks to refer to Rihanna's song 'Diamonds' and omit them when referring to the Diamonds sequence in *Girlhood*.
5 In the previous chapter, I described James's use of melancholy as a method to subvert resilience norms. In short, I argued melancholy did not align with the modes of resilience produced by *The Hunger Games*. For James's analysis of Rihanna's 'Diamonds', however, melancholy makes much more sense – as literally the sounds produced are melancholic. I outline this to explain that I am not discounting melancholy altogether but merely expanding on James's theoretical project.
6 In 2009, Chris Brown pleaded guilty and was subsequently charged with assault for his violent attack on then-girlfriend Rihanna (Duke 2014). For analysis of the media response to Brown's violence within a neoliberal, postfeminist and post-racial context, see Rodier and Meagher (2014).
7 EDM refers to electronic dance music, with EDM-pop typically used to describe a subgenre that emerged in the 2010s in which artists like Skrillex, David Guetta and Calvin Harris mix the conventions of pop music (song structure and melody) with those of EDM (heavy bass, soars and drops).
8 For further discussion on the complexities of the relationship between relationality and individual autonomy, see Ruti (2017: 81–3).
9 This trope spans many genres, usually with a naive or strait-laced protagonist becoming infatuated with a more popular girl or group of girls who lead her astray, sometimes for comic effect as in *Mean Girls* or with the devastating consequences seen in *Thirteen* (2003, Hardwicke) as thirteen-year-old protagonist Tracy's friendship with rebellious Evie leads to petty crime, drug abuse and self-harm.

6 Feel-bad femininity in *Catch Me Daddy*

1 The men in pursuit of Laila operate in two groups, divided along racial lines: in the first, Laila's brother Zaheer is working with three other British Pakistani men, while the second comprises two White British men. In an interview (*Film 4* 2014), Wolfe explains that his inspiration for the film was a news article about so-called 'honour crimes', which are traditionally concerned with female sexual impurity and family shame. Although the film does not refer to honour crimes explicitly, these discourses tacitly underpin the narrative.

2 Adapted from Margaret Atwood's eponymous 1985 novel.
3 While Simone's is a cover of the original by British songwriters Anthony Newley and Leslie Bricusse, it remains perhaps the most iconic version. Written originally for Newley and Bricusse's stage musical, *The Roar of the Greasepaint – the Smell of the Crowd* (1964), the song is used to mark the victory of a Black male character against his White oppressor (Cheal 2020), which lends further support to Iversen's critique.
4 Following James, it becomes clear that it is precisely *because* of the men pursuing Laila that she is provided with the opportunity to overcome. In other words, the creation of a resilient heroine necessarily depends upon an object or obstacle for her to defeat.
5 Berlant's concept of flat affect describes a process of withholding emotions solicited by dominant affective structures.
6 Enelow's analysis includes Jennifer Lawrence in *Winter's Bone* (Granik 2010) and *The Hunger Games* (Ross 2012) as well as Rooney Mara in *The Girl with the Dragon Tattoo* (Fincher 2011) and *Carol* (Haynes 2015), Oscar Isaac in *Inside Llewyn Davis* (Coen and Coen 2013) and Michael B. Jordan in *Fruitvale Station* (Coogler 2013).
7 While Hanich's interpretation that 'weeping does not, by definition, involve sounds; it is inaudible' (2008: 30) would suggest that sound is the crucial marker of difference between weeping and crying, Koestler does also describe the breathing patterns of weeping as 'a series of short, deep, gasping inspirations, i.e. sobs' ([1964] 1989: 272), which seems unlikely to be entirely silent. It is a minor distinction to draw, but it is probably more accurate to say that Hanich is interested in the silent weeping of cinemagoers rather than suggesting that weeping is silent by definition.
8 The film *Vive L'Amour* (Ming-liang 1994) includes a comparable six-minute medium close-up of protagonist Lin Mei-mei crying. Although Song Hwee Lim describes the scene as 'an unrelenting soundtrack of female sobbing that borders on the unbearable' (2014: 125), it uses similar techniques to those of *Girlhood*, such as obscuring Lin Mei-mei's face with her hair and thereby protecting the audience from having to fully witness her distress. This correspondence in the aesthetics of crying across genres further supports Hanich's argument regarding its social undesirability and capacity for (perceived) self-dissolution.

9 Further analysis of this series might interrogate the degree to which staging scenes of suffering agency in fiction gradually comes to naturalize our grasp and our experience of circumstances in which there are no good choices, resulting in suffering beginning to seem inevitable.
10 The school of anti-relational negativity is contentious within the field of queer theory. In the 2006 *PMLA* summary of the Modern Language Association conference forum, Tim Dean, Halberstam and José Muñoz strongly disputed Edelman's antisocial thesis. Muñoz's (2009) work on queer utopianism provides an important alternative perspective, asserting that queerness is in fact 'an insistence on potentiality or concrete possibility for another world' (2009: 1).
11 We might also be cautious of doing so in light of the persistent historical association between femininity and negativity. Elaine Showalter (1985) explains how by the end of the nineteenth century hysteria was widely recognized as a uniquely feminine condition in psychiatry and literature (129), and that in the Victorian era women were perceived as innately 'childlike, irrational, and sexually unstable' (73). Sara Mills complains that 'many [feminists] have paradoxically gone on to celebrate the traits or behaviour that we have been assigned, as if these traits were in some sense inherent, rather than socially constructed, as if we might as well make the most of what we have got' (1987: 189). In this respect, a theoretical imperative to embrace negativity is hardly innovative. Frustratingly, the connection between femininity and negativity proves remarkably durable, as thirty years after Mills's critique Ruti designates 'queer theory's depictions of "feminine" masochism, passivity, submission' as 'a flimsy excuse for misogyny' (2017: 188).
12 This speaks to a concern with the viability and sustainability of social and cultural scripts, practices, ways of living, ideologies and affective structures, as opposed to the alignment of any given individual with those socially dominant norms.

Conclusion

1 The anti-relational school of thought within queer theory originates with Leo Bersani's *Homos* (1995), in which he argues that 'the most politically disruptive aspect of ... gay desire is a redefinition of sociality so radical

that it may appear to require a provisional withdrawal from relationality itself' (1995: 7), positioning queerness as intrinsically anti-relational. Extending Bersani's formulation, Edelman (2004) links queerness to the Lacanian concept of death-driven jouissance and self-undoing. See Chapter 6 for further detail on Edelman's arguments, and Lorenzo Bernini's *Queer Apocalypses: Elements of Antisocial Theory* (2017) gives insight into the anti-relational strand of queer theory.

2 Despite the entrenched associations between agency and voice, the power of silence has long been part of feminist traditions. For example, Mary M. Dalton and Kirsten James Fatzinger interrogate 'the prevailing metaphor linking voice to power' (2003: n.p.) in the film *The Piano* (Campion 1993), in which the protagonist Ada chooses 'not to speak, rather than to speak and not be heard' (n.p.). Intersecting with Ruti and Mulder's discussion, Dalton and Fatzinger find silence, in particular circumstances, to be 'a tool of defiance' (n.p.), a strategic opting out of social systems that restrict one's ability to participate on equal terms.

3 It is worth considering Audre Lorde's unequivocal scepticism of the power of silence: 'I was going to die, if not sooner than later, whether or not I had ever spoken myself. My silences had not protected me. Your silence will not protect you' (1984: 41). Although she acknowledges that speech has a unique capacity to make subjects vulnerable (particularly racialized subjects, within the context of Lorde's writing on systemic racism), for Lorde it is always worth speaking up, simply 'because the machine will try to grind you into dust anyway, whether or not we speak. We can sit in our corners mute forever while our sisters and our selves are wasted, while our children are distorted and destroyed, while our earth is poisoned; we can sit in our safe corners mute as bottles, and we will still be no less afraid' (Lorde 1984: 42).

References

500 Days of Summer (2009), [Film] Dir. Mark Webb, USA: Fox Searchlight Pictures.

A Cinderella Story (2004), [Film] Dir. Mark Rosman, USA: Warner Brothers Pictures.

Aapola, S., Marnina Gonick and Anita Harris (2005), *Young Femininity: Girlhood, Power, and Social Change*. Basingstoke: Palgrave Macmillan.

Abbott, S., and Deborah Jermyn (eds) (2009), *Falling in Love Again: Romantic Comedy in Contemporary Cinema*. London: I.B. Tauris.

Adriaens, F. (2009), 'Post Feminism in Popular Culture: A Potential for Critical Resistance?' *Politics and Culture*, 4. Available online: https://politicsandculture.org/2009/11/09/post-feminism-in-popular-culture-a-potential-for-critical-resistance/ (accessed 28 April 2016).

Adriaens, F., and Sofie Van Bauwel (2011), '*Sex and the City*: A Postfeminist Point of View? Or How Popular Culture Functions as a Channel for Feminist Discourse', *Journal of Popular Culture*, 47(1): 174–95.

Ahmed, S. ([2004] 2012), *The Cultural Politics of Emotion*. London: Routledge.

Ahmed, S. (2010), *The Promise of Happiness*. Durham, NC: Duke University Press.

Ahmed, S. (2017), *Living a Feminist Life*. Durham, NC: Duke University Press.

Anderson, J. A. (2015), 'Toward a New Fantastic: Stop Calling It Science Fiction', *Los Angeles Review of Books*, 24 December. Available online: https://lareviewofbooks.org/article/toward-a-new-fantastic-stop-calling-it-science-fiction (accessed 13 April 2016).

Annie Hall (1977), [Film] Dir. Woody Allen, USA: United Artists.

Appropriate Behaviour (2014), [Film] Dir. Desiree Akhavan, USA: Parkville Pictures.

Arthurs, J. (2003), '*Sex and the City* and Consumer Culture: Remediating Postfeminist Drama', *Feminist Media Studies*, 3(1): 83–98.

Assassination Nation (2018), [Film] Dir. Sam Levinson, USA: BRON Studios.

Atwood, M. ([1985] 1996), [Novel] *The Handmaid's Tale*, London: Vintage.

Augé, M. (1995), *Non-Places: Introduction to an Anthropology of Supermodernity*, trans. John Howe. London: Verso.

Aurther, K., and M. Donnelly (2021), 'Let's Talk about the Knockout Ending of "Promising Young Woman"', *Variety*, 16 January. Available online: https://variety.com/2021/film/news/promising-young-woman-ending-spoilers-2-1234885400/ (accessed 24 April 2021).

Bachelorette (2012), [Film] Dir. Leslye Headland, USA: The Weinstein Company.

Bande de Filles [Girlhood] (2014), [Film] Dir. Céline Sciamma, France: Pyramide Distribution.

Banet-Weiser, S. (2014), 'Am I Pretty or Ugly? Girls and the Market for Self-Esteem', *Girlhood Studies*, 7(1): 83–101. Available online: https://doi.org/10.3167/ghs.2014.070107 (accessed 7 May 2021).

Banet-Weiser, S. (2018), *Empowered: Popular Feminism and Popular Misogyny*. Durham, NC: Duke University Press.

Basic Instinct (1992), [Film] Dir. Paul Verhoeven, USA: TriStar Pictures.

Bastién, A. J. (2017), 'In Its First Season, *The Handmaid's Tale*'s Greatest Failing Is How It Handles Race', *Vulture*, 14 June. Available online: https://www.vulture.com/2017/06/the-handmaids-tale-greatest-failing-is-how-it-handles-race.html (accessed 24 April 2021).

Battle Royale (2000), [Film] Dir. Kinji Fukasaku, Japan: Toei Company.

Becker Stevens, A. (2013), 'Did "Girls" Romanticize a Rapist?' *Ms. Magazine Blog*, 20 March. Available online: http://msmagazine.com/blog/2013/03/20/did-girls-romanticize-a-rapist (accessed 13 April 2016).

Begum, N. (1992), 'Disabled Women and the Feminist Agenda', *Feminist Review*, 40: 70–84.

Bell, K. (2013), '"Obvie, We're the Ladies!" Postfeminism, Privilege, and HBO's Newest *Girls*', *Feminist Media Studies*, 13(2): 363–6. Available online: https://doi.org/10.1080/14680777.2013.771886 (accessed 7 May 2021).

Berlant, L. (2008), *The Female Complaint: The Unfinished Business of Sentimentality in American Politics*. Durham, NC: Duke University Press.

Berlant, L. (2011), *Cruel Optimism*. Durham, NC: Duke University Press.

Berlant, L. (2012), 'On Her Book *Cruel Optimism*', *Rorotoko*, 5 June. Available online: http://rorotoko.com/interview/20120605_berlant_lauren_on_cruel_optimism (accessed 13 April 2016).

Berlant, L. (2013), 'Interview with Lauren Berlant', *Society and Space*, 22 March. Available online: https://societyandspace.com/2013/03/22/interview-with-lauren-berlant (accessed 13 April 2016).

Berlant, L. (2015), 'Structures of Unfeeling: *Mysterious Skin*', *International Journal of Politics, Culture, and Society*, 28: 191–213. Available online: https://doi.org/10.1007/s10767-014-9190-y (accessed 7 May 2021).

Berlant, L. (2017), 'Big Man', *Social Text Online*, 19 January. Available online: https://socialtextjournal.org/big-man/ (accessed 16 August 2018).

Berlant, L., and Lee Edelman (2013), *Sex, or the Unbearable*. Durham, NC: Duke University Press.
Bernini, L. (2017), *Queer Apocalypses: Elements of Antisocial Theory*. Basingstoke: Palgrave Macmillan.
Bernstein, A. (2019), 'Sympathy for the Devil: How The Handmaid's Tale Finally Goes Too Far', *Guardian*, 5 June. Available online: https://www.theguardian.com/tv-and-radio/2019/jun/05/sympathy-for-the-devil-how-the-handmaids-tale-finally-goes-too-far (accessed 24 April 2021).
Bersani, L. (1995), *Homos*. Cambridge, MA: Harvard University Press.
Bertagna, J. (2002), [Novel] *Exodus*, Basingstoke: Palgrave Macmillan.
Bertagna, J. (2007), [Novel] *Zenith*, Basingstoke: Palgrave Macmillan.
Bertagna, J. (2011), [Novel] *Aurora*, Basingstoke: Palgrave Macmillan.
Blankenship, M. (2009), 'The Movie "Precious" Tells Two Stories at Once', *Huffington Post*, 9 November. Available online: https://www.huffpost.com/entry/the-movie-precious-tells_b_350924 (accessed 24 April 2021).
Blevins, K. (2018), 'bell hooks and Consciousness-Raising: Argument for a Fourth Wave of Feminism', in J. R. Vickery and T. Everbach (eds), *Mediating Misogyny Gender, Technology, and Harassment*, 91–108. Switzerland: Springer International (Palgrave Macmillan).
Blue Jasmine (2013), [Film] Dir. Woody Allen, USA: Sony Pictures Classics.
Bolin, A. (2014), 'The Oldest Story: Toward a Theory of a Dead Girl Show', *LA Review of Books*, 28 April. Available online: https://lareviewofbooks.org/article/oldest-story-toward-theory-dead-girl-show/#! (accessed 26 August 2018).
Bordwell, D. (1999), 'The Art Cinema as a Mode of Film Practice', in L. Braudy and M. Cohen (eds), *Film Theory and Criticism*, 716–24. Oxford: Oxford University Press.
Boyle, K. (2019), *#MeToo, Weinstein and Feminism*. Switzerland: Springer International (Palgrave Macmillan).
Brabon, B. A. (2013), '"Chuck Flick": A Genealogy of the Postfeminist Male Singleton', in J. Gwynne and N. Muller (eds), *Postfeminism and Contemporary Hollywood Cinema*, 116–30. Basingstoke: Palgrave Macmillan.
Bradbury-Rance, C. (2013), 'Querying Postfeminism in Lisa Cholodenko's *The Kids Are All Right*', in J. Gwynne and N. Muller (eds), *Postfeminism and Contemporary Hollywood Cinema*, 27–43. Basingstoke: Palgrave Macmillan.
Brennan, T. (2004), *The Transmission of Affect*. Ithaca, NY: University of Cornell Press.
Bridesmaids (2011), [Film] Dir. Paul Feig, USA: Universal Pictures.

Bridget Jones' Diary (2001), [Film] Dir. Sharon Maguire, USA: Miramax.
Broad City (2014–19), [TV programme] USA: Comedy Central, 22 January.
Broad, K. R. (2013), 'The Dandelion in the Spring: Utopia as Romance in Suzanne Collins's *The Hunger Games* trilogy', in B. Basu, K. Broad and C. Hintz (eds), *Contemporary Dystopian Fiction for Young Adults: Brave New Teenagers*, 117–30. New York: Routledge.
Bronfen, E. (1992), *Over Her Dead Body: Death, Femininity and the Aesthetic*. Manchester: Manchester University Press.
Brown, W. (2005), *Edge Work: Critical Essays on Knowledge and Politics*. Princeton, NJ: Princeton University Press.
Burkeman, O. (2013), 'Gillian Flynn on Her Bestseller *Gone Girl* and Accusations of Misogyny', *Guardian*, 1 May. Available online: https://www.theguardian.com/books/2013/may/01/gillian-flynn-bestseller-gone-girl-misogyny (accessed 25 August 2018).
Bushnell, C. (1997), *Sex and the City*. New York: Warner Books.
Butler, J. ([1990] 2010), *Gender Trouble: Feminism and the Subversion of Identity*. New York: Routledge.
Butler, J. (1991), 'Imitation and Gender Insubordination', in D. Fuss (ed.), *Inside/Out: Lesbian Theories, Gay Theories*, 13–31. London: Routledge.
Butler, J. (1993), *Bodies That Matter: On the Discursive Limits of 'Sex'*. New York: Routledge.
Butler, J., E. Laclau and S. Žižek (2000), *Contingency, Hegemony, Universality: Contemporary Dialogues on the Left*. London: Verso.
Cappello, N. (2014), 'How "Gone Girl" Is Misogynistic Literature', *Huffington Post*, 9 July. Available online: https://www.huffingtonpost.com/nile-cappello/how-gone-girl-is-misogynistic_b_5572288.html (accessed 25 August 2018).
Carol (2015), [Film] Dir. Todd Haynes, USA and UK: The Weinstein Company and StudioCanal.
Carstensen, L., et al. (2008), 'Poignancy: Mixed Emotional Experience in the Face of Meaningful Endings', *Journal of Personality and Social Psychology*, 94(1): 158–67. Available online: https://doi.org/10.1037/0022-3514.94.1.158 (accessed 21 August 2021).
Catastrophe (2015–19), [TV programme] UK: Channel 4, 19 January.
Catch Me Daddy (2014), [Film] Dir. Daniel Wolfe, UK: Film4.
Cecire, N. (2015), 'Resilience and Unbreakability' [blog post], 26 April. Available online: http://natalia.cecire.org/pop-culture/resilience-and-unbreakability/ (accessed 11 September 2018).

Cefalu, P. (2009), 'What's So Funny about Obsessive-Compulsive Disorder?' *PMLA*, 124(1): 44–58. Available online: https://doi.org/10.1632/pmla.2009.124.1.44 (accessed 21 August 2021).

Chafe, W. H. (2012), 'The American Narrative: Is There One and What Is It?' *Daedalus*, 141(1): 11–17.

Chamberlain, P. (2017), *The Feminist Fourth Wave: Affective Temporality*. Switzerland: Springer International (Palgrave Macmillan).

Chanter, T. ([1997] 2013), 'Can the Phallus Stand, or Should It Be Stood Up?' in T. Dufresne (ed.), *Returns of the 'French Freud': Freud, Lacan, and Beyond*, 43–66. New York: Routledge.

Cheal, D. (2020), 'Feeling Good – Nina Simone's anthem of liberation', *Financial Times*, 3 February. Available online: https://ig.ft.com/life-of-a-song/feeling-good.html (accessed 10 December 2021).

Chen, E. Y. (2010), 'Neoliberal Self-Governance and Popular Postfeminism in Contemporary Anglo-American Chick Lit', *Concentric: Literary and Cultural Studies*, 36(1): 243–75.

Chewing Gum (2015–17), [TV programme] Channel 4, 13 October.

Chion, M. (1994), *Audio Vision: Sound on Screen*. New York: Columbia University Press.

Clough, P. T. (2007), 'Introduction', in P. T. Clough and J. Halley (eds), *The Affective Turn: Theorizing the Social*, 1–33. Durham, NC: Duke University Press.

Cochrane, K. ([2013] 2014), *All the Rebel Women: The Rise of the Fourth Wave Feminist*. London: Simon & Schuster.

Cohan, S. (2007), 'Camp, Postfeminism, and the Fab Five's Makeovers of Masculinity', in D. Negra and Y. Tasker (eds), *Interrogating Postfeminism: Gender and the Politics of Popular Culture*, 176–200. Durham, NC: Duke University Press.

Colling, S. (2017), *The Aesthetic Pleasures of Girl Teen Film*. London: Bloomsbury.

Collins, S. (2008), [Novel] *The Hunger Games*, New York: Scholastic.

Collins, S. (2009), [Novel] *Catching Fire*, New York: Scholastic.

Collins, S. (2010), [Novel] *Mockingjay*, New York: Scholastic.

Crazy Ex-Girlfriend (2015–19), [TV programme] The CW, 12 October.

Cronin, A. M. (2000), 'Consumerism and Compulsory Individuality: Women, Will and Potential', in S. Ahmed et al. (eds), *Transformations: Thinking through Feminism*, 273–87. London: Routledge.

Cvetkovich, A. (2012), *Depression: A Public Feeling*. Durham, NC: Duke University Press.

Dalton, M. M., and K. J. Fatzinger (2003), 'Choosing Silence: Defiance and Resistance without Voice in Jane Campion's *The Piano*', *Women and Language*, 26(2): 34–9.

Darling, O. (2020), '"The Moment You Realise Someone Wants Your Body": Neoliberalism, Mindfulness and Female Embodiment in *Fleabag*', *Feminist Media Studies*. Available online: https://doi.org/10.1080/14680 777.2020.1797848 (accessed 24 April 2021).

Davies, H., and C. O'Callaghan (eds) (2016), *Gender and Austerity in Popular Culture: Femininity, Masculinity and Recession in Film and Television*. London: I.B. Tauris.

Day, S. K., M. A. Green-Barteet and A. L. Montz (2014), *Female Rebellion in Young Adult Dystopian Fiction*. Surrey: Ashgate.

De Lauretis, T. (1984), *Alice Doesn't: Feminism, Semiotics, Cinema*. Basingstoke: Macmillan Press.

Dean, T. (2006), 'The Antisocial Homosexual', *PMLA*, 121(3): 826–8.

Death Race (1975), [Film] Dir. Paul Bartel, USA: New World Pictures.

DeCarvalho, L. J. (2013), 'Hannah and Her Entitled Sisters: (Post)feminism, (Post)recession, and *Girls*', *Feminist Media Studies*, 2(13): 367–70.

Dejmanee, T. (2016), 'Consumption in the City: The Turn to Interiority in Contemporary Postfeminist Television', *European Journal of Cultural Studies*, 19(2): 119–33.

Delaroche, P. (1855), [Oil on canvas] *The Young Martyr*, France: Louvre.

Deleuze, G. (1994), *Difference and Repetition*, trans. P. Patton. New York: Columbia University Press.

Deleyto, C. (2009), *The Secret Life of Romantic Comedy*. Manchester: Manchester University Press.

Doane, M. A. (1991), *Femmes Fatales: Feminism, Film Theory, Psychoanalysis*. New York: Routledge.

Dobbins, A. (2014), 'Yes, *Gone Girl* Has a Woman Problem', *Vulture*, 3 October. Available online: http://www.vulture.com/2014/10/yes-gone-girl-has-a-woman-problem.html (accessed 26 August 2018).

Dobson, J. (2017), 'Dis-Locations: Mapping the Banlieue', in D. Forrest, G. Harper and J. Rayner (eds), *Filmurbia: Mapping the Suburbs*, 29–48. Basingstoke: Palgrave Macmillan.

Dogville (2003), [Film] Dir. Lars Von Trier, Denmark: Zentropa.

Douce France (1995), [Film] Dir. Malik Chibane, France: MKL Distribution.

Dow, B. J. (2003), 'Ellen, Television, and the Politics of Gay and Lesbian Visibility', in Toby Miller (ed.), *Television: Critical Concepts in Media and Cultural Studies Volume 1*, 252–71. London: Routledge.

Drinking Buddies (2013), [Film] Dir. Joe Swanberg, USA: Magnolia Pictures.

Driscoll, C. (2002), *Girls: Feminine Adolescence in Popular Culture and Cultural Theory*. New York: Columbia University Press.

Du Maurier, D. ([1938] 2015), [Novel] *Rebecca*, London: Virago.

Dubrofsky, R. E., and E. D. Ryalls (2014), 'The Hunger Games: Performing Not-Performing to Authenticate Femininity and Whiteness', *Critical Studies in Media Communication*, 31(5): 395–409. Available online: https://doi.org/10.1080/15295036.2013.874038 (accessed 21 August 2021).

Duke, A. (2014), 'Brown Sentenced for Rihanna Assault; Other Incidents Surface', *CNN*, 26 August. Available online: http://edition.cnn.com/2009/CRIME/08/25/chris.brown.sentencing/index.html (accessed 12 September 2018).

DuPlessis, R. B. (1985), *Writing beyond the Ending: Narrative Strategies of Twentieth-Century Women Writers*. Bloomington: Indiana University Press.

Duschinsky, R., and E. Wilson (2015), 'Flat Affect, Joyful Politics and Enthralled Attachments: Engaging with the Work of Lauren Berlant', *International Journal of Politics, Culture, and Society*, 28(3): 179–281. Available online: https://doi.org/10.1007/s10767-014-9189-4 (accessed 21 August 2021).

Dyer, R. (2007), *Pastiche*. New York: Routledge.

Eco, U. (1992), 'Postmodernism, Irony, the Enjoyable', in P. Brooker (ed.), *Modernism/Postmodernism*, 225–8. London: Routledge.

Edelman, L. (2004), *No Future: Queer Theory and the Death Drive*. Durham, NC: Duke University Press.

Ehrenreich, B. (2009), *Bright-Sided: How Positive Thinking Is Undermining America*. London: Picador.

Electrelane (2007), 'To the East', Track 2 on *No Shouts, No Calls* [Spotify]. London: Too Pure.

Electrelane, and J. B. Almogáver (2004), 'Oh Sombra!' Track 6 on *The Power Out* [Spotify]. London: Beggars Banquet.

Elephant (2003), [Film] Dir. Gus Van Sant, USA: Fine Line Features.

Elliott, J. (2013), 'Suffering Agency Imagining Neoliberal Personhood in North America and Britain', *Social Text*, 115, 31(2): 83–101.

Enelow, S. (2016), 'The Great Recession: American Movie Acting Today', *Film Comment*, 6 September. Available online: https://www.filmcomment.com/article/american-movie-acting-today/ (accessed 13 September 2018).

État des lieux [Inner City] (2005), [Film], Dir. Jean-François Richet, France: MKL Distribution.

Ewing, E. L. (2020), 'I'm a Black Scholar Who Studies Race. Here's Why I Capitalize "White"', *Medium*, 2 July. Available online: https://zora.medium.com/im-a-black-scholar-who-studies-race-here-s-why-i-capitalize-white-f94883aa2dd3 (accessed 7 May 2021).

Faludi, S. (1991), *Backlash: The Undeclared War against American Women*. New York: Crown.

Farrimond, K. (2013), 'The Slut That Wasn't: Virginity, (Post)Feminism and Representation in Easy A', in J. Gwynne and N. Muller (eds), *Postfeminism and Contemporary Hollywood Cinema*, 44–59. Basingstoke: Palgrave Macmillan.

Farrimond, K. (2017), *The Contemporary Femme Fatale: Gender, Genre and American Cinema*. New York: Routledge.

Fatal Attraction (1987), [Film] Dir. Adrian Lyne, USA: Paramount.

Feinberg, L. (1993), [Novel] *Stone Butch Blues*, Ann Arbor, MI: Firebrand Books.

Fielding, H. (1996), [Novel] *Bridget Jones' Diary*, London: Picador.

Film4 (2014), '*Catch Me Daddy* on Film 4', *28th Leeds International Film Festival Catalogue*, November 5. Available online: https://issuu.com/martingrund/docs/liff_2014_catalogue_final_hi-res_fo (accessed 12 September 2018).

Fish Tank (2009), [Film] Dir. Andrea Arnold, UK: BBC Films.

Fisher, M. (2014), 'Fading Privilege: *Girls*', *New Humanist*, 3 June. Available online: https://newhumanist.org.uk/articles/4667/fading-privilege-girls (accessed 17 August 2018).

Fleabag (2016–19), [TV programme], UK: BBC Three, 21 July.

Fleetwood, N. R. (2012), 'The Case of Rihanna: Erotic Violence and Black Female Desire', *African American Review*, 45(3): 419–35.

Flynn, G. ([2012] 2013), [Novel] *Gone Girl*, London: Orion Books.

Ford, T. C. (2018), 'The Complexity of Black Girlhood Is at the Heart of *The Hate U Give*', *Atlantic*, 19 October. Available online: https://www.theatlantic.com/entertainment/archive/2018/10/the-hate-u-give-movie-starr-carter-black-girlhood/573319/ (accessed 7 May 2021).

Fradley, M. (2013), 'Hell Is a Teenage Girl? Postfeminism and Contemporary Teen Horror', in J. Gwynne and N. Muller (eds), *Postfeminism and*

Contemporary Hollywood Cinema, 204–21. Basingstoke: Palgrave Macmillan.

Framke, C. (2015), '*Broad City*: "Knockoffs"', *AV Club*, 4 February. Available online: https://tv.avclub.com/broad-city-knockoffs-1798182737 (accessed 7 May 2021).

Freaky Friday (2003), [Film] Dir. Mark Waters, USA: Buena Vista Pictures.

Freeman, E. (2010), *Time Binds: Queer Temporalities, Queer Histories*. Durham, NC: Duke University Press.

Freud, S. (1917), *Mourning and Melancholia*, 14th edn. London: Vintage.

Friedan, B. ([1963] 2010), *The Feminine Mystique*. London: Penguin.

Fruitvale Station (2013), [Film] Dir. Ryan Coogler, USA: The Weinstein Company.

Gal, S. (1991), 'Between Speech and Silence', in M. di Leonardo (ed.), *Gender at the Crossroads of Knowledge: Feminist Anthropology in the Postmodern Era*, 175–203. Berkeley: University of California Press.

Genz, S. (2017), '"I Have Work ... I Am Busy ... Trying to Become Who I Am": Neoliberal Girls and Recessionary Postfeminism', in M. Nash and I. Whelehan (eds), *Reading Lena Dunham's Girls: Feminism, Postfeminism, Authenticity, and Gendered Performance in Contemporary Television*, 17–30. Basingstoke: Palgrave Macmillan.

Genz, S., and B. A. Brabon (eds) (2009), *Postfeminism: Cultural Texts and Theories*. Edinburgh: Edinburgh University Press.

Gerhard, J. (2005), '*Sex and the City*: Carrie Bradshaw's Queer Postfeminism', *Feminist Media Studies*, 5(1): 37–49.

Gilbert, S. (2017), 'What Was Missing from the *Girls* Finale', *Atlantic*, 17 April. Available online: https://www.theatlantic.com/entertainment/archive/2017/04/girls-finale-latching/523233/ (accessed 7 May 2021).

Gilbert, S. (2018), '*The Handmaid's Tale* and the Suffering of Women', *Atlantic*, 25 April. Available online: https://www.theatlantic.com/entertainment/archive/2018/04/the-handmaids-tale-season-two/558809/ (accessed 7 May 2021).

Gill, R. (2007), 'Postfeminist Media Culture: Elements of a Sensibility', *European Journal of Cultural Studies*, 10(2): 147–66.

Gill, R. (2008), 'Culture and Subjectivity in Neoliberal and Postfeminist Times', *Subjectivity*, 25: 432–45.

Gill, R. (2016), 'Post-postfeminism? New Feminist Visibilities in Postfeminist Times', *Feminist Media Studies*, 16(4): 610–30. Available online: https://doi.org/10.1080/14680777.2016.1193293 (accessed 21 May 2021).

Gill, R. (2017), 'The Affective, Cultural and Psychic Life of Postfeminism: A Postfeminist Sensibility 10 Years on', *European Journal of Cultural Studies*, 20(6): 606–26. Available online: https://doi.org/10.1177/1367549417733003 (accessed 21 May 2021).

Gill, R., and C. Scharff (eds) (2011), *New Femininities: Postfeminism, Neoliberalism and Subjectivity*. Basingstoke: Palgrave Macmillan.

Girls (2012–17), [TV programme] USA: HBO, 15 April.

Glee (2009–15), [TV programme] USA: Fox, 19 May.

Gonick, M. (2006), 'Between "Girl Power" and "Reviving Ophelia": Constituting the Neoliberal Girl Subject', *National Women's Studies Association*, 18(2): 1–23.

Gonick, M., E. Renold, J. Ringrose and L. Weems (2009), 'Rethink-ing Agency and Resistance: What Comes after Girl Power?' *Girlhood Studies*, 2(2): 1–9.

Goodley, D., K. Liddiard and K. Runswick-Cole (2017), 'Feeling Disability: Theories of Affect and Critical Disability Studies', *Disability & Society*, 33(2): 197–217. Available online: https://doi.org/10.1080/09687599.2017.1402752 (accessed 9 December 2021).

Gordon, A. M., and H. Vera (2003), *Screen Saviors: Hollywood Fictions of Whiteness*. Boston, MA: Rowman and Littlefield.

Gorton, K. (2007), 'Theorizing Emotion and Affect: Feminist Engagements', *Feminist Theory*, 8(3): 333–48. Available online: https://doi.org/10.1177/1464700107082369 (accessed 9 December 2021).

Gottschall, K., S. Gannon, J. Lampert and K. McGraw (2013), 'The Cyndi Lauper Affect: Bodies, Girlhood and Popular Culture', *Girlhood Studies*, 6(1): 30–45.

Grady, C. (2021), 'The Angry Women of Carey Mulligan', *Vox*, 9 February. Available online: https://www.vox.com/culture/22263001/carey-mulligan-variety-controversy-promising-young-woman (accessed 10 December 2021).

Grady, C., and E. VanDerWerff (2017), 'The Handmaid's Tale Season 1, Episode 4: "Nolite Te Bastardes Carborundorum" Sends Offred Some Words of Wisdom', *Vox*, 3 May. Available online: https://www.vox.com/culture/2017/5/3/15523626/handmaids-tale-episode-4-recap-nolite-te-bastardes-carborundorum (accessed 24 April 2021).

Grant, C., and L. Waxman (2011), 'Introduction: The Girl in Contemporary Art', in C. Grant and L. Waxman (eds), *Girls! Girls! Girls! In Contemporary Art*, 1–16. Chicago: Intellect.

Grant, R., and M. Nash (2015), 'Twenty-Something *Girls* v. Thirty-Something *Sex and The City* Women', *Feminist Media Studies*, 15(6): 976–91. Available online: https://doi.org/10.1080/14680777.2015.1050596 (accessed 21 May 2021).

Grant, R., and M. Nash (2017), 'From Sex and the City to Girls: Paving the Way for "Post? Feminism"', in M. Nash and I. Whelehan (eds), *Reading Lena Dunham's Girls: Feminism, Postfeminism, Authenticity, and Gendered Performance in Contemporary Television*, 61–74. Basingstoke: Palgrave Macmillan.

Grdešić, M. (2013), '"I'm Not the Ladies!": Metatextual Commentary in *Girls*', *Feminist Media Studies*, 13(2): 355–8. Available online: https://doi.org/10.1080/14680777.2013.771878 (accessed 21 May 2021).

Greil, M. (2006), 'Picturing America', *Threepenny Review*, 29 August. Available online: https://www.threepennyreview.com/samples/marcus_f06.html (accessed 26 August 2018).

Gwynne, J. (2013), *Erotic Memoirs and Postfeminism: The Politics of Pleasure*. Basingstoke: Palgrave Macmillan.

Gwynne, J., and N. Muller (eds) (2013), *Postfeminism and Contemporary Hollywood Cinema*. Basingstoke: Palgrave Macmillan.

Halberstam, J. (2005), *In a Queer Time and Place: Transgender Bodies, Subcultural Lives*. New York: New York University Press.

Halberstam, J. (2006), 'The Politics of Negativity in Recent Queer Theory', *PMLA*, 121(3): 824–5.

Halberstam, J. (2011), *The Queer Art of Failure*. Durham, NC: Duke University Press.

Hamad, H. (2013), 'Hollywood Fatherhood: Paternal Postfeminism in Contemporary Popular Cinema', in J. Gwynne and N. Muller (eds), *Postfeminism and Contemporary Hollywood Cinema*, 99–114. Basingstoke: Palgrave Macmillan.

Handyside, F. (2015), 'Girlhood, Postfeminism and Contemporary Female Art-House Authorship: The "Nameless Trilogies" of Sofia Coppola and Mia Hansen-Løve', *Alphaville: Journal of Film and Screen Media*, 10: 1–18.

Handyside, F. (2016), 'Emotion, Girlhood, and Music in *Naissance des pieuvres* (Céline Sciamma, 2007) and *Un amour de jeunesse* (Mia Hansen-Løve, 2011)', in F. Handyside and K. Taylor-Jones (eds), *International Cinema and the Girl: Local Issues, Transnational Contexts*, 121–34. Basingstoke: Palgrave Macmillan.

Handyside, F., and K. Taylor-Jones (2016), 'Introduction', in F. Handyside and K. Taylor-Jones (eds), *International Cinema and the Girl: Local Issues, Transnational Contexts*, 1–18. Basingstoke: Palgrave Macmillan.

Hanich, J. (2008), 'A Weep in the Dark: Tears and the Cinematic Experience', in R. J. Poole and I. Saal (eds), *Passionate Politics: The Cultural Work of American Melodrama from the Early Republic to the Present*, 27–45. Newcastle: Cambridge Scholars.

Harlow, R. (2003), '"Race Doesn't Matter, but …": The Effect of Race on Professors Experiences and Emotion Management in the Undergraduate College Classroom', *Social Psychology Quarterly*, 66(4): 348–63. Available online: https://doi.org/10.2307/1519834 (accessed 7 May 2021).

Harris, A. (2004), *Future Girl: Young Women in the Twenty-First Century*. New York: Routledge.

Harris, C. (2012), 'Sweet Nothing (featuring Florence Welch)', Track 10 on *12 Months* [Spotify], London: Deconstruction.

Harvey, A. (2011), [Novel] *Haunting Violet*, London: Bloomsbury.

Harvey, D. (2005), *A Brief History of Neoliberalism*. Oxford: Oxford University Press.

Hasinoff, A. A. (2012), 'Sexting as Media Production: Rethinking Social Media and Sexuality', *New Media & Society*, 15(4): 1–17. Available online: http://doi.org/10.1177/1461444812459171 (accessed 21 May 2021).

Haskell, M. ([1974] 2016), *Reverence to Rape: The Treatment of Women in the Movies*. Chicago: University of Chicago Press.

Healy, A. M., and A. Zolli (2012), *Resilience: Why Things Bounce Back*. New York: Simon & Schuster.

Henderson, M., and A. Taylor (2019), *Postfeminism in Context: Women, Australian Popular Culture, and the Unsettling of Postfeminism*. London: Routledge.

Henry, A. (2004), 'Orgasms and Empowerment: *Sex and the City* and the Third Wave Feminism', in K. Akass and Janet McCabe (eds), *Reading Sex and the City*, 65–82. London: I.B. Tauris.

Hess, A. (2013), 'Was That a Rape Scene in *Girls*?' *Slate*, 11 March. Available online: http://www.slate.com/blogs/xx_factor/2013/03/11/girls_adam_and_natalia_sexual_assault_and_verbal_consent_on_hbo_s_girls.html (accessed 13 April 2016).

Hess, A. (2014), 'The Psycho Bitch, from *Fatal Attraction*'s Single Woman to *Gone Girl*'s Perfect Wife', *Slate*, 6 October. Available online: http://www.slate.com/blogs/xx_factor/2014/10/06/

psycho_bitch_the_trope_evolves_from_fatal_attraction_s_alex_forrest_ to_gone.html (accessed 26 August 2018).

Higbee, W. (2007), 'Re-Presenting the Urban Periphery: Maghrebi-French Filmmaking and the "Banlieue" Film', *Cineaste*, 33(1): 38–43.

Higbee, W. (2018), '"Beyond Ethnicity" or a Return to Type?: *Bande de filles/ Girlhood* (Sciamma, 2014) and the Politics of Blackness in Contemporary French Cinema', in K. A. Kleppinger and L. Reeck (eds), *Post-Migration and Postcoloniality in Contemporary French Culture*, 166–82. Liverpool: Liverpool University Press.

Hill, S. (2020), *Young Women, Girls and Postfeminism in Contemporary British Film*. London: Bloomsbury.

Hochschild, A. (1979), 'Emotion Work, Feeling Rules, and Social Structure', *American Journal of Sociology*, 85(3): 551–75. Available online: http://www.jstor.org/stable/2778583 (accessed 7 May 2021).

Hodkin, M. (2011), [Novel] *The Unbecoming of Mara Dyer*, New York: Simon & Schuster.

Holden, S. (2015), 'Aimless Adventures of a Hip Narcissist: Desiree Akhavan's "Appropriate Behavior"', *New York Times*, 15 January. Available online: https://www.nytimes.com/2015/01/16/movies/desiree-akhavans-appropriate-behavior.html (accessed 17 September 2018).

Holm, N. (2017), 'The Politics of Deadpan in Australasian Satire', in J. M. Davis (ed.), *Satire and Politics: The Interplay of Heritage and Practice*, 103–24. Basingstoke: Palgrave Macmillan.

hooks, b. (2000), *Feminist Theory: From Margin to Center*. London: Pluto Press.

Hu, J. (2012), 'Reality Hunger: On Lena Dunham's "Girls"', *Los Angeles Review of Books*, 28 April. Available online: https://lareviewofbooks.org/article/reality-hunger-on-lena-dunhams-girls (accessed 17 August 2018).

Huehls, M. (2016), *After Critique: Twenty-First-Century Fiction in a Neoliberal Age*. New York: Oxford University Press.

Huijg, D. (2021), [Conference presentation] '"Tools, Tips and Tricks": An Analysis of Gendered Neuronormativity in Self-Help Literature about and for ADHD Women', *Feminist Perspectives on Neurodiversity and Neuronormativity*, 29 January.

I Hate Suzie (2020–present), [TV programme] Sky Atlantic, 27 August.

I May Destroy You (2020), [TV programme] BBC1, 8 June.

Insecure (2016–21), [TV programme] USA: HBO, 23 September.

Inside Llewyn Davis (2013), [Film] Dir. Ethan Coen and Joel Coen, France: StudioCanal.

Iversen, K. (2017), 'On the Strange Use of Nina Simone Songs in "The Handmaid's Tale"', *Nylon*, 14 June. Available online: https://www.nylon.com/articles/handmaids-tale-hulu-music-songs-choices-nina-simone (accessed 24 April 2021).

Jacey, H. (2010), *The Woman in the Story: Writing Memorable Female Characters*. Studio City, CA: Michael Wiese Productions.

Jackson, A. Y. (2010), 'Deleuze and the Girl', *International Journal of Qualitative Studies in Education*, 23(5): 579–87. Available online: https://doi.org/10.1080/09518398.2010.500630 (accessed 21 May 2021).

Jackson, S. (2016), 'They've Always Got Flat Tummies and It Really Bugs Us', in J. Coffey, S. Budgeon and H. Cahill (eds), *Learning Bodies: The Body in Youth and Childhood Studies*, 69–84. New York: Springer.

Jagose, A. (1996), *Queer Theory: An Introduction*. New York: New York University Press.

James, R. (2013a), 'Rihanna's Melancholic Damage', [blog post] *It's Her Factory*, 24 March. Available online: https://www.its-her-factory.com/2013/03/rihannas-melancholic-damage/ (accessed 12 September 2018).

James, R. (2013b), 'Melancholic Damage', *New Inquiry*, 30 May. Available online: https://thenewinquiry.com/melancholic-damage/ (accessed 12 September 2018).

James, R. (2015), *Resilience and Melancholy: Pop Music, Feminism, Neoliberalism*. Winchester: Zero Books.

Jameson, F. (1990), *Postmodernism, or, the Cultural Logic of Late Capitalism*. Durham, NC: Duke University Press.

Jansen, L., and M. Westphal (2017), 'Rihanna Works Her Multivocal Pop Persona: A Morpho-Syntactic and Accent Analysis of Rihanna's Singing Style', *English Today*, 1–10. Available online: https://doi.org/10.1017/S0266078416000651 (accessed 21 May 2021).

Jermyn, D. (2004), 'You Can't Keep a Dead Woman Down: The Female Corpse and Textual Disruption in Contemporary Hollywood', in E. Klaver (ed.), *Images of the Corpse: From the Renaissance to Cyberspace*, 153–68. Madison: University of Wisconsin Press.

Jolly, M. (2001), 'Coming Out of the Coming Out Story: Writing Queer Lives', *Sexualities*, 4(4): 475–97. Available online: https://doi.org/10.1177/136346001004004005 (accessed 21 May 2021).

Kamińska, A. (2020), 'Failing Adulthood, Queering Girlhood: Perpetual Adolescence in *Broad City* and *Girls*', *Journal of Popular Culture*, 53(5): 1046–65.

Kanai, A. (2019), *Gender and Relatability in Digital Culture: Managing Affect, Intimacy and Value*. London: Palgrave Macmillan.

Kanai, A., and A. Dobson (2019), 'Making Do on Not Much: High Energy Striving, Femininity and Friendship in *Broad City*', *Culture Unbound*, 11 (3–4): 517–33.

Kearney, M. C. (2006), *Girls Make Media*. New York: Routledge.

Kearney, M. C. (2009), 'Coalescing: The Development of Girls' Studies', *National Women's Studies Association*, 21(1): 1–28.

Keller, J., and M. Ryan (2014), 'Call for Papers: Problematizing Postfeminism'. Available online: http://arcyp.ca/archives/4244 (accessed 22 February 2016).

Kennedy, C. (2021), 'Promising Young Woman Has Surprising Roots Back to Shakespeare', *Digital Spy*, 16 April. Available online: https://www.digitalspy.com/movies/a36129663/promising-young-woman-shakespeare-tragedy-ending/ (accessed 24 April 2021).

Kennedy, M. (2019), *Tweenhood: Femininity and Celebrity in Tween Popular Culture*. London: Bloomsbury.

Kermode, J. (2015), 'Sex, Lies and Cinema: Desiree Akhavan on *Appropriate Behaviour*', *Eye for Film*, 24 June. Available online: https://www.eyeforfilm.co.uk/feature/2015-06-24-interview-with-desiree-akhavan-about-appropriate-behaviour-feature-story-by-jennie-kermode (accessed 17 August 2018).

Kilbourne, J. (1999), *Can't Buy My Love: How Advertising Changes the Way We Think and Feel*. New York: Touchstone.

Killing Eve (2018–present), [TV programme] BBC Three, 15 September.

Koestler, A. ([1964] 1989), *The Act of Creation*. London: Penguin.

Kotsko, A. (2010), *Awkwardness*. Winchester: Zero Books.

Kristeva, J. ([1941] 1980), *Desire in Language: A Semiotic Approach to Literature and Art*, ed. L. S. Roudiez, trans. T. Gora, A. Jardine and L. S. Roudiez. New York: Columbia University Press.

Krutnik, F. (1998), 'Love Lies: Romantic Fabrication in Contemporary Romantic Comedy', in P. W. Evans and C. Deleyto (eds), *Terms of Endearment: Hollywood Romantic Comedy of the 1980s and 1990s*, 15–36. Edinburgh: Edinburgh University Press.

Kurian, A. (2017), 'Decolonizing the Body: Theoretical Imaginings on the Fourth Wave Feminism in India', in S. Jha and A. Kurian (eds), *New Feminisms in South Asia: Disrupting the Discourse*, 1–27. New York: Routledge.

La Boum [The Party] (1980), [Film] Dir. Claude Pinoteau, France: Gaumont Film Company.

La Haine (1995), [Film] Dir. Mathieu Kassovitz, France: Canal+.

LaBelle (1974), 'It Took a Long Time', Track 4 on *Nightbirds* [Spotify], New York: Epic.

Lacan, J. [1973] 1981, *The Seminar of Jacques Lacan, Book XVII: The Other Side of Psychoanalysis*, ed. J. Miller, trans. A. Sheridan. New York: Norton.

Lavalley, R., and K. Robinson Johnson (2020), 'Occupation, Injustice, and Anti-Black Racism in the United States of America', *Journal of Occupational Science*, 27(s1): 1–13. Available online: https://doi.org/10.1080/14427591.2020.1810111 (accessed 7 May 2021).

Levin, A. (2020), 'Finding the "Herstorical" Narrative in Angie Thomas's *The Hate U Give*', *English Studies in Africa*, 63(1): 148–66. Available online: https://doi.org/10.1080/00138398.2020.1780762 (accessed 24 March 2021).

Lewis, D. L. (2012), 'Exceptionalism's Exceptions: The Changing American Narrative', *Daedalus*, 141(1): 101–17.

Lies, E. (2013), '*Girls*' Season 2 Review: Things Get Dark', *Vulture*, 20 March. Available online: http://www.vulture.com/2013/03/girls-season-2-review-things-get-dark.html (accessed 10 September 2018).

Light Asylum (2010), 'Dark Allies', Track 3 on *In Tension* [Spotify], New York: Mexican Summer.

Lim, S. H. (2014), *Tsai Ming-liang and a Cinema of Slowness*. Honolulu: University of Hawai'i Press.

Lindop, S. (2015), *Postfeminism and the Fatale Figure in Neo-Noir Cinema*. Basingstoke: Palgrave Macmillan.

Littler, J. (2013), 'Meritocracy as Plutocracy: The Marketising of "equality" under Neoliberalism', *New Formations: A Journal of Culture/Theory/Politics*, 80(1): 52–72.

Lorde, A. (1984), *Sister Outsider*. Berkeley, CA: Ten Speed Press.

Lotz, A. D. (2006), *Redesigning Women: Television after the Network Era*. Chicago: University of Illinois Press.

Love Actually (2003), [Film] Dir. Richard Curtis, USA: Universal Pictures.

Love, H. (2007), *Feeling Backwards: Loss and the Politics of Queer History*. Cambridge, MA: Harvard University Press.

Lübecker, N. (2015), *The Feel-Bad Film*. Edinburgh: Edinburgh University Press.

Lucas, D. A. (2018), *Affect Theory, Genre, and the Example of Tragedy: Dreams We Learn*. London: Palgrave Macmillan.

Lyons, M. (2013), 'On *Girls*, Adam, Rape, and Consent', *Vulture*, 12 March. Available online: http://www.vulture.com/2013/03/on-girls-adam-rape-and-consent.html (accessed 13 April 2016).

Macón, C. (2021), 'White Scarves and Green Scarves. The Affective Temporality of #QueSeaLey [#MakeItLaw] as Fourth-Wave Feminism', in C. Macón, M. Solana and N. L. Vacarezza (eds), *Affect, Gender and Sexuality in Latin America*, 41–62. Switzerland: Springer International (Palgrave Macmillan).

Madhok, S., A. Phillips and K. Wilson (2013), 'Introduction', in S. Madhok, A Phillips and K. Wilson (eds), *Gender, Agency, and Coercion*. Basingstoke: Palgrave Macmillan.

Maher, J. (2018), 'Torture Born: Babies, Bloodshed and the Feminist Gaze in Hulu's *The Handmaid's Tale*', *Communication Culture & Critique*, 11: 209–11.

Marie Antoinette (2006), [Film] Dir. Sofia Coppola, USA: Columbia Pictures.

Marks, E. (1979), 'Lesbian Intertextuality', in G. Stambolian and E. Marks (eds), *Homosexualities and French Literature: Cultural Contexts/Critical Texts*, 353–77. New York: Cornell University Press.

Marnie (1964), [Film] Dir. Alfred Hitchcock, USA: Universal Pictures.

Marston, K. (2018), *Postfeminist Whiteness: Problematising Melancholic Burden in Contemporary Hollywood*. Edinburgh: Edinburgh University Press.

Martin, B. (1998), 'Lesbian Identity and Autobiographical Difference(s)', in S. Smith and J. Watson (eds), *Women, Autobiography, Theory: A Reader*, 380–92. Madison: University of Wisconsin Press.

Martin, R., and P. Sunley (2015), 'On the Notion of Regional Economic Resilience: Conceptualization and Explanation', *Journal of Economic Geography*, 15(1): 1–42. Available online: https://doi.org/10.1093/jeg/lbu015 (accessed 21 May 2021).

Mason, P. (2012), 'The Graduates of 2012 Will Survive Only in the Cracks of Our Economy', *Guardian*, 1 July. Available online: https://www.theguard

ian.com/commentisfree/2012/jul/01/graduates-2012-survive-in-cracks-economy (accessed 17 August 2018).

McAndrews, M. B. (2021), 'On the Disempowerment of Promising Young Woman', *RogerEbert.com*, 13 January. Available online: https://www.rogerebert.com/features/on-the-disempowerment-of-promising-young-woman (accessed 24 April 2021).

McNeill, I. (2017), ' "Shine Bright Like a Diamond": Music, Performance and Digitextuality in Céline Sciamma's *Bande de filles* (2014)', *Studies in French Cinema*, 1–15. Available online: https://doi.org/10.1080/14715880.2017.1345187 (accessed 13 May 2018).

McNeill, W. H. (1995), *Keeping Together in Time: Dance and Drill in Human History*. Cambridge, MA: Harvard University Press.

McRobbie, A. (2008), *The Aftermath of Feminism*. London: Sage.

McRobbie, A. (2020), *Feminism and the Politics of Resilience: Essays on Gender, Media and the End of Welfare*. Cambridge: Polity.

Meagher, M., and K. Rodier (2014), 'In Her Own Time: Rihanna, Post-Feminism, and Domestic Violence', *Women: A Cultural Review*, 25(2): 176–93. Available online: https://doi.org/10.1080/09574042.2014.944416 (accessed 21 August 2021).

Mean Girls (2004), [Film] Dir. Mark Waters, USA: Paramount.

Meeks, C. ([2006] 2011), 'Gay and Straight Rites of Passage', in S. Seidman, N. Fischer and C. Meeks (eds), *Introducing the New Sexuality Studies*, 2nd edn, 57–64. New York: Routledge.

Menta, A. (2021), 'In Defense of the "Promising Young Woman" Ending', *Decider*, 15 January. Available online: https://decider.com/2021/01/15/promising-young-woman-ending-explained-defense/ (accessed 24 April 2021).

Meredith, L. S. et al. (2011), 'Promoting Psychological Resilience in the U.S. Military', *RAND: The Centre for Military Health Policy Research*. Available online: https://www.rand.org/content/dam/rand/pubs/monographs/2011/RAND_MG996.pdf (accessed 11 September 2018).

Merry, S. (2015), ' "Appropriate Behavior" Movie Review: Desiree Akhavan Comes of Age', *Washington Post*, 15 January. Available online: https://wapo.st/2JO3AbZ (accessed 10 September 2018).

Merskin, D. (2011), 'A Boyfriend to Die For: Edward Cullen as Compensated Psychopath in Stephanie Meyer's Twilight', *Journal of Communication Inquiry* 35(2): 157–78. Available online: https://doi.org/10.1177/0196859911402992 (accessed 21 August 2018).

Meyer, S. (2005–8), [Novel] *Twilight Saga*. New York: Little, Brown.
Millais, J. E. (1851–2), [Oil on canvas] *Ophelia*, UK: Tate Britain.
Mills, S. (1987), 'The Male Sentence', *Language and Communication* 7(3): 189–98.
Mitchell, A. M. (2016), 'Beyoncé as Aggressive Black Femme and Informed Black Female Subject', in A. Trier-Bieniek (ed.), *The Beyoncé Effect: Essays on Sexuality, Race and Feminism*, 40–54. Jefferson, NC: McFarland.
Modleski, T. ([1988] 2005), *The Women Who Knew Too Much: Hitchcock and Feminist Theory*, 2nd edn. New York: Routledge.
Modleski, T. (1999), *Old Wives' Tales: Feminist Re-visions of Film and Other Fiction*. London: I.B. Tauris.
Monaghan, W. (2016), *Queer Girls, Temporality and Screen Media: Not 'Just a Phase'*. Basingstoke: Palgrave Macmillan.
Montemurro, B. (2004), 'Charlotte Chooses Her Choice: Liberal Feminism on *Sex and the City*', *Scholar and Feminist Online*, 3(1). Available online: http://sfonline.barnard.edu/hbo/montemurro_01.htm (accessed 24 May 2018).
Morris, W. (2014), 'If U Seek Amy: The Grim Grossness of David Fincher's "Gone Girl"', *Grantland*, 3 October. Available online: http://grantland.com/hollywood-prospectus/david-fincher-gone-girl-movie-review/ (accessed 26 August 2018).
Morris, W., and J. Wortham (2021), [Podcast] 'Still Processing', *New York Times*, 1 April. Transcript available online: https://www.nytimes.com/2021/04/01/podcasts/still-processing-promising-young-women-oscars.html?showTranscript=1 (accessed 14 April 2021).
Moss, G. (2014), 'On Gillian Flynn's "Cool Girl": She Does Exist in Reality, and to Suggest Otherwise Is Sexist and Infuriating', *Bustle*, 8 October. Available online: https://www.bustle.com/articles/43382-on-gillian-flynns-cool-girl-she-does-exist-in-reality-and-to-suggest-otherwise-is-sexist (accessed 26 August 2018).
Mulholland Falls (1996), [Film] Dir. Lee Tamahori, USA: MGM.
Mulvey, L. (1975), 'Visual Pleasure and Narrative Cinema', *Screen*, 16(3): 6–18.
Mulvey, L. (2006), *Death 24x a Second: Stillness and the Moving Image*. London: Reaktion Books.
Muñoz, J. E. (2006), 'Thinking beyond Antirelationality and Antiutopianism in Queer Critique', *PMLA*, 121(3): 825–6.
Muñoz, J. E. (2009), *Cruising Utopia: The Then and There of Queer Futurity*. New York: New York University Press.

Munro, E. (2013), 'Feminism: A fourth wave?' *Political Insight*, 4(2): 22–5.

Munt, S. R. (2007), *Queer Attachments: The Cultural Politics of Shame*. Farnham: Ashgate.

Mykhnenko, V. (2016), 'Resilience: A Right-Wingers' Ploy?' in S. Spring, K. Birch and J. MacLeavy (eds), *The Handbook of Neoliberalism*, 190–206. New York: Routledge.

Naissance des pieuvres [Water Lilies] (2007), [Film] Dir. Céline Sciamma, France: Haut et Court.

Neale, S. (1980), *Genre*. London: British Film Institute.

Nealon, J. (2002), 'Empire of the Intensities: A Random Walk Down Las Vegas Boulevard', *Parallax*, 8(1): 78–91.

Needham, G. (2009), 'Scheduling Normativity: Television, the Family, and Queer Temporality', in G. Davis and G. Needham (eds), *Queer TV: Theories, Histories, Politics*, 143–58. London: Routledge.

Negra, D. (2008), *What a Girl Wants?: Fantasizing the Reclamation of Self in Postfeminism*. London: Routledge.

Negra, D., and Y. Tasker (2005), 'Postfeminism and Contemporary Media Studies', *Cinema Journal*, 44(2): 107–10.

Negra, D., and Y. Tasker (eds) (2007), *Interrogating Postfeminism: Gender and the Politics of Popular Culture*. Durham, NC: Duke University Press.

Negra, D., and Y. Tasker (2013), 'Neoliberal Frames and Genres of Inequality: Recession-Era Chick Flicks and Male-Centred Corporate Melodrama', *European Journal of Cultural Studies*, 16(3): 344–61.

Negra, D., and Y. Tasker (2014), 'Introduction. Gender and Recessionary Culture', in D. Negra and Y. Tasker (eds), *Gendering the Recession: Media and Culture in an Age of Austerity*. Durham, NC: Duke University Press.

Nelson, R. (2007), *State of Play: Contemporary 'High-End' TV Drama*. Manchester: Manchester University Press.

Nelson, R. A. (2011), [Novel] *Throat*, New York: Penguin Random House.

Neocleous, M. (2013), 'Resisting Resilience', *Radical Philosophy*, 178(1). Available online: https://www.radicalphilosophy.com/commentary/resisting-resilience (accessed 17 September 2018).

Ngai, S. (2005), *Ugly Feelings*. Cambridge, MA: Harvard University Press.

Nussbaum, E. (2013), 'Difficult Women: How "Sex and the City" Lost Its Good Name', *New Yorker*, 29 July. Available online: https://www.newyorker.com/magazine/2013/07/29/difficult-women (accessed 26 August 2018).

Oliver, L. (2011), [Novel] *Delirium*. New York: HarperCollins.

Oliver, L. (2012), [Novel] *Pandemonium*. New York: HarperCollins.

Oliver, L. (2013), *Requiem*. New York: HarperCollins.
Olsen, G. (2011), *Envy*. New York: Splinter.
Orgad, S., and R. Gill (2018), 'The Amazing Bounce-Backable Woman: Resilience and the Psychological Turn in Neoliberalism', *Sociological Research Online*, 1–19. Available online: https://doi.org/10.1177/1360780418769673 (accessed 7 May 2021).
Parpart, J. L. (2010), 'Choosing Silence: Rethinking Voice, Agency and Women's Empowerment', in R. Ryan-Flood and R. Gill (eds), *Secrecy and Silence in the Research Process: Feminist Reflections*, 15–29. New York: Routledge.
Parry, D. C., C. W. Johnson and F. A. Wagler (2019), 'Fourth Wave Feminism: Theoretical Underpinnings and Future Directions for Leisure Research', in D. C. Parry (ed.), *Feminisms in Leisure Studies: Advancing a Fourth Wave*, 1–12. London: Routledge.
Petersen, A. H. (2012), 'That Teenage Feeling: *Twilight*, Fantasy, and Feminist Readers', *Feminist Media Studies*, 12(1): 51–67.
Petersen, A. H. (2014), 'The Problem with "Gone Girl" Is That There's No "Cool Girl"', *Buzzfeed*, 3 October. Available online: https://www.buzzfeed.com/annehelenpetersen/gone-girl-no-cool-girl?utm_term=.vkDkpdWaX#.ydLNvbE37 (accessed 26 August 2018).
Pipher, M. ([1994] 2005), *Reviving Ophelia: Saving the Selves of Adolescent Girls*. New York: Riverhead Books.
Plotz, B. (2020), *Fat on Film: Gender, Race and Body Size in Contemporary Hollywood Cinema*. London: Bloomsbury.
Pollard, T. (2010), 'Tragedy and Revenge', in E. Smith and G. A. Sullivan Jr (eds), *The Cambridge Companion to English Renaissance Tragedy*, 58–72. Cambridge: Cambridge University Press.
Poniewozik, J. (2012), 'Lena Dunham Interview, Part One: What *Girls* Is Made Of', *TIME*, 12 April. Available online: http://entertainment.time.com/2012/04/12/lena-dunham-interview-part-one-what-girls-is-made-of (accessed 13 April 2016).
Precious (2009), [Film] Dir. Lee Daniels, USA: Lionsgate.
Projansky, S. (2001), *Watching Rape: Film and Television in Postfeminist Culture*. New York: New York University Press.
Projansky, S. (2007), 'Mass Magazine Cover Girls: Some Reflections on Postfeminist Girls and Postfeminism's Daughters', in D. Negra and Y. Tasker (eds), *Interrogating Postfeminism: Gender and the Politics of Popular Culture*, 40–72. Durham, NC: Duke University Press.

Projansky, S. (2014), *Spectacular Girls: Media Fascination and Celebrity Culture*. New York: New York University Press.

Promising Young Woman (2020), [Film] Dir. Emerald Fennell, USA: Focus Features.

Puar, J. K. (2007), *Terrorist Assemblages: Homonationalism in Queer Times*. Durham, NC: Duke University Press.

Pulcini, Robert, and Shari Springer Berman (20123), *Girl Most Likely*. Canada: Lionsgate.

Rebecca (1940), [Film] Dir. Alfred Hitchcock, USA: United Artists.

Reid, R. (2018), 'Why I'm Turning Off the Handmaid's Tale and Its Needless Torture Porn', *Telegraph*, 30 May. Available online: https://www.telegraph.co.uk/women/life/turning-handmaids-tale-needless-torture-porn/ (accessed 24 April 2021).

Ren, N. S. (2011), [Novel] *Imaginary Girls*, New York: Penguin Random House.

Renold, E., and J. Ringrose (2013), 'Feminisms Re-Figuring "Sexualisation", Sexuality and "the Girl"', *Feminist Theory*, 14(3): 247–54.

Retallack, H., J. Ringrose and E. Lawrence (2016), '"Fuck Your Body Image": Teen Girls' Twitter and Instagram Feminism in and around School', in J. Coffey, S. Budgeon and H. Cahill (eds), *Learning Bodies: The Body in Youth and Childhood Studies*, 85–104. New York: Springer.

Rihanna (2012), 'Diamonds', Track 2 on *Unapologetic*. New York: Def Jam.

Riley, S., A. Evans, S. Elliott, C. Rice and J. Maracek (2017), 'A Critical Review of Postfeminist Sensibility', *Social and Personality Psychology Compass*, 11: 1–12. Available online: https://doi.org/10.1111/spc3.12367 (accessed 14 December 2020).

Ringmar, E. (2017), 'What Are Public Moods?' *European Journal of Social Theory*, 21(4): 1–17. Available online: https://10.1177/1368431017736995 (accessed 7 May 2021).

Ringrose, J. (2011), 'Beyond Discourse?: Using Deleuze and Guattari's Schizoanalysis to Explore Affective Assemblages, Heterosexually Striated Space, and Lines of Flight Online and at School', *Educational Philosophy and Theory*, 43(6): 598–618.

Ringrose, J. (2013), *Postfeminist Education? Girls and the Sexual Politics of Schooling*. New York: Routledge.

Ringrose, J., and L. Harvey (2015), 'Boobs, Back-Off, and Small Bits: Mediated Body Parts, Sexual Reward and Gendered Shame in Teens' Networked Images', *Continuum: Journal of Media and Cultural Studies*, 29(2): 205–17.

Ringrose, J., R. Gill, S. Livingstone and L. Harvey (2012), 'A Qualitative Study of Children, Young People and "Sexting": A Report Prepared for the NSPCC', *National Society for the Prevention of Cruelty to Children*. Available online: https://library.nspcc.org.uk/HeritageScripts/Hapi.dll/search2?CookieCheck=43361.7124496181&searchTerm0=C604 (accessed 18 September 2018).

Rivers, N. (2017), *Postfeminism(s) and the Arrival of the Fourth Wave: Turning Tides*. Switzerland: Springer International (Palgrave Macmillan).

Rooney, D. (2014), '*Appropriate Behavior*: Sundance Review', *Hollywood Reporter*, 18 January. Available online: http://www.hollywoodreporter.com/review/appropriate-behavior-sundance-review-672264 (accessed 27 August 2018).

Rowles, D. (2012), 'HBO's "Girls" and Our Resentment toward Privileged, White America', *Pajiba*, 24 April. Available online: http://www.pajiba.com/think_pieces/hbos-girls-and-our-resentment-toward-privileged-white-america.php (accessed 30 April 2016).

Ruti, M. (2017), *The Ethics of Opting Out: Queer Theory's Defiant Subjects*. New York: Columbia University Press.

Ryan, C. (2010), [Novel] *The Dead-Tossed Waves*, New York: Random House.

Sandywell, B. (1999), 'Specular Grammar: The Visual Rhetoric of Modernity', in I. Heywood and B. Sandywell (eds), *Interpreting Visual Culture: Explorations in the Hermeneutics of the Visual*, 31–58. London: Routledge.

Saner, E. (2014), 'The *Gone Girl* Backlash: What Women Don't Want', *Guardian*, 7 October. Available online: https://www.theguardian.com/film/2014/oct/07/gone-girl-backlash-david-fincher-misogynist-feminist (accessed 26 August 2018).

Schoene, B. (2017), 'Contemporary American Literature as World Literature: Cruel Cosmopolitanism, Cosmopoetics, and the Search for a Worldlier American Novel', *Anglia*, 135(1): 86–104. Available online: https://doi.org/10.1515/ang-2017-0006 (accessed 26 August 2018).

Schoonover, K. (2012), 'Wastrels of Time: Slow Cinema's Laboring Body, the Political Spectator, and the Queer', *Journal of Cinema and Media*, 53(1): 65–78. Available online: https://doi.org/10.1353/frm.2012.0007 (accessed 26 August 2018).

Search Party (2016–present), [TV programme] TBS, 21 November.

Sebold, A. (2002), [Novel] *The Lovely Bones*, New York: Little, Brown.

Seidel, E. (2020), '*Fleabag, Jane the Virgin*, and Feminist Media on Television's Textual Edges', *Cinephile*, 14(1): 6–12.

Seidman, S., C. Meeks and F. Traschen (1999), 'Beyond the Closet? The Changing Social Meaning of Homosexuality in the United States', *Sexualities*, 2(1): 9–34. Available online: https://doi.org/10.1177/136346099002001002 (accessed 10 September 2018).

Sex and the City (1998–2004), [TV programme] USA: HBO, 6 June.

Shaviro, S. (2010, *Post Cinematic Affect*. Winchester: Zero Books.

Shaw, K. (2015), *Crunch Lit*. London: Bloomsbury.

Shepard, I., and I. Wojik-Andrews (2014), 'Are the -Isms Ever in Your Favor?: Children's Film Theory and The Hunger Games', in S. P. Connors (ed.), *The Politics of Panem: Challenging Genres*, 189–202. Rotterdam: Sense.

Shepherd, J. E. (2012), 'Why I'm Deeply Skeptical of HBO's Super-Hyped Show "Girls"', *Alternet*, 11 April. Available online: http://www.alternet.org/story/154957/why_i'm_deeply_skeptical_of_hbo's_super-hyped_show_'girls' (accessed 30 April 2016).

Sheth, F. (2009), *Toward a Political Philosophy of Race*. Albany: State University of New York.

Shields Dobson, A. (2015), *Postfeminist Digital Cultures: Femininity, Social Media, and Self-Representation*. Basingstoke: Palgrave.

Shields, S. A. (2002), *Speaking from the Heart: Gender and the Social Meaning of Emotion*. Cambridge: Cambridge University Press.

Shields, S. A., and L. R. Warner (2007), 'The Perception of Crying in Women and Men: Angry Tears, Sad Tears, and the "Right Way" to Cry', in U. Hess and P. Philippot (eds), *Group Dynamics and Emotional Expression*, 92–117. Cambridge: Cambridge University Press.

Showalter, E. (1985), *The Female Malady: Women, Madness, and English Culture, 1830–1980*. London: Penguin.

Shutter Island (2010), [Film] Dir. Martin Scorsese, USA: Paramount.

Siegel, L. (2002), 'Relationshipism', *The New Republic*, 18 November. Available online: https://newrepublic.com/article/66593/relationshipism (accessed 10 December 2021).

Simone, N. (1965), 'Feeling Good', Track 7 on *I Put a Spell on You* [Spotify], New York: Philips.

Smith, A. (2015), 'Introduction', in C. Nally and A. Smith (eds), *Twenty-First Century Feminism Forming and Performing Femininity*. Switzerland: Springer International (Palgrave Macmillan).

Smith, P. (1975), 'Land: Horses / Land of a Thousand Dances / La Mer (De)', Track 7 on *Horses*, New York: Arista Records.

Sobchak, V. (2012), 'Fleshing Out the Image: Phenomenology, Pedagogy, and Derek Jarman's "Blue"', in J. Carel and G. Tuck (eds), *New Takes in Film-Philosophy*, 191–206, Basingstoke: Palgrave Macmillan.

Sorry to Bother You (2018), [Film] Dir. Boots Riley, USA: Cinereach.

Spiers, E. (2018), *Pop-Feminist Narratives: The Female Subject under Neoliberalism in North America, Britain, and Germany*. Oxford: Oxford University Press.

Springer, K. (2007), 'Divas, Evil Black Bitches, and Bitter Black Women: African American Women in Postfeminist and Post-Civil-Rights Popular Culture', in D. Negra and Y. Tasker (eds), *Interrogating Postfeminism: Gender and the Politics of Popular Culture*, 249–76, Durham, NC: Duke University Press.

Srnicek, N. (2012), 'Navigating Neoliberalism: Political Aesthetics in an Age of Crisis', paper presented at *The Matter of Contradiction: Ungrounding the Object*, Vassivière, France, 8–9 September.

Stacey, J. (2015), 'Crossing Over with Tilda Swinton – the Mistress of "Flat Affect"', *International Journal of Politics, Culture, and Society*, 28(3): 243–71.

Steck, P. A. (c.1894–5), [Oil on canvas] *Ophelia Drowning*, France: Paris Musées.

Stevens, D. (2021), '*Promising Young Woman*'s Flaws Run Deeper Than Its Ending', *Slate*, 17 February. Available online: https://slate.com/culture/2021/02/promising-young-woman-movie-review-carey-mulligan-ending.html (accessed 24 April 2021).

Stilwell, R. (2007), 'The Fantastical Gap between Diegetic and Nondiegetic', in D. Goldmark, L. Kramer and R. Leppert (eds), *Beyond the Soundtrack: Representing Music in Cinema*, 184–202. Berkeley: University of California Press.

StreetDance (2010), [Film] Dir. Max Giwa and Dania Pasquini, UK: BBC Films.

Sturges, F. (2018), 'Cattleprods! Severed Tongues! Torture Porn! Why I've Stopped Watching the Handmaid's Tale', *Guardian*, 16 June. Available online: https://www.theguardian.com/tv-and-radio/2018/jun/16/handmaids-tale-season-2-elisabeth-moss-margaret-atwood (accessed 24 April 2021).

Suderman, P. (2015), '*The Hunger Games* Movies Succeeded Because They Were Perfect for Millennials', *Vox*, 23 November. Available online: https://

www.vox.com/2015/11/23/9785962/hunger-games-millennials (accessed 11 September 2018).

Suebsaeng, A. (2012), ' "Girls": What the Hell Was HBO Thinking?' *Mother Jones*, 11 April. Available online: http://www.motherjones.com/mixed-media/2012/04/tv-review-girls-hbo-lena-dunham (accessed 30 April 2016).

Tan, S. S. M. (2014), 'Worse Games to Play?: Deconstructing Resolution in The Hunger Games', in S. P. Connors (ed.), *The Politics of Panem: Challenging Genres*, 29–43. Rotterdam: Sense.

Taylor, A. (2011), ' "The Urge towards Love Is an Urge towards (Un)death": Romance, Masochistic Desire and Postfeminism in the Twilight Novels', *International Journal of Cultural Studies*, 15(1): 31–46. Available online: https://doi.org/10.1177/1367877911399204 (accessed 27 April 2018).

Taylor, S. (2015), 'Arrested Development: Can Funny, Female Characters Survive Script Development Processes?' *Philament*, 20: 61–77.

Tazi, M., and K. Oumlil (2020), 'The Rise of Fourth-Wave Feminism in the Arab region? Cyberfeminism and Women's Activism at the Crossroads of the Arab Spring', *CyberOrient*, 14(1): 44–71.

The 100 (2014–20), [TV Programme] USA: The CW, 19 March.

The Big Bang Theory (2007–19), [TV programme] USA: CBS, 24 September.

The Birds (1963), [Film] Dir. Alfred Hitchcock, USA: Universal Pictures.

The Fits (2015), [Film] Dir. Anna Rose Holmer, USA: Oscilloscope Laboratories.

The Girl with the Dragon Tattoo (2011), [Film] Dir. David Fincher, USA: Columbia Pictures.

The Handmaid's Tale (2017–present), [TV programme] Hulu, 26 April.

The Hate U Give (2018), [Film] Dir. George Tillman Jr., USA: 20th Century Fox.

The Hunger Games (2012), [Film] Dir. Gary Ross, USA: Lionsgate.

The Maltese Falcon (1941), [Film] Dir. John Huston, USA: Warner Brothers.

The Mindy Project (2012–17), [TV programme] USA: Hulu, 25 September.

The Piano (1993), [Film] Dir. Jane Campion, UK: Entertainment Film Distributors.

The Roar of the Greasepaint – the Smell of the Crowd (1964), [Theatrical Production] L. Bricusse and A. Newley. Nottingham: Theatre Royal, 3 August.

The Running Man (1987), [Film] Dir. Paul Michael Glaser, USA: Tristar Pictures.

The Virgin Suicides (1999), [Film] Dir. Sofia Coppola, USA: Paramount Classics.

There's Something about Mary (1998), [Film] Dir. Bobby Farrelly and Peter Farrelly, USA: 20th Century Fox.

Thirteen (2003), [Film] Dir. Catherine Hardwicke, USA: Fox Searchlight Pictures.

Thomas, A. (2017), [Novel] *The Hate U Give*, New York: Balzer & Bray.

Thornton, M. (2013), 'Foreign Film Week: Growing Up Queer: "Water Lilies" (2007) and "Tomboy" (2011)', *Bitch Flicks*, 22 March. Available online: http://www.btchflcks.com/2013/03/foreign-film-week-growing-up-queer-water-lilies-2007-and-tomboy-2011.html#.W5kZXyXwaUk (accessed 12 September 2018).

Thumim, N. (2012), *Self-Representation and Digital Culture*. Basingstoke: Palgrave Macmillan.

Trainwreck (2015), [Film] Dir. Judd Apatow, USA: Universal Pictures.

Twin Peaks (1990–1), [TV programme] USA: ABC, 8 April.

Two Weeks Notice (2002), [Film] Dir. Marc Lawrence, USA: Warner Brothers.

Un amour de jeunesse [Goodbye First Love] (2011), [Film] Dir. Mia Hansen-Løve, France: Les films du losange.

Unbreakable Kimmy Schmidt (2015–19), [TV programme] Netflix, 6 March.

VanArendonk, K. (2019), '*Fleabag* Breaks the Fourth Wall and Then Breaks Our Hearts', *Vulture*, 23 May. Available online: https://www.vulture.com/2019/05/fleabag-season-2-fourth-wall-ending.html (accessed 10 December 2021).

VanDerWerff, E. (2014), '*Gone Girl* Is the Most Feminist Mainstream Movie in Years', *Vox*, 6 October. Available online: https://www.vox.com/2014/10/6/6905475/gone-girl-feminist-movie-david-fincher (accessed 25 August 2018).

VanDerWerff, E. (2018), 'The Handmaid's Tale Season 2 Was Masterful. But It May Have Broken the Show', *Vox*, 11 July. Available online: https://www.vox.com/culture/2018/7/11/17555532/the-handmaids-tale-season-2-review-recap-finale (accessed 10 December 2021).

VanDerWerff, E. (2021), 'A Close Read of Promising Young Woman's Brilliant, Divisive Ending', *Vox*, 15 January. Available online: https://www.vox.com/

culture/22229324/promising-young-woman-ending-explained-review-carey-mulligan (accessed 24 April 2021).

Vincendeau, G. (2005), *La Haine: French Film Guide*. London: I.B. Tauris.

Vincendeau, G. (2015), 'Minority Report', *Sight and Sound*, 25(6): 27.

Viruet, P. (2016), '*Girls* Recap: One Wedding, No Funerals', *Vulture*, 21 February. Available online: http://www.vulture.com/2016/02/girls-recap-season-5-episode-1.html (accessed 10 September 2018).

Vive L'Amour (1994) [Film] Dir. Tsai Ming-liang, USA: Strand Releasing.

Wanzo, R. (2016), 'Precarious Girl Comedy: Issa Rae, Lena Dunham, and Abjection Aesthetics', *Camera Obscura: Feminism, Culture, and Media Studies*, 2(31): 27–59.

Wearing, S. (2007), 'Subjects of Rejuvenation: Aging in Postfeminist Culture', in D. Negra and Y. Tasker (eds), *Interrogating Postfeminism: Gender and the Politics of Popular Culture*, 277–310. Durham, NC: Duke University Press.

Wechter, M., and E. Berland (1992), 'Fatal/Fetal Attraction: Psychological Aspects of Imagining Female Identity in Contemporary Film', *Journal of Popular Culture*, 26(3): 35–45. Available online: https://doi.org/10.1111/j.0022-3840.1992.2603_35.x (accessed 13 September 2021).

Weedon, C. (1987), *Feminist Practice and Poststructural Theory*. Cambridge: Blackwell.

Westerfeld, S. (2005), [Novel] *Uglies*, London: Simon & Schuster.

Whelehan, I. (2010), 'Remaking Feminism: Or Why Is Postfeminism So Boring?' *Nordic Journal of English Studies*, 9(3): 155–72.

When Harry Met Sally (1989), [Film] Dir. Rob Reiner, USA: MGM.

White, R. (2018), *Television Comedy and Femininity: Queering Gender*. London: Bloomsbury.

Whitham, B. (2013), 'From Security to Resilience? (Neo)liberalism, War and Terror after 9/11', *Resilience: International Policies, Practices and Discourses*, 1(3): 219–29. Available online: https://doi.org/10.1080/21693293.2013.842345 (accessed 7 May 2021).

Williams, A. A., Z. Bryant and C. Carvell (2018), 'Uncompensated Emotional Labor, Racial Battle Fatigue, and (In)civility in Digital Spaces', *Sociology Compass*, 13(2): 1–12. Available online: https://doi.org/10.1111/soc4.12658 (accessed 7 May 2021).

Willmore, A. (2021), 'The Queasy Ending of *Promising Young Woman*', *Vulture*, 15 January. Available online: https://www.vulture.com/arti

cle/the-queasy-ending-of-promising-young-woman.html (accessed 10 December 2021).

Winter's Bone (2010), [Film] Dir. Debra Granik, USA: Roadside Attractions.

Woods, F. (2019), 'Too Close for Comfort: Direct Address and the Confessional Comic Woman in *Chewing Gum* and *Fleabag*', *Communication Culture & Critique*, 12: 194–212.

Woolf, V. ([1925] 1953), [Novel] *Mrs. Dalloway*, New York: Harvest Books.

Young Adult (2011), [Film] Dir. Jason Reitman, USA: Paramount.

Yuneun, C. L. (2011), 'Cool Postfeminism: The Celebrity Stardom of Sofia Coppola', in S. Holmes and D. Negra (eds), *In the Limelight and under the Microscope: Forms and Functions of Female Celebrity*, 174–98. New York: Continuum.

Žižek, S. (2005), 'Neighbours and Other Monsters: A Plea for Ethical Violence', in S. Žižek, E. L. Santner and K. Reinhard (eds), *The Neighbour: Three Inquiries in Political Theology*, 134–90. Chicago: University of Chicago Press.

Index

adulthood
  coming of age 115, 206
  distinction between girl and
    woman 16, 32
  normative adult
    subjectivity 99, 101
  and normative
    femininity 74, 85, 99
  rejection of normative adult
    milestones 99, 101
  see also femininity
affect 152–3, 181, 198, 204, 210
  affective masking 136–7, 145, 166
  affective or cognitive
    mapping 12–13
  affect theory 2, 9–15, 20–2, 43,
    62–4, 81, 88, 96, 102–3, 120, 133,
    145–6, 204, 210
  crying 181–6, 192, 223 n.8
  emotion management 42–3, 133,
    136–7, 181–6 (*see also* 'feeling
    rules')
  feel-bad 22–3, 26–8, 32, 34,
    45, 54–5, 169–71, 175,
    181–2, 187, 190–2, 195–6,
    200–3, 207
  feel-bad femininity (*see under*
    femininity)
  and femininity 26, 175, 195
  'flat affect' (*see under* Berlant,
    Lauren)
  girl studies 15–17, 20, 145–6, 204
  'manly emotion' 181
  and resilience 119, 152–8, 162–3,
    166, 169, 171, 175–86, 195,
    204, 210
  resilient affect (*see under*
    resilience)
  see also affect *under* postfeminism;
    Ahmed, Sara; Berlant, Lauren;
    Colling, Samantha; genre;
    Hochschild, Arlie; Kanai, Akane
agency 44, 46, 174, 182, 190, 208
  Butler, Judith 37–9
  defiant agency 38–9, 116, 124,
    126, 128–30, 132, 134, 142, 172,
    208, 211
  female agency 22, 132, 135, 137,
    156, 195, 197–9
  kinetic agency 175–80
  narrative agency 25, 48–9, 106,
    132, 154, 157, 164, 173–4,
    177–8, 197–9
  and postfeminism 25, 27, 39, 41,
    44, 65, 115, 194, 211–12
  and resilience 22, 25–7, 115, 124–6,
    128–9, 132, 173–5, 180, 182, 191,
    193–5, 201, 209, 211
  suffering agency 116, 124–5,
    128–9, 175, 186–8
  see also Cool Girl figure *under Gone
    Girl*; dead girl figure *under Gone
    Girl*; de Lauretis, Teresa; Ruti,
    Mari; Elliott, Jane; resilience
Ahmed, Sara 11–12, 34–6, 60, 87–9,
  93–4, 97
  feminist killjoy 43–44
  'happiness scripts' 1, 36, 46, 50, 111
Anderson, Joshua Adam 64, 88
Appropriate Behaviour (Akhavan
  2014) 91, 152
  and *Broad City* 98
  coming out 101–5
  and *Fleabag* 109
  generic belonging vs. isolation 83–4,
    86–90, 92–3, 98, 111, 204
  and *Girlhood* 152, 206
  and *Girls* 24, 83, 87, 204
  and *Gone Girl* 89
  normativity 96–7, 206

Index

and postfeminism 24, 84, 87, 93, 203–4
queer temporality 84–5, 87, 94, 97–9, 106, 111, 152
queerlinearity 94–5, 97–9, 106
see also Ahmed, Sara; Freeman, Elizabeth; queer
Augé, Marc 149–50, 165

Bachelorette (Headland 2012) 32–3
Banet-Weiser, Sarah 3, 6, 16, 18
Berlant, Lauren 61, 191
  affect 2, 80–1, 198
  attachment 10, 13, 70–1
  'crisis ordinariness' 81, 135, 219 n.5
  'cruel optimism' 10–11, 56, 62–3, 79–80, 82
  and Edelman, Lee 120, 192
  fantasy 11, 60, 62, 75, 80, 124
  'flat affect' 102–3, 181
  genre 13–15, 50–1, 63–4, 80, 119, 127, 203
  impasse 8, 12–13, 21, 24, 70–1, 75, 78, 82
  'the good life' 10–11, 60, 80, 87
  sovereignty 124
  see also affect; postfeminism
Brabon, Benjamin 5
  see also Genz, Stéphanie and Brabon, Benjamin
Broad City (Glazer and Jacobson 2014–19) 25, 83, 98–101
Broad, Katherine R. 140, 205
Bridget Jones' Diary (Maguire 2001) 9, 40–1
Butler, Judith
  agency 37–9, 52
  queer theory 105

Catch Me Daddy (Wolfe 2014)
  agency 173–80, 182, 186–8, 190–1, 193–5, 201, 208
  feel-bad femininity 26, 175, 181–2, 185–7, 191–2, 195, 205, 207

  'feel-bad film' 26, 169–71, 190, 192
  resilience 26, 169, 173–5, 178, 180, 185–7, 191–5, 201, 205, 207–8
  social viability 26–7, 175, 179–80, 187, 191–5, 201, 205, 207
  see also de Lauretis, Teresa; Edelman, Lee; Lübecker, Nikolaj; queer negativity *under* girls; resilient affect *under* resilience
Cecire, Natalia 122, 124, 205
Colling, Samantha 7
  affective approach to postfeminism 21, 147, 151, 164
  'double coding 74–5, 77
  ideological approach to postfeminism 10, 20(*see also* Handyside, Fiona and Taylor-Jones, Kate)
  neoliberalism 58
coming of age 150, 205
  in *Broad City* 98
  girlhood 1–2, 16, 22–3, 25, 54, 115, 130, 132, 141–5, 173–4, 208
  as impeded 23, 50, 53–4, 71–23, 174, 194, 196
  and postfeminism 2, 16–17, 22–3, 25–6, 50, 53–4, 54–7, 71–4, 143
  quest narratives 26, 174 (*see also* de Lauretis, Teresa)
  and relationality 165
  and resilience 1–2, 22–3, 26, 115, 130, 132, 141–3, 169, 171
  and social viability 24, 130, 206
  and survival 130, 141
  and transformation 23, 54, 57, 71, 73, 143–5, 158
  and Whiteness 132
  see also adulthood; *Appropriate Behaviour*; *Catch Me Daddy*; *Girlhood*; *Girls*; *The Hunger Games*
Cool Girl figure
  see under Gone Girl

'cruel optimism'
   see under Berlant, Lauren

de Lauretis, Teresa 26, 45, 173–4
dead girl figure
   see under Gone Girl
death
   and agency 48–9
   death drive 191–4
   death match genre 118–19
   as a method of undermining resilience 123–4, 126–32, 194
   (*see also* melancholy *under* James, Robin)
   and perfection 47–8, 201
   and social viability 46, 49, 128–9, 194
   suicide 46, 48–50, 128–9, 169, 171, 181, 190, 194
Dejmanee, Tisha 8, 63
desire
   and fantasy 11, 52, 62
   and feminine fulfilment 23, 55, 57, 81
   and generic convention 87, 111, 204
   'inner directive' 40, 44, 126, 129–35, 173
   male desire 43, 173–4
   and narrative catharsis 169–70, 197
   normative desire 38–40, 43–44, 51, 80–1, 126, 128, 173–4, 211
   and postfeminism 35, 80
   and resilient agency 26
   and social viability 34, 39–40, 55, 126, 128, 130, 133–4
   see also Lacan, Jacques; Ruti, Mari
Dobson, Julia 147, 150, 165
Driscoll, Catherine 15–16
Dunham, Lena 70

Edelman, Lee
   anti-social queer theory 27, 120, 191–3, 206–8
   and Berlant, Lauren 120, 192

Elliott, Jane 116, 124–5, 128–9, 175, 186, 190
   see also suffering agency *under* agency

fantasy
   and coherent subjectivity 26–7, 46, 49, 52, 124, 185, 192, 206
   and 'cruel optimism' 11, 13, 62, 74–5, 78
   and postfeminism 44, 47, 52, 77, 79–80, 148, 209
   and 'the good life' 43, 60, 62, 74–5, 197
Farrimond, Katherine 5, 48–9
'feeling rules' 12, 133
   gendered feeling rules 12
   racialized feeling rules 137–8
   see also Hochschild, Arlie; Kanai, Akane
female subjectivity 2, 44, 50, 135, 204
   Black female subjectivity 25, 135–40, 148, 157, 164 (*see also* Black girlhood *under* girls; Black girlhood *under* resilience)
   see also femininity
femininity
   and adulthood 74, 85, 99, 101, 115, 206
   feel-bad femininity 26, 175, 181–2, 185–6, 191–2, 195–7, 207
   feminine good life 15, 43
   'girlness' 16, 32
   normative 1, 7, 19, 27, 31, 33–4, 40–4, 46, 49, 51, 73–4, 80, 108, 194, 210–11
   postfeminism 3, 7, 11, 23, 27, 31, 33–5, 37, 40–4, 46, 49, 68, 70, 80–1, 87, 116, 176, 180–1, 211–12
   and resilience 1, 17, 25, 115–6, 118, 142, 169, 174–6, 180–1, 184–5, 194, 205, 209–10

traditional 1, 19, 23–4, 27, 43–4, 116–18, 175, 178, 180–1, 185, 192, 204–5, 210–11
  and transformation 27, 51, 180
  White femininity 42–3, 46
  see also Cool Girl; death; female subjectivity; Whiteness
feminism
  and agency 37
  fourth-wave feminisms 5–6
  and postfeminism 3–4, 8, 64, 68, 71, 80
  and resilience 18
Fisher, Mark 60, 65–6, 69
Fleabag (Waller-Bridge 2016–19) 83, 106–10
Freeman, Elizabeth
  'chrononormativity' 84–5, 95, 97

genre
  and Berlant, Lauren 13–15, 50–5, 63–5, 78–81, 119, 127, 203
  and coming-of-age 2, 25, 57–8, 72, 115, 142, 144, 158, 166, 208
  and coming out 87, 101–6
  feel-bad postfeminism 1, 22–3, 27, 174, 195–7, 200
  generic belonging vs. isolation 83, 86–8, 98, 111, 204
  and postfeminism 2–3, 14–15, 22–4, 27, 32, 34–5, 40, 50–5, 56, 63–5, 70–1, 77, 79–82, 83–4, 110, 163, 202–3, 211–12
  and resilience 115, 153, 203–5, 209–10
  see also postfeminism as a genre under postfeminism
Genz, Stéphanie 7
  see also Genz, Stéphanie and Brabon, Benjamin
Genz, Stéphanie and Brabon, Benjamin 3–4, 9, 63
Gill, Rosalind 35
  postfeminism and affect 9, 14

postfeminism and choice 31, 204
postfeminism and empowerment 23
postfeminism and feminism 3, 5–7
postfeminism and neoliberalism 3, 17, 64
postfeminism and self-maintenance 57, 204
postfeminism as a sensibility 3–4, 7, 14, 57
postfeminist femininity 41, 46 (see also Cool Girl figure under Gone Girl; Gill, Rosalind and Scharff, Christina)
resilience 17 (see also Gill, Rosalind and Orgad, Shani)
Gill, Rosalind and Orgad, Shani 17–19, 115
Gill, Rosalind and Scharff, Christina 31, 64
Girlhood/Bande de Filles (Sciamma 2014)
  and *Appropriate Behaviour* 152, 206
  and *Catch Me Daddy* 169, 174–7, 181–5, 191
  coming of age 143–6, 150, 154, 158, 162, 169, 174
  French national context 142–3, 146
  and *Girls* 158, 203
  girlhood interiority 144, 146, 155–6, 159–60, 163–6, 176
  and *Gone Girl* 158, 167
  music 143, 145, 147, 151–8, 162–4, 175–6
  postfeminism 148, 158, 163, 167
  and relationality 101, 146–50, 154–7, 159–61, 163–8, 203
  and resilience 25, 115, 142, 147, 152–63, 166–9, 175, 181–5, 191
  space 144–5, 147–50, 159, 161–3, 165–6, 177
  and *The Hate U Give* 150, 153

Index

and *The Hunger Games* 143–4, 153, 166, 174, 183–4, 191
transformation 144–5, 154, 157–8, 203
see also relational resilience *under* resilience; resilient affect *under* resilience; transformative resilience *under* resilience;
girls
  affect theory 20, 145–6, 204
  agency of 124, 128–9, 131–2, 135, 137, 156–7, 164, 174–180, 182, 186–91, 193–5, 201, 208–9, 211
  'at risk' girl 15, 159–60, 163
  Black girlhood 25, 116, 134–7, 146, 150, 171
  'can-do' girl 15, 159–60
  'future girl' 17, 130
  girl studies 15, 20, 31, 210
  as 'hypervisible' 31
  as idealized subjects 16–17, 185, 201
  and postfeminism 9, 11, 15, 20–1, 27, 31, 204
  and queer negativity 191–5, 208–9
  and resilience 1–2, 17, 19, 26, 115–41, 142–68, 169–201, 210
  and women 16, 203
  see also Colling, Samantha; coming of age; Cool Girl; dead girl figure *under Gone Girl*; 'girlness' *under* femininity; Handyside, Fiona; Harris, Anita
Girls (Dunham 2012–17)
  and *Appropriate Behaviour* 83, 87–8, 98, 101, 105, 204
  'cruel optimism' 24, 56–7, 62, 70, 78–9, 81–3, 88
  and middle-class precarity 59–62, 65–70
  postfeminism 24, 56–7, 62–5, 67, 70–1, 74–5, 77–82, 158, 203
  postfeminist impasse 24, 56–7, 63, 70–5, 78–80, 82, 199, 203–3, 205–6

'the good life' 60, 62–5, 71, 73, 78, 87, 98, 206
rom-com run 75–9, 110
and *Sex and the City* 57, 65–70, 88
see also Berlant, Lauren; postfeminism
Gone Girl (Flynn 2012) 205–6
  agency 27, 37–9, 41, 44, 46, 48–9, 106
  and *Appropriate Behaviour* 89, 105
  and *Catch Me Daddy* 194
  Cool Girl figure 1, 23–4, 31–2, 34–5, 39–46, 50, 52
  dead girl figure 45–51, 194
  feel-bad postfeminism 1, 22–3, 32, 34, 45, 54–5, 205
  and *Girlhood/Bande de Filles* 158, 167
  and girls 31–2, 35, 42, 45–9, 54
  and postfeminism 1–2, 23–4, 27, 31–6, 39–42, 45–6, 50–6, 158, 204
  and postfeminist impasse 32, 105, 201
  and social viability 27, 32, 34, 36, 38–40, 45–9, 51, 53–5, 203
  see also Whiteness
Grady, Constance, 172, 196

Halberstam, Jack 12, 84, 106, 208
Handyside, Fiona 15–16, 145–6, 164, 166
Handyside, Fiona and Taylor-Jones, Kate 6–7, 31, 142
happiness
  see under Ahmed, Sara
Harris, Anita 15, 17, 64, 130, 159–60
Henderson, Marg, and Taylor, Anthea 4, 7–8
Hochschild, Arlie 133, 136
  see also feeling rules
Holm, Nicholas 102–3
Huehls, Mitchum 21, 143–5, 208–9

impasse
  see under Berlant, Lauren

James, Robin 132, 193
  intensified trauma 134–5, 139
  melancholy 122–4, 126–7, 129, 131, 152–4
  neoliberalism 19, 26, 115, 118, 120–3, 125, 191
  overcoming identity-based oppression 19, 26, 116, 121, 132, 152, 157, 162, 174–6, 179–80, 191, 193
  overcoming trauma 19, 25, 115–16, 118, 121–2, 123, 125, 129, 139, 152, 162, 192
  in relation to queer negativity 191–2
  resilience and femininity 19, 25, 115–16, 118–19, 130, 174–5, 179–80, 185, 191–2, 209
  resilience discourse in pop music 19, 119, 152–4, 204
  see also resilience

Kamińska, Aleksandra 98–9, 101
Kanai, Akane 7
  feeling rules 12, 133
  resilience 19
Kanai, Akane and Shields Dobson, Amy 98–9, 101

Lacan, Jacques 38, 44, 126, 215 n.4, 215 n.5
  see also desire; Ruti, Mari; Žižek, Slavoj
Levin, Adam 138–9
Lübecker, Nikolaj 23, 26, 169–71, 191–2, 198

Marston, Kendra 24, 34, 51
McNeill, Isabelle 146, 151, 155, 160, 164

McRobbie, Angela
  girls 160
  neoliberalism 3–4, 64
  postfeminism 1, 3–4, 9, 33, 41, 64
  resilience 17–19, 115
Monaghan, Whitney 84–5, 105
Morris, Wesley and Wortham, Jenna 196, 198
Mulvey, Laura 42, 53

Needham, Gary 73, 75, 85, 87, 198
Negra, Diane 11
  see also Negra, Diane and Tasker, Yvonne
Negra, Diane and Tasker, Yvonne 4, 7, 9, 15, 20, 32, 64–5, 202
neoliberalism
  affective mapping 13
  and agency 38, 124–5, 187–7
  economic precarity 7, 18, 32, 66, 99
  and femininity 17, 27, 42, 64, 108
  and postfeminism 3, 14, 17, 20–1, 27, 42, 58, 60–4, 108, 208
  and resilience 2, 17–19, 20, 26, 115–16, 118, 120–2, 125, 130, 191
  and 'the good life' 60
normativity 39, 51, 80, 82, 84–5, 95–7
  see also adulthood; femininity; 'chrononormativity' under Freeman, Elizabeth; queerlinearity under queer

Orgad, Shani
  see Gill, Rosalind and Orgad, Shani

Petersen, Anne Helen 34, 93
post-2008 recession 119
  middle-class precarity 33–4, 65–7, 87(see also under Girls)
  postfeminism 7, 9, 32–4, 65–7, 202
  resilience 17–18, 115
  see also Genz, Stephanié; Negra, Diane and Tasker, Yvonne

postfeminism
  and affect 2, 7, 9–11, 13–15, 22–3, 34, 45, 54–5, 61–2, 65, 80–1, 84, 88, 142, 202–5, 209, 212
  Australian postfeminism 4, 8
  and coming of age 2, 23–26, 32, 50, 53–4, 56–8, 71, 73, 194, 196–7, 203, 208
  complicity/liberation binary 20–2, 167–8, 208–10
  economic precarity 7, 61, 65, 67, 87, 202
  feel-bad postfeminism 1, 22–3, 27–8, 34, 55, 174, 195–7, 200–2, 204
  and feminism 3, 6, 8, 64, 71
  as a genre 14–15, 50, 63–4, 83, 203
  and girls 15–16, 19–20, 26, 31–2, 54, 142, 148, 163, 167, 203–4, 208–9
  as an ideology 10, 14–15, 20, 203
  and neoliberalism 3, 14, 17, 20–1, 27, 42, 58, 60–4, 108, 208
  and normativity 35–6, 39–44, 46, 55–6, 73–4, 79–82, 84, 87, 93, 110–11, 116–17, 167, 194, 202, 204, 208, 210–11
  postfeminist aspiration 7, 23, 32–6, 45–6, 50, 65–7, 70–1, 79–81, 105, 201–2
  postfeminist empowerment 2–3, 7–9, 13, 15, 17, 22–5, 27, 31–6, 40–1, 43–5, 50–2, 57–8, 65, 83, 87, 93, 110–11, 115–17, 125, 163, 167, 194, 199, 201–5, 209–12
  postfeminist fantasy 11, 23, 43–5, 50, 56–7, 65, 70–1, 77–82, 148, 201, 203, 205, 209
  postfeminist impasse 8, 16–17, 21, 24, 32, 55, 57, 63, 70–1, 74–5, 78–80, 82, 105, 199–201, 203, 208–9
  as 'potentially redundant' 5–7, 20
  as a relation of cruel optimism 11, 24, 33, 56–7, 60, 62–3, 70–1, 81–2, 87–8, 111, 201, 203, 205
  and resilience 17–19, 22–3, 25–8, 115–16, 118, 130, 142, 167–8, 180, 194–5, 201–5, 208–12
  as a sensibility 7, 14–15, 203 (*see also under* Gill, Rosalind)
  and subjectivity 2, 31–2, 37, 50–4, 62–4, 71, 142, 158, 167, 203, 209
  and transformation 25, 27, 31–2, 41, 52, 55–8, 71, 73, 143, 158, 163, 167, 203–4, 209
  see also Cool Girl; McRobbie, Angela; Gill, Rosalind; Genz, Stéphanie; social viability
Projansky, Sarah 3, 9, 15–16, 20, 32
Promising Young Woman (Fennell 2021) 196–201

queer
  affect theory 10, 12
  anti-relational queer theory 27, 120, 191–3, 208
  bisexuality 86, 94, 99, 101, 103
  coming-out narrative 86–7, 92–4, 101–5
  intersectionality with race 93–4
  queer theory 10, 28, 106, 120, 191–3, 208
  queerlinearity 94–5, 97–9, 106, 152, 207
  sexuality 86, 92–4, 98–9
  temporality 84–5, 87, 94, 97–9, 106, 111, 152
    see also Butler, Judith; Halberstam, Jack; Monaghan, Whitney; sexuality

race
  Ahmed, Sara 43, 93–4
  in *The Hate U Give* 135–9
  'melancholic migrant' 43

and postfeminism 4
post-racial fantasy 43
post-racial politics in *The Hunger Games* 25, 130-2
systemic racism 120, 193, 208
see also racialized feeling rules *under* 'feeling rules'; Black female subjectivity *under* female subjectivity; Whiteness
resilience
   and aesthetics 19, 115, 119, 152-3, 155, 157, 160, 163, 166-7, 172-80, 186, 204-5, 207-8
   and agency (*see* resilience *under* agency)
   and Black girlhood 25, 132, 135-9, 171
   and 'cruel optimism' 19
   defiant resilience 116, 119, 125-6, 128-30, 132, 134, 142, 147, 204, 208-9
   and femininity 1, 17, 25, 27, 115-16, 118, 142, 169, 174-6, 180-1, 184-5, 194, 205, 209-10
   in *Girlhood/Bande de Filles* 25, 115, 142, 147, 152-63, 166-9, 175, 181-5, 191
   and girls 1-2, 17, 19, 26, 115-41, 142-68, 169-201, 210
   McRobbie, Angela 17-19, 115
   and neoliberalism 2, 17-19, 20, 26, 115-16, 118, 120-2, 125, 130, 191
   and overcoming 1-2, 19, 25-7, 115-16, 118, 121-3, 125-6, 129, 134, 140-2, 147, 152-3, 156-8, 166, 174-5, 178-87, 190-7, 199, 205, 208-10
   and postfeminism 17-19, 22-3, 25-8, 115-16, 118, 130, 142, 167-8, 180, 194-5, 201-5, 208-12
   in *Precious* 171
   relational resilience 25-6, 115, 142, 147-50, 156-7, 163, 165-8, 204, 209
   resilient affect 175, 181-86, 210
   and social viability 17, 19, 22, 26-7, 116, 127-8, 137, 147, 175, 179, 191, 193-5, 201, 205
   in *The Handmaid's Tale* 171-3
   in *The Hate U Give* 25, 116, 134-41
   in *The Hunger Games* 1-2, 25, 115-16, 118-19, 121, 123, 126-31, 134-5, 139-41, 143, 191
   transformative resilience 25-6, 115, 142-4, 157-64, 167-8, 204, 209
   in *Unbreakable Kimmy Schmidt* (Fey and Carlock 2015-19) 115
   and Whiteness 25, 132, 135, 137-9, 173
   see also 'feeling rules'; 'future girl' *under* girls; James, Robin; Kanai, Akane
Retallack, Hanna, Ringrose, Jessica, and Lawrence, Emilie 5, 8-9, 20, 64
Ringmar, Eric 12, 96, 147-8
romantic comedy 51, 88
   and postfeminism 36
   and *Promising Young Woman* 197, 201
   rom-com run 57, 71, 75-81, 110
   and 'the good life' 65
   see also Girls (Dunham 2012-17); *Sex and the City* (Star 1998-2004)
Ruti, Mari 40, 147, 157, 166
   agency 37-40, 44, 126, 129-30, 210-11
   antisocial queer theory 120, 193, 207-8
   defiant agency 38-9, 44, 116, 124, 126, 129-30, 132-3, 193, 210-11, 215 n.4, 215 n.5
   critique of Butler 37-9

critique of Edelman 120, 193, 207–8
opposition of power 37–8
silence as a mode of resistance 210–11
see also agency; Butler, Judith; Edelman, Lee

Scharff, Christina
  see Gill, Rosalind and Scharff, Christina
Schoene, Berthold 21, 199, 209
Schoonover, Karl 97–9
Sex and the City (Star 1998–2004) 9, 36, 57, 65–70, 84, 88, 93
sexuality
  bisexuality 86, 94, 99, 101, 103
  heteronormativity 33, 35, 46, 73, 93, 98–101, 104–6, 108, 110, 192, 206
  heterosexuality 35, 46, 73, 99–101, 104, 106, 108, 110
  homonormativity 93, 214 n.8
Shields Dobson, Amy 31, 210
  see also Kanai, Akane and Shields Dobson, Amy
Shields, Stephanie and Warner, Leah 181, 184
social class
  in *Appropriate Behaviour* 86–7, 92, 95
  in *Girls* 60–1
  in *Gone Girl* 33, 46
  middle-class 33, 60–1, 196
  working-class 175
social viability
  and femininity 19, 40, 42, 108, 116, 175, 179, 183, 194, 201
  loss of social viability 127, 182–3, 191, 199, 207, 211
  and neoliberalism 17, 24, 123, 187, 108
  and postfeminist empowerment, 22, 24, 27, 34, 36, 39–40, 46–7, 49, 51, 53, 55, 116, 193–4, 201, 203, 205–6
  and postfeminist resilience 17, 19, 22, 26–7, 116, 127–8, 137, 147, 174–5, 179, 191, 193–5, 201, 205
  risking one's social viability 38–40, 55, 123–124, 126, 130, 142, 147, 192–3, 199, 207, 209, 211
  socially unviable practices 123–4, 126, 129–30, 132
  and suicide 46, 48–50, 128–9, 190, 194
  see also Cool Girl; dead girl figure *under Gone Girl*; Edelman, Lee; Lacan, Jacques; James, Robin, normativity; postfeminism; resilience; Ruti, Mari
subjectivity
  see female subjectivity

Tan, Susan S. M. 139–40
Tasker, Yvonne
  see Negra, Diane and Tasker, Yvonne
The Handmaid's Tale (Miller 2017–present) 171–3
The Hate U Give (Tillman Jr 2018) 25, 116, 134–41, 150, 153, 199
  novel by Thomas, Angie 137, 139
The Hunger Games (Collins 2008–10) 153, 166, 206
  and girlhood coming of age 1–2, 115, 130, 141, 143–4, 174, 205
  and postfeminism 1–2, 25, 139, 205
  post-racial politics 25, 130–2
  and resilience 1–2, 25, 115–16, 118–19, 121, 123, 126–31, 134–5, 139–41, 143, 191
  and social viability 127, 183–4
  and Whiteness 25, 124, 132, 173
  see also resilience, Whiteness
The Virgin Suicides (Coppola 1999) 34, 49

transformation
  see under postfeminism
  see also transformative resilience
    under resilience
trauma
  and coming of age 141, 196
  overcoming trauma 19, 25, 115–16,
    118, 121–3, 125–6, 129, 134,
    140–2, 147, 152, 156–8, 166, 192,
    196, 199
  and resilience 19, 25, 115–16, 118,
    122–6, 129, 132, 134–5, 138,
    140, 210
  socially inflicted trauma 19, 118,
    120, 122, 124–6, 147, 196
  and social viability 118, 142, 199
  systemic racism 120, 137–8
  see also intensified trauma *under*
    James, Robin
Twilight (Meyer 2005–8) 84, 93

VanArendonk, Katherine 107–8, 110
VanDerWerff, Emily 172, 196, 200

Whelehan, Imelda 5–6
When Harry Met Sally (Reiner
  1989) 75, 77
Whiteness 143, 198–9
  anti-Black racism 135–7
  'classic idealized white femininity'
    42–3, 54
  in *Girlhood/Bande de
    Filles* 160, 162
  in *Gone Girl* 33–4, 46
  and resilience 25, 132, 135,
    137–9, 173
  in *The Hate U Give* 136–9, 199
  in *The Hunger Games* 25, 124,
    132, 173
  White supremacy 124, 136–7

Žižek, Slavoj 37–8, 126, 128, 215 n.4

Printed in the USA
CPSIA information can be obtained
at www.ICGtesting.com
LVHW010144060124
768267LV00002B/82